**Ctrl+
Alt+
CHAOS**

How
Teenage
Hackers
Hijack the
Internet

Ctrl+
Alt+
CHAOS

To Lina,

Joe Tidy

Elliott&Thompson

First published 2025 by
Elliott and Thompson Limited
2 John Street
London WC1N 2ES
www.eandtbooks.com

Represented by:
Authorised Rep Compliance Ltd.
Ground Floor, 71 Lower Baggot Street
Dublin, D02 P593
Ireland
www.arccompliance.com

ISBN: 978-1-78396-876-3

Copyright © Joe Tidy 2025

The Author has asserted his rights under the Copyright, Designs and Patents Act, 1988, to be identified as Author of this Work.

All rights reserved. No part of this publication may be reproduced, stored in or introduced into a retrieval system, or transmitted, in any form, or by any means (electronic, mechanical, photocopying, recording or otherwise) without the prior written permission of the publisher. Any person who does any unauthorised act in relation to this publication may be liable to criminal prosecution and civil claims for damages.

Every effort has been made to trace and contact all copyright holders. Where we have been unable to do this, we have included all the information we have about the provenance of 'The Hacker's Manifesto'. For the symbols of the hacker gangs, there is no copyright information. We will make good any omissions or rectify any mistakes brought to our attention.

9 8 7 6 5 4 3 2 1

A catalogue record for this book is available from the British Library.

Typesetting: Marie Doherty
Printed by CPI Group (UK) Ltd, Croydon, CR0 4YY

This book is dedicated to victims of cybercrime and the people who work hard to protect our lives online.

Contents

//Preface   ix

//1   An accidental arrest   1
//2   Ransom_man strikes   7
//3   I got the email   27
//4   The rise of Zeekill   49
//5   Hacking for retweets   55
//6   Hacking for power – and bitcoins   73
//7   Zeekill arrested   99
//8   Addicted to hacking   109
//9   Hacking to harm   131
//10 Christmas is cancelled   153
//11 Vastaamo implodes   171
//12 Untouchable Hacker God caged   181
//13 The baton passed   201

Acknowledgements   225
Endnotes   227
Index   233

//Preface

As a television reporter I'm used to my bosses making outrageous requests. But this was surely the most ridiculous yet.

'I want a lizard. On air tonight,' my news editor said, adding the chilling words: 'Ryley's called – make it happen.'

When John Ryley – the head of Sky News – gives you a mission it's one you have to accept. But this was surely mission impossible?

By 'lizard' he meant a member of the Lizard Squad hacking crew who were making global headlines after carrying out a cyber attack that was spoiling Christmas for about a hundred million people around the world.

Lizard Squad – a gang of anonymous teens known only by their social media handles – had successfully brought the Xbox Live and PlayStation Network services to their knees. Anyone trying to connect to the online systems of either of these games giants was met with the error message: 'Page not found'. So that meant no playing against your mates, no downloading new games and no registering your shiny new console.

This type of cyber attack would be disruptive at the best of times, but this was Christmas Day 2014 – a peak time for millions of children, parents and everyone in between to fire up their exciting new gaming gifts and play.

Lizard Squad's attack was a top story around the world and one of those rare occasions when a cyber attack was seen to have an immediate and obvious impact on society. Tens of millions of people were instantly impacted, and a tsunami of them turned to social media to vent their anger and confusion. They were met with a group of kids bragging about their hacking handiwork. People started asking: how on earth was it possible for these teenage boys to humble tech giants like Sony and Microsoft?

I was left with a different question: how was I going to find and interview one of these lizards for a Sky News TV report that evening?

A frantic seven-hour search across every recess of the internet led me to a seventeen-year-old called Julius Kivimäki. An infamous figure in the anarchist teenage hacking scene, he was calling himself 'Ryan'. But he would go on to have dozens of other aliases, including 'The Untouchable Hacker God' and 'Zeekill'.

As the clock ticked down to our deadline, my video editor and I anxiously waited for this teenager to come online as promised. Just in time, he called on Skype. With a smirk, public enemy number one for gamers all over the world popped up on my screen. I was shocked at how young he looked. He had a shaved head, soft facial features and deadpan eyes. He was utterly unremorseful and arrogant in manner. I did my best to hold him to account but found the experience surreal – he didn't seem to give a damn, making himself chuckle throughout the interview. Lizard Squad had decided to carry out the hacks on a whim, he said, boasting that the whole thing took him and three others about six hours to pull off. 'I can't really say I feel bad about it,' he said with a broad smile.

His arrogance was like a red rag to a bull to the cybersecurity world and the hordes of angry people who had been affected. The video racked up more than a million views on YouTube. More importantly, from my point of view, the top brass at Sky News were placated.

But that day, and that interview, sparked my now decade-long obsession with cybersecurity.

//PREFACE

Back then crime had been a major part of my beat as a general Home Affairs reporter, and I'd covered everything from murders to drug busts. But never before had I come across such brazen and boastful criminals. And never before had I interviewed someone like Julius – so nihilistic and so cocky.

I came to appreciate the power that cyber criminals can wield from their keyboards and I've been hooked on hackers ever since. I made it my business to report on every subsequent major cyber attack, first for Sky News and then in my current role at BBC News. I've been lucky enough to travel the world covering cybersecurity stories and making documentaries as the BBC's first Cyber Correspondent. I've traversed Russia in search of the world's most wanted cyber criminals. I've unmasked Ukraine's civilian hacking force. I've hung out at the Argentinian beach house of the first millionaire ethical hacker. And I've put tough questions to authorities in Saudi Arabia as they hosted a cybersecurity conference in an effort to become trusted global players in the burgeoning industry.

You can see why the Saudis want a slice. It's estimated that the cybersecurity industry is now worth $200 billion,[1] with huge growth on the horizon. Companies and consultants charge terrified organisations top dollar for the latest and greatest software to stop hackers. But time and again people fail to address one of the biggest elephants in the room. Often the culprits aren't super cyber spies. They're bored, lonely and unsupervised teenage boys who team up to cause mayhem from their bedrooms, often situated thousands of miles apart from each other and all without knowing each other's real names.

I've never met a female cyber criminal. I'm sure there are some out there, but the testosterone-filled subculture of teen hacking appears to deter girls from falling onto this dark path. For better or worse.

It's boys who rise up from the depths of the internet every few years to wreak havoc. They've been doing it since the dawn of

xi

hacking in the 1970s. What is it about teenage boys that makes them so easily attracted to a life of cybercrime and how are they able, time and time again, to fool the smartest minds in cyber? It's a cycle we've failed to stop, and each new teen gang is more serious and sinister than the last. But the 2010s period in which Lizard Squad and others were running riot also saw a dangerous and seemingly irreversible shift in the nature of this cycle.

The hackers featured in this book are now grown men. Some have served prison sentences. Some have found well-paid and respectable jobs in cybersecurity. Others are living lavish lifestyles funded by cryptocurrency that they may or may not have acquired during their hacking days. In writing about their activities, I've chosen to omit identifiable details to protect those among them who are still under the radar. Doing so is a difficult decision which I've often faced in my job, but I think it's justified to get the full stories from the horses' mouths. But one thing that quickly became evident in the process of researching the book is that this community of hackers is a vipers' nest of backstabbing and hatred. Even now when these characters are in their twenties and thirties, they remain prone to exaggeration and routinely lie about things they did and didn't do. And their readiness to argue with each other and trade nasty abuse is something I have found shocking. For the purposes of this book, I've made clear which of their various competing stories are backed up with hard evidence and which claims are just that – claims. In particular I've leaned heavily on court records to help me navigate my way through this shifting world of liars and wannabes.

Julius Kivimäki will be our focus. He is the thread that runs through so much of the period covered by the book – from 2014 through to the present day – and where he went, others have sadly followed. Through his dark story we'll learn how teenage hacking culture is shaped by young men and how it can turn innocent computer obsessives into callous cyber criminals.

//PREFACE

It's hard to find a cyber criminal quite as callous as Kivimäki. He is arguably the most hated hacker in history. Not just by the gamers he angered over Christmas 2014 but by the many other victims (including fellow hackers) he harmed along the way. In 2022, for example, eight years after I interviewed him for Sky News, he was linked to probably the most shocking cyber attack in history – the hacking of the mental health records of 33,000 people in Finland and a subsequent attempt to extort money from the victims to keep the records unpublished. Everyone in this small country of just 5.5 million people knows someone who was affected by this attack.

Some will say we shouldn't give hackers like Kivimäki any more of the attention they crave. But in these pages I hope to shine a spotlight that reveals for the first time how the stories of these wayward characters can be drawn together to tell the full picture and find the otherwise obscured patterns that might help us answer the biggest question of all – how can we stop teenage boys becoming cyber criminals?

This book is not aimed at glamorising this troubling corner of criminality – it's designed to focus an unflinching light on these immature, misguided and cruel boys and to learn lessons from their stories.

And it all starts with a stroke of luck that led French police to Julius Kivimäki in the early hours of 3 February 2023 . . .

//1
An accidental arrest
2023

It was just getting light as the patrol car rolled up the cobbled intersection to 1 Promenade Saint-Nicolas. The six-storey building wraps around a pretty little park and children's play area in Courbevoie – a leafy corner on the northern fringes of Paris. Far from any nightlife hotspots, this is a place for families and business people. 'Bustling during the day but usually peaceful at night' is how one of the residents described it to me. The alert to police came from a woman worried about a friend of hers who lived there. A group of them had been out drinking at a nightclub and her friend had had a big argument with her partner. He was angry and drunk, she told the call handler. Her friend had not been picking up her phone since they returned home and she was terrified something had happened. The police took the report seriously and turned up at the apartment shortly after the call came in at 7 a.m.

They knocked and waited in the corridor but no one answered. They knocked again and nothing. Again, and still silence. Then, according to local news reports,[1] the officers got their battering ram out and were readying to smash the door in when a young woman opened it.

She was fine. Perhaps a little hungover and upset, but any police fears of domestic violence were quickly laid to rest. They found her husband in bed and woke him up. Then, as a matter of protocol, they asked to see some ID. He dug around for his documents and handed over a passport that declared him to be a Romanian citizen called Asan Amet. It seemed an unlikely name for this six-foot-three, blond-haired, green-eyed man so one of the officers radioed the station to run some checks while the other made small talk in the apartment.

Then alarm bells rang.

The name 'Asan Amet' was flagged up as one of the fake identities used by one of Europe's most wanted criminals. This baby-faced man had been charged in Finland with 'computer-related crime, racketeering and extortion'.

Police cuffed him and led him outside to their car as residents walked past on their way to work or on the school run. Another team came to search the apartment, finding signs of a resourceful and well-connected criminal: he had two other Romanian photo ID cards under the same fake name and there were also images on his wife's phone of four other drivers' licences, each one bearing his picture but each one a fake – including one from Britain and one from Arizona.

With the fugitive in the back of their patrol car, the police drove down the narrow streets towards the River Seine. The Eiffel Tower was visible in the overcast skyline that lay ahead on the long straight road to the city centre. The officers probably couldn't wait to talk about the morning's unexpected success. The man sitting in cuffs behind them was a huge target.

His real name was Aleksanteri Julius Tomminpoika Kivimäki.

#

Some 2,600 km away in Helsinki, the silence in the offices of Finland's Cybercrime Centre was broken by four sounds in quick succession. First came the ding of a text message. Then a chuckle. Then another ding. And then an almighty shout of 'JOOOO!', which is the Finnish for 'Yeeeeees!'

AN ACCIDENTAL ARREST

The first ding was Detective Chief Inspector Marko Leponen receiving a text from a colleague informing him of the arrest. The chuckle was him laughing it off as a bad joke and sending a sarcastic reply. The second ding was the confirmation that the news was real. And that exultant 'JOOOO!' was the chirpy middle-aged cyber cop shouting out in delight. Congratulations exploded around the station. Everyone knew how hard Marko had worked over the previous couple of years to find the hacker behind the Vastaamo cyber attack. They knew too that he had been waiting for news of this arrest for months – ever since he had identified Kivimäki as the prime suspect and arranged for him to be remanded 'in absentia' on 27 October 2022.

That notice released by Helsinki District Court had been the biggest talking point of the cyber world at the time. It read: 'A European arrest warrant has been issued against the suspect. He can be arrested abroad under this warrant. After that the police will request his surrender to Finland. An Interpol notice will also be issued against the suspect, who is a Finnish citizen and about 25 years of age.'

The reason it sparked so much interest was simple: the Vastaamo cyber attack of October 2020 was one of the most impactful and cruel hacks in history – and remains so to this day. Not only did it affect 33,000 innocent and vulnerable people, including children, it exposed them to the most grotesque form of blackmail, with their therapy notes used as a bargaining chip and then callously published online for the world to see. It also destroyed a growing Finnish company that had been doing important work in mental health. Even grizzled cyber professionals who thought they'd seen it all were stunned by the incident and desperate to see the criminal brought to justice.

Although the police didn't initially name the twenty-five-year-old suspect, they didn't need to. Kivimäki AKA The Untouchable Hacker God AKA Zeekill AKA Ryan was a notorious figure with a long history of causing cyber chaos. Marko and his team had been certain he would eventually be found, but they had been forced to put their faith in the ability of foreign police forces to see through Kivimäki's bank of false identities. They couldn't believe their luck when the call came in from France so quickly.

Messages of congratulation came flooding into the Helsinki Cyber Crime centre from other police forces around the world. 'Everyone was rooting for us to get Kivimäki,' Marko recalls. He cancelled all of his other case work and scrambled a team to go to France and bring the fugitive back to Finland. They would do the lengthy and complex paperwork needed to organise the extradition while Marko and his detectives would begin working towards the most important trial of their careers and the biggest criminal case in Finland's history. No expense or police officer's time was spared. Everyone wanted to see justice done.

The anger felt by the police towards this young man long predated the Vastaamo hack. His chosen alias of The Untouchable Hacker God was all too appropriate. Kivimäki had been on the force's radar for more than ten years. He had been a serial offender since the age of thirteen. With a click of his mouse he had repeatedly disrupted the lives of millions of people and done profound harm to some individuals too. But until now he'd largely got away with it. Not only that, he had bragged about his crimes and taunted the police for years in social media posts and press interviews. This was their chance to right a wrong and put him behind bars.

A couple of days after Kivimäki's extradition from France came his opening interrogation. Seeing his quarry for the first time face to face, Marko Leponen was surprised by how polite and cooperative he was. But the interview was also extremely tense. It took place in a small room with Marko and three fellow officers facing off against Kivimäki and his lawyer. The detective had prepared for this moment mentally and been willing it to happen for months, but was still amazed that they finally had Kivimäki in custody. He could sense Kivimäki found it all strange too. 'It was very surreal.'

AN ACCIDENTAL ARREST

There's always a huge amount riding on the first interrogation of a suspect. For the detectives it is less about extracting evidence and more about building a workable connection and relationship with the accused. For that reason, Marko himself took the decision to leave the room after the first introductions had been made. He knew that he had a slim chance of building any rapport with Kivimäki because the hacker saw him as the agent of his doom; it was Marko who had been the figurehead of the Vastaamo investigation and who had arranged for him to be arrested in absentia. It was a good decision. One of his fellow detectives built up a strong connection with Kivimäki from the off. Over the course of the next eight months, that's how it worked: Marko would stay out of the room unless he was needed for a specific topic and would instead receive detailed feedback on each interview from his officers and via the recorded tapes.

The detectives called Kivimäki in from his prison cell for interviews around a dozen times, sometimes questioning him for eight hours in a day as they tried to break through his guard and find the truth. He was always polite and cooperative, but also wily and careful. He liked to talk. He seemed to enjoy discussing everything cyber and computers – but only on his terms. He had a very good memory for detail until it came to anything potentially incriminating – for example, how much money he had amassed in bitcoin. 'I can't remember' or 'I can't answer that' were his responses when Marko or others tried to press him on important details.

Marko could never work out who the real Kivimäki was under that politeness. He would skirt around subjects and avoid any outright lies with clever turns of phrase. Working out *how* Kivimäki answered became more important than what he actually said. Detectives slowly identified a pattern to his evasive language that helped them gain clues about what he was – and wasn't – lying about.

Another thing gradually became clear in Marko's mind: Kivimäki would never admit that he had committed the crime. No matter how solid the case was against him or how strong the evidence, he would never confess. And the evidence was extremely compelling thanks in large part to the way events had played out over the three chaotic days in October 2020 when the Vastaamo hack became public and shocked the world.

//2
Ransom_man strikes
October 2020

The post landed on the anonymous Finnish website Ylilauta at just after 2 a.m. on Wednesday 21 October 2020. The user ID was 114398433 – a jumble of random numbers assigned by the message board site. But the poster would quickly become known as 'ransom_man'. He posted in English:

> Hello Finnish colleagues,
> We have hacked the psychotherapy clinic 'vastaamo.fi' and taken tens of thousands of patient records including extremely sensitive session notes and social security numbers. We requested a small payment of 40 bitcoins (nothing for a company with yearly revenues close to 20 million euros), but the CEO has stopped responding to our emails. We are now starting to gradually release their patient records, 100 entries every day.
> You can view the data at http://3wnug3445ja7qj47.onion.pet/
>
> Enjoy!
>
> Press contact: vastaamopress@tutanota.com

Vastaamo's name was instantly recognisable to Finns as a safe and reliable place to go to for mental health support. It was Finland's largest commercial therapy provider and one of the crown jewels of the country's home-grown social enterprise start-ups. The company was launched in 2009 to address the shortage of mental health provision in Finland and had become extremely popular and successful. Its bright green speech bubble logo began popping up on buildings in towns and cities across the country and it grew fast to become a recognised and trusted brand. By 2020 Vastaamo had clinics in twenty-seven locations across the small nation and employed 300 people – mostly psychotherapists, psychologists and psychiatrists. As well as offering fast appointment booking and online therapy, the company provided free online services to promote mental health and prevent mental health problems, which were used annually by more than half a million Finns.

So anyone who happened to be online when ransom_man posted his threat about publishing Vastaamo's data would instantly have felt the hairs rise on the back of their neck. If they'd clicked on ransom_man's link they would have seen the innermost secrets of one hundred Vastaamo patients laid bare: multiple note entries written by therapists detailing the intimate struggles of their clients, alongside the patients' phone numbers, social security numbers and email addresses, all readable in plain text. And according to ransom_man, this was just the start.

It's not clear what sort of response the criminal was hoping for by posting his threat. Perhaps a hero's welcome. Or digital high fives. Or shocked excitement. He got none of it. Just forty-five seconds later an anonymous user replied to his thread: 'Go to shower, sleep and work in the morning. Oh and KYS.'

KYS is the internet acronym for 'kill yourself'. It's reserved for the nastiest responses on the chaotic Ylilauta message threads. It's a site where almost anything goes but even still, ransom_man must have been taken aback.

Ylilauta is a Finnish-language copy of the notorious international online cesspit 4chan – a site famous for purveying some of the most heinous and offensive conspiracy theories of recent times thanks to its almost non-existent moderation. The Finnish site calls itself an image board but most of the content is just text. People start a conversation thread and hundreds more chime in, in Finnish or English.

Somehow it's one of the most popular websites in Finland. According to the people behind it, it gets around 100 million page views a month from a dedicated 2.5 million visitors, most of whom are based in Finland. Huge for such a small country. But I would guess those numbers are over generous. Its homepage proudly states it is a 'privacy-oriented anonymous discussion board where you are free to discuss almost anything'. Sending messages requires neither registration nor a username.

'The tone on Ylilauta, as also in 4chan, is irreverent, mock-everything, everything is ironic and I am a cool edge-lord above caring,' says Finnish Urban Philosophy Professor Veikko Eranti in a research paper about the website.[1] Analysis suggests most of the site's users are young, male and often leaning to the alt-right in politics. According to Eranti's research, race, sexual assault and immigration are common themes of discussion. Users like to split the world into 'us' and the 'normies'. If you're an outsider then you must be a 'hippie' or a 'feminazi'. A scan of the homepage at the time of writing this book gives an idea of the sort of content and discussion points you can find there: homophobic slurs, transphobic labels, stories about being bullied or depressed and many many Pepe the Frog cartoons (Pepe is commonly used by the alt-right or antagonistic trolls). According to a study commissioned by the Finnish government, which took a two-month snapshot of internet usage in 2021, Ylilauta was responsible for the most hate speech across all message boards and social media in the country.[2] Of the 300,000 examples of hate speech recorded, 285,000 – or 96 per cent – of the messages were on the site.

So you'd think ransom_man's bombshell hack would have gone down well with such an anarchic community. But post after post showed that stealing the psychotherapy notes of tens of thousands of mental health patients and publishing them online was a bridge too far even for Ylilauta users. Comments cascaded under ransom_man's post in a mixture of Finnish and English.

'You could've done anything with your life and you hacked a psychotherapy clinic and posted about it on a Finnish forum for frogs. Look at your life and how pathetic it is.'

'Hide all the contact information posts, I'm not fucking interested in anyone's problems.'

'This is sensitive information for those concerned. It would piss me off if my name popped up.'

As the thread gained traction, people joined in their droves to have their say and ask questions. A few minutes into the discussion, one user posted a picture of a screaming white cat accompanied by a bizarre message in capital letters – 'ALERT WARNING ALERT WARNING ALERT WARNING' – and some nonsensical conspiracy theory about false flags and the media. No one seemed to pay any attention to it, brushing the post off as a case of so-called 'shitposting' – the practice of trying to derail the conversation thread with nonsense content.

Ransom_man tried to keep his cool and get the conversation back to his hack. He posted more information, including a screenshot of his failed negotiations with Ville Tapio, the boss of Vastaamo. 'This is how the CEO of the company feels about protecting their patient data', he wrote.

But it backfired instantly: 'How big a spinner do you have to be to demand a €400k ransom for something like this? Nobody would pay that,' came one of the responses.

The thread descended into a mixture of aggressive insults hurled at the hacker and the usual stream of random stuff that people post to get attention. The forum's users fired off critical questions asking ransom_man why he would blackmail an innocent CEO, challenging his research into Vastaamo's finances, arguing that he didn't know the difference between a company's turnover and profit. Ransom_man replied with the firm's public financial records in an attempt to win the respect of the baying online mob. He was met with insults: one user called him a 'Grade A low-level asshole'; another dismissed him as a 'script kiddie' – the ultimate insult to a hacker. It implies that the hacker has made use of pre-written off-the-shelf 'scripts' and is not talented enough to write their own hacking programmes.

Looking now at the hundreds of interactions between the hacker and his uncooperative audience, it's almost amusing to see the disdain that the Ylilauta users have for him and his need for recognition. *Almost* amusing, until you remember what is at stake here – the highly sensitive therapy records of tens of thousands of innocent and vulnerable people. Amongst all the mayhem there were a small number of users who seemed genuinely worried. 'These are my infos mate, please can you delete them?' one person pleaded.

Eventually people started reporting ransom_man's post for being evidence of criminal activity and soon the moderators of Ylilauta deleted his thread. But there was another site with fewer qualms about illegal activity.

Torilauta means 'market board' in Finnish. Before the Finnish language site was shut down later in 2020, it was the go-to place for buying and selling illegal goods like drugs. It was a so-called 'darknet' website, housed on a part of the internet that is far off the beaten track of Google, Facebook and other mainstream sites. The darknet is the portion of the internet that can only be accessed through specialist software that protects a user's identity, concealing their true location by sending their internet traffic through a series of different routers placed around the world. One such software package is called The Onion Router (Tor) and it's true that peeling back its layers of protection to find the real person surfing the darknet requires a complex and eyewatering amount of work. Interestingly Tor was created in 2002 by the US government's Naval Research Laboratory to allow US spies to use the internet without risk of identification. They needed to spread the software far and wide to make it a truly effective way for spooks to carry out their work around the world, so they gave the technology away and have continued to fund its development through the nonprofit Tor Project. Tor has been used by privacy nerds, activists and whistleblowers ever since. But it's also been a gift that keeps on giving for all sorts of criminals who use it to remain anonymous while launching websites selling all manner of illegal products and services.

Cyber criminals especially love the darknet. They routinely use it to leak, sell and extort their stolen data. Established cybercrime gangs maintain their own darknet 'leak sites' that they use to name and shame organisations they've hacked into. Once the hackers get inside an organisation they'll poke and prod around its computer network looking for valuable or incriminating data to download. Customer records or sensitive internal documents are always seized upon as they can be used as bargaining chips in the forthcoming negotiation. Sometimes the hackers will install malicious software called ransomware to scramble the company's data and make it unreadable and useless. This can often plunge modern companies back to the dark ages of using pen and paper to carry out everyday business. The hackers usually direct the victim to their darknet leak site – sometimes with a sinister note that flashes up on staff computer screens. On these sites, they begin the extortion. Small samples of the stolen data are shared next to an organisation's logo and a big red countdown timer ticks away to pile on the pressure. If the victim doesn't pay the ransom (normally in bitcoin) within the set time frame, then the hackers will publish all the data to the darknet leak site and refuse to provide the digital antidote to the ransomware poison that has scrambled the data. To pay or not to pay – that is the question so many companies around the world are faced with when they are hit by these cyber attacks.

It's all part of the everyday extortion tactics used by organised cybercrime groups. And it works. According to cybersecurity company Sophos, 46 per cent of victim organisations paid a ransom to hackers in 2023,[3] with a median payment of around $400,000 (so ransom_man had obviously done his research). The ones who don't pay have to live with the inevitable embarrassment, commercial impact and potential litigation as their details are published for all to see on the darknet leak site. The leak sites of the most prolific gangs have hundreds of victims all displayed in rows like gravestones. Not only are they free to access for other criminals, or nosy sleuths, they often come with a click number showing exactly how many times the data has been ogled over.

These gangs can be as bold and arrogant as they like on their darknet sites as there's not much the police can do to shut them down.

Ransom_man didn't have his own darknet website on which to leak and publicise the Vastaamo hack, but he correctly guessed that Torilauta was the next best thing. The site's administrators didn't give a damn about the illegality or immorality of his posts and happily kept his thread alive. Interestingly though, the users of Torilauta were equally as unfriendly to him as the Ylilauta community had been. 'What is this bullshit?' came the first response. 'Hopefully you kill yourself one day,' someone else replied. 'There is plenty of room behind the sauna for guys like you,' wrote another, referencing a Finnish euphemism used when taking animals for slaughter on a farm.

So even on a criminal darknet forum, ransom_man got a tough reception. But none of this seemed to bother him. This was never about winning favour with fellow miscreants online. Causing a monumental stink and getting attention was the plan. He wanted his threats known far and wide. He wanted to cause panic and force the otherwise uncooperative Vastaamo executives to crack and pay his ransom. Notice, for example, that he included a press contact email address at the bottom of his announcement. He wanted his extortion to make headlines. And within hours of posting on Ylilauta, Torilauta and a Finnish section of the mainstream social site Reddit, he'd succeeded.

Every newsroom in Finland scrambled to cover the story. A day later when, true to his threat, he released another hundred patient records, the outcry went international. BBC News, CNN, the *Guardian*, Associated Press, *Wired*, the *Financial Times* and many others began covering the situation. This second leak came at around 1 a.m. on 22 October. Posted under the username 'ransom_manHIbGCf', it read: 'We have still not heard back from the company, so we have released 100 more records.'

Another file – a letter – was also added to the website under the name 'oooreadme.txt'. In it once again ransom_man tried to put pressure on Vastaamo's CEO Ville Tapio to pay: 'We're not asking for much,' it said. 'Approximately 450,000 euros which is less than 10 euros per patient.' (The maths here is a bit confusing to read after the fact: in the end the total number of victims was around 33,000, but at this stage ransom_man and everyone looking at the breach had overestimated the numbers as being more like 45,000.)

There were now 200 therapy patients who had had their innermost secrets published online. Reading their records was as easy as loading up the Tor browser and typing in ransom_man's address. And many people did. Some users of Twitter (as the site was then called) ran a live thread about the situation, adding new tweets every time the story developed. It became clear that these first patients had not been chosen at random. They weren't just scraped from the top of the pile or scooped up alphabetically. The hacker had handpicked the most salacious and dramatic ones to inflict the most harm possible. Some of the patients were children.

On the Torilauta thread, some people started getting worried about their own privacy. One Vastaamo patient offered to pay ransom_man privately to delete their records. Ransom_man agreed, demanding $600 in bitcoin. It's not known if the money was sent. Another user begged him to delete their patient notes, sharing on the public message board: 'I have discussed with my therapist very private things and will literally kill myself if they are released.' Ransom_man didn't reply.

By now police and appalled cybersecurity experts from all over the world were investigating the hack and logging every move ransom_man made. Many began scratching their heads about his strange behaviour. Hand-picking patient records and choosing the worst ones was cruel and unusual – but it was also very time-consuming. Not at all the sort of thing you'd expect from a well-drilled and dispassionate hacking gang who would usually try the quickest and easiest methods of extortion and move on to the next victim if they weren't getting their own way.

Like clockwork, ransom_man posted again the next day – 23 October – just after midnight. Clearly getting angry that his plan wasn't working, he posted the Vastaamo CEO's home address alongside the next one hundred patient records. One onlooker on the Torilauta thread asked him if there were any politicians or celebrities in the published files. Ransom_man replied with a screenshot of the email addresses of six Finnish police officers. 'Hehe,' he wrote.

But later that night, at around 2 a.m., he made possibly the biggest blunder in the history of cybercrime.

#

Mikko Hypponen is the most famous cybersecurity expert in Finland and well known around the world. He's given three extremely popular TED Talks and is a major social media influencer with 230,000 followers on X. His posts and analysis on cyber issues reach global audiences. With his distinctive long blond ponytail and thin-rimmed glasses, he is the face of global cybersecurity company WithSecure – one of Finland's most successful tech firms. So naturally, when the Vastaamo hack kicked off in his native country, his phone blew up. In his semi-autobiographical book *If It's Smart It's Vulnerable*, he recounts those manic days of never-ending phone calls and press appearances. News organisations around the world and friends of friends in Finland begged to get time with him.

On that third day, Friday 23 October, he was in the green room waiting area at Finnish TV channel MTV preparing to go on set. Overnight ransom_man had published his third batch of records and people were getting extremely anxious. The news team wanted to ask Mikko what victims could do, if anything, to stop their deepest and darkest secrets from being exposed on the internet. Before his slot on the news show at 7.20 a.m. Mikko logged onto ransom_man's Tor server from his iPad and found the latest folder of a hundred more victims. But he was also surprised to see a new file called 'vastaamo.tar'.

A 'tar' file is a type that contains lots of other files, like a zip folder. What caught Mikko's attention was the size of this new file. Up to that point, the attacker had only been sharing text files of less than 100 kilobytes (KB) in size but the vastaamo.tar file was a massive 10.9 gigabytes (GB). Mikko was called onto the television set before he had a chance to delve any deeper. But all the time he was being interviewed by the concerned news presenters he was desperate to investigate and discover what the huge file could contain. What new devilry could ransom_man be up to? By the time he got back online to check the Tor link again, the file was gone. In fact, no one was able to connect to any of ransom_man's files at all after 11.45 a.m. when everything mysteriously went offline.

However, some fast-fingered people lurking on the Torilauta forum had been able to download some of it. They were surprised by what they found. After uploading the latest batch of a hundred patient records, ransom_man had helpfully put all three of the released batches into one file for easy referencing. 'There's a vastaamo.tar in the directory that you can use for a bulk download,' he said, adding a download link. But instead of only uploading the 300 patient records he had accidentally uploaded the entire stolen Vastaamo database.

Ransom_man's next (and last) post on the forum came eight hours later, presumably after a monumental bout of self-flagellation:

whoopsie :D
enjoy big tar

But his flippant post belies just how bad this was for him. Not only had he accidentally given away all his bargaining chips, he'd also inadvertently handed over a treasure trove of clues about himself to investigators. He had uploaded the entire home directory of his computer. It was like forwarding someone your entire email inbox and all the files and folders on your desktop instead of just the one email you wanted to share.

'It contained information the attacker absolutely did not want to publish: server user logs, passwords, source codes,' Mikko recalls. Vastaamo.tar included several leads and usable evidence, which made it far more likely that the hacker would be caught.

Ransom_man had one piece of luck though: his Tor server had run out of storage space so the tar file was only downloadable for one hour and forty-one minutes until the darknet website stopped working. Connecting to websites and servers via the darknet is very slow because of the way users' traffic is bounced around various parts of the world to obscure the origin of senders and receivers. With increased privacy comes what can often be a painfully slow connection. Think about the early days of the internet when it could take a full minute to load up a page. On the darknet, that's not an uncommon experience, so very few people, if any, actually managed to download the entire 10.9GB folder.

On the Torilauta thread one person said they'd only had time to download 1GB. Another said they had grabbed a paltry 16 megabytes (MB). Unfortunately for Vastaamo's victims, the patient data was contained in the first portion of the folder and, as it was only in the form of text files, it was relatively quick to download. If you'd managed to grab more than 500MB, you would have the full patient notes of all the victims. For investigators – and there were a lot of them in both the public and private sector at this stage – getting hold of as much of the tar archive as possible became the focus.

Mikko's firm, WithSecure, took an early decision not to download any of the ransom_man data. The company's Head of IT Security put out a notice to staff explicitly telling them not to access or save the files even though they were obviously professionally curious. This prohibition was made out of an abundance of caution both legally and morally, but in retrospect, Mikko thinks it was a mistake. They should have gathered as much evidence as they could to help search for answers about the hack while also ensuring that none of the patient data was ever accessed internally.

But there was another company that had quietly been investigating the Vastaamo hack long before it had hit the newsfeeds and they'd been patiently watching, waiting and hoping that ransom_man would slip up.

#

Antti Kurittu didn't believe it at first. He was sitting in front of his computer with his first cup of coffee of the day and easing himself into the cold and dark Helsinki morning when he saw the torrent of emails from colleagues. With his large curly auburn beard and bald head, Antti looks like he should be sailing the seas as a Scandi Viking, but he's far more comfortable, and equally formidable, in front of a PC as a cyber expert. Skim-reading the messages, he saw that his team at cybersecurity company Nixu were celebrating: ransom_man had messed up big time. Three days earlier they had set up an automatic scraper bot to check every hour for any new posts or file uploads from ransom_man and download them just in case something like this happened. While the team had been asleep, their bot had diligently slurped up as much of the data as it could before the server went down: around 1.1GB of the 10.9GB folder. It doesn't sound like a lot but it's one of the largest publicly known copies of vastaamo.tar. The police got a smidge more at 1.2GB. And the largest came in at 2.1GB, which was handed to police by an unnamed person or organisation who presumably had a rapid internet connection – and a lot of luck.

'What the fuck!' Antti said out loud through hurried slurps of his coffee as he clicked and scrolled his way through the tar folders. The jokes and memes flowed between his team chats as the rest of the experts celebrated a rare moment of utter stupidity from an otherwise calculating cyber criminal. More and more nuggets of gold were unearthed in the data and shared amongst the team with theories beginning to emerge about what the information could tell them about who ransom_man was.

But Antti has been investigating cybercrime long enough to be suspicious. Of EVERYTHING. He had a nagging feeling that it was all too good to be true. Slick cyber criminals can run for years fully in the public eye without ever giving away a crumb of evidence as to their locations or identities. Could this be some sort of diversion tactic or a plant to throw them off the real trail?

Such doubts, however, were slowly dissolved throughout the day as he and his team took a deep dive into vastaamo.tar. There were so many breadcrumbs leading to so many clues that this couldn't have been deliberate. 'The more I looked into it, the more it looked like a deliciously horrible OpSec failure,' he says. (OpSec is shorthand for Operational Security, which in the context of cybercrime boils down to the art of staying anonymous and therefore off the authorities' radar.)

Ransom_man had made a major OpSec mistake just three days into his public Vastaamo extortion, and had so far not made a penny for his troubles. Antti had been hoping that the criminal or criminals would mess up and was over the moon that he and his team were ready to capitalise when they did: 'I've always said that OpSec isn't hard – it's impossible, everyone makes mistakes.' But even Antti had never imagined such a magnificent self-own from the hacker.

So how was it that Antti and his team were so well prepared and in the know about the hack? Well, while the cyber world, and especially the general public, had been stunned by the unfolding Vastaamo extortion, Antti had quietly been expecting it, and dreading it. His firm had been called in by Vastaamo weeks earlier, when ransom_man had first started trying to blackmail the company directly over email. While the company executives tried to stall for time, Nixu's incident response team had been investigating how the data was stolen, whether the criminal was telling the truth about how much patient data he had, and how they could stop any further attacks.

It was on 28 September, three weeks before ransom_man published his threats online that Ville Tapio, the CEO of Vastaamo, had received the first email from the hacker. It had been a busy Monday full of meetings and Ville saw the email in the evening as he sat down to relax. As CEO of a famous company, he was used to getting spam but immediately he knew this email was different. The message was mostly written in English with some broken Finnish at the top saying: 'Good day. I'm a hacker. I have copied the Vastaamo database.' Then it read:

> I have attached a small sample of your patient database to this email. If you reply within the next 6 hours we are prepared to offer you a very special discount. Any price you'll pay us will be small compared to the damage that would be inflicted to your business if we release this information on the internet. We have over a gigabyte of your most sensitive patient data.

If you have any questions or difficulty understanding what's happening, I'm here to help.

The email was sent not just to Ville but to the two IT executives listed on the company website. Both had also seen the email and were already investigating. Ville ordered them to come to his house urgently for a meeting. Over pizza they discussed the situation and confirmed that the sample of data attached to the hacker's email was genuine. The next day, as Ville and the pair worked out what to do and how to respond, they also started looking for answers as to how the breach had happened but couldn't work it out. Then, when the hacker sent another email urging them to reply, Ville called Antti Kurittu and the team at Nixu to begin a deep search of Vastaamo's activity logs to find out how the hacker had got in.

So, weeks before ransom_man reared his ugly head online, Antti and his team had the unenviable job of trying to figure out what had happened while also keeping everything a secret, knowing the horror that would unfold if and when everything went public. Antti knew the stakes were extremely high, so before he accepted the assignment from Vastaamo he demanded Nixu be allowed to share all their findings with police, the National Cyber Security Center (NCSC) and data protection authorities. Vastaamo immediately agreed, so the first call that day was with the police and NCSC. As a former cyber police officer himself, Antti was hoping to open up a free-flowing information channel with the cops. Both sides – the private sector and public – could complement each other brilliantly, he thought. But it wasn't to be – the flow of information and updates went only in one direction. So he and his team quietly got on with their work while waiting and hoping that ransom_man wouldn't leak the patient data.

Meanwhile Vastaamo was in chaos. Daily meetings were scheduled to discuss progress with the police and the NCSC. Ville Tapio responded to the blackmailer on 30 September to ask what his demands were. A payment of 40 bitcoins – roughly 450,000 euros at the time – came the reply. The hacker again gave Ville six hours to reply. At this point the police assumed full control of the communication, setting up email accounts under Ville's name to continue the conversation. On 14 October they sent 0.01 bitcoin to the hacker's cryptocurrency wallet address. It was pitched as a test for a larger amount to be sent but was actually a tactic to aid their investigations. The police never had any intention of paying but hoped to string the hacker along to allow them to find out as much as possible about him and prepare – a common tactic in ransom negotiations. But it was of course futile.

Coincidentally, Antti's report was delivered to Vastaamo on the same day that ransom_man posted his first threat online – 21 October 2020. Nixu's verdict into how the hack happened was scathing. Vastaamo had made monumental cybersecurity mistakes. Forensic analysis showed the patient database had been breached at least twice – once in 2018 and again in 2019. Its IT defences were pitiful and Antti and his team submitted urgent recommendations for what Vastaamo should do to improve them – some of which were very basic. The report would go on to be referenced in subsequent court decisions and criminal convictions against both the company and its CEO.

As part of the agreement, the report, which was paid for by Vastaamo itself, was kept under wraps. But that didn't stop Antti and other staff at Nixu getting hounded by the press for answers and updates when the extortion went public. The company was forced to issue a press release amidst the furore. 'Nixu's task is not to look for the culprits, and Nixu has not provided Vastaamo with crisis communication services,' it politely clarified.

Even though their work was effectively done, the Nixu team remained professionally curious about the case and continued to watch and analyse every move ransom_man made. And so it was that Antti and his team quietly set up their scraper bot. Catching ransom_man was obviously not Antti's job, but like many Finns he was fired up and wanted this anonymous hacker brought to justice. One hunch grew stronger the deeper he dug into the vataamo.tar. Wherever ransom_man was in the world, Antti thought that he had probably been born in Finland. While all of ransom_man's public messages were posted in English, many things, such as where the breach was first publicised, pointed towards an intimate knowledge of the Finnish language and internet scene.

Not only that – one name kept creeping into Antti's mind over and over again – Julius Kivimäki. He knew Kivimäki all too well. Before working for Nixu, Antti had led a criminal investigation into the talented and prolific young hacker, but he tried to silence that voice in his head. It couldn't be Julius. It was too obvious.

#

Across the city on that same morning Marko Leponen was in a race against ransom_man.

His officers were a few steps ahead of Antti, and his team had worked from the early hours to mine the giant tar folder for information. They struck gold by finding an IP address for a server that ransom_man was using. An IP or 'Internet Protocol' address is a unique numerical identifier for a device on the internet that also contains information on the device's physical location.

Amazingly, the IP address for ransom_man's server led to a hosting company about a thirty-minute drive from the police station. Hosting companies rent out computers as servers that can be used for the remote storage of data in the same way that your own computer files can be stored on Google Drive or Apple's iCloud. This particular hosting company had been paid a monthly fee by ransom_man to host whatever content he wanted to save. Quickly Marko's team was able to identify which server was owned by the criminal and get some basic details on its size. It was a monster. Where vastaamo.tar was 10.9GB, this server contained hundreds of thousands of gigabytes of data. But ransom_man knew that police would be following his trail so he had already started deleting files fast.

Marko had to act quickly or miss the chance to gather potentially crucial evidence. He dispatched one team by car to go and physically seize the server and ordered another to get the hosting company on the phone as quickly as possible. The hosting company, unaware that they had played a part in this major cyber criminal enterprise, were shocked by the police call but sprang into action. An engineer ran across the warehouse through shelves stacked to the rafters with noisy servers all busily whirring through various tasks for customers around the world. He located the computer being rented by ransom_man, took it off the shelf and unplugged its internet cable to cut it off from the outside world. At 11.45 a.m. ransom_man was disconnected. He was like a cornered drug dealer unable to flush any more of his cocaine down the toilet. Marko's officers arrived minutes later to seize the computer. The evidence was secured and there was nothing the hacker could do about it, wherever he was in the world.

Unfortunately, someone (Marko still doesn't know who) also pulled out the server's power lead. This triggered a booby trap left by ransom_man, which automatically scrambled everything on the computer. Marko was briefly devastated – encrypted files are impossible to read unless you have the key to unscramble them. But the panic was short lived: the vastaamo.tar folder – the gift that kept on giving – also contained ransom_man's key to reverse the encryption process. So, with the computer safely back at the cyber lab, Marko's team was able to use the key to decrypt most of the remaining data.

What was inside the servers turned out to be invaluable. It turbo-charged Marko's case and led to some of the most important pieces of evidence against ransom_man. But Marko is sure that he and his team would have still caught ransom_man even without his giant slip-up. 'The thing about cyber criminals is that we often think they are masterminds of everything. In my experience they are masterminds when they carry out their hacks, yes – but not masterminds in operational security. It's hard to cover your tracks.'

With ransom_man's server in custody and Marko's team dissecting it for further evidence, Marko could finally breathe a sigh of relief. The three days since the hack had gone online had been exhausting and public pressure to deal with the case had been immense. Now he'd had a breakthrough and couldn't help but smile and start to relax. Until his phone rang, bringing him crashing back down to earth and reminding him of the bigger picture.

'Detective, please help, I'm one of the victims and my records are on the internet. What can I do?' the caller said, in tears. Marko tried his best to comfort them, even though the bitter truth was that it was too late. 'I felt utterly helpless in that moment because there was nothing I could do. I couldn't help them, but I also didn't want to be completely honest and tell them that their data is gone now and will be on the internet forever.' The lives of 33,000 people were about to be ripped apart on the internet and there was nothing Marko could do to stop it. He hung up and tried to get his head back into the case. But then came another call. Another victim. Then another. And another. Marko realised that somehow his phone number had been leaked online. Over the next few days the calls kept coming:

'What am I going to do when my husband finds out what I told my therapist? My marriage is going to fall apart.'

'What can I do to stop my work colleagues finding out what I said about them?'

Marko did his best to reassure and calm down as many people as he could. The emotional burden of hearing from distraught victims and not being able to offer any answers caused him to break down and cry himself. He stopped answering calls and got a new phone number. Before he switched SIM cards he estimates he had received more than 200 phone calls.

He hunkered down with his team and took a step back from press interviews and conferences.

But ransom_man wasn't done with inflicting pain yet. His next move, which came only hours after his big mistake, was one of the most shocking in the history of cybercrime.

//3
I got the email
2020

It's estimated that there are 3 million saunas in Finland. Not bad for a country of only 5.5 million people. They are everywhere – in homes, garages, outhouses, gyms, leisure centres and even government buildings. Some think this helps explain why in 2024, for the seventh year running, Finland was deemed the world's happiest country by the World Happiness Report. As the *Economist* jokingly put it, the real reason the country is so content is that 'the Finns sweat out their negative thoughts'.[1]

Traditionally, Saturday night is sauna night. And throughout this particular Saturday in October 2020 Tiina Parikka had been looking forward to sweating out her worries in her home sauna. As the principal of the Finnish School of Watchmaking – a prestigious academy offering degrees to watchmakers and micromechanics – life was always hectic for this middle-aged woman with warm eyes and bobbed blonde hair. But the latest wave of the Covid-19 pandemic was sweeping through the country, and the school had had its first confirmed case of the virus on campus that day. Tiina had therefore spent her Saturday organising contact tracing, putting in place more stringent social distancing measures and deep cleaning the labs. But, by late in the evening she'd done everything she could, and was finally able to climb into the sauna with her husband to relax.

Cooling off in her bathrobe afterwards she checked her emails, only to feel all the warmth and relaxation in her body drain immediately away. She had received a chilling message from ransom_man:

> Dear Mrs Parikka,
>
> As you probably already know from the news, we have hacked into the medical records of Vastaamo, we are contacting you because you have used the therapy and/or psychiatric services of Vastaamo. As the management of this company has refused to take responsibility for its own mistakes, we regrettably have to ask you to pay to keep your personal data safe. Please follow the instructions below to send bitcoins to our address. If we receive €200 worth of bitcoins within 24 hours, your data will be permanently deleted from our servers. If we do not receive this payment within 24 hours, you will have another 48 hours to acquire and send us €500 worth of bitcoins. If we do not receive our money even after this period, your details will be made available for all to see, including your name, address, telephone number, social security number, and your detailed medical history, including transcripts of your conversations with a therapist/psychiatrist at the Vastaamo.

The email ended with detailed instructions on how to buy and send bitcoin using a Finnish bitcoin exchange service. Bitcoin has, for a long time, been the payment method of choice for cyber criminals. It's a bankless form of money. Anyone can send bitcoins from one digital wallet to another without the need for financial authorities getting involved with all their pesky due diligence and anti-money-laundering checks. In fact, once you have figured out the process, sending bitcoin is almost as easy as sending someone an email. First you need to sign up to an exchange website where you can purchase bitcoin using any traditional currency such as euros, dollars or rupees. Then you need to set up a digital wallet in which to store your bitcoin. Once that is done you can send that bitcoin to anyone as long as you have their unique wallet address, which is made up of a long jumble of random numbers and letters. For cyber criminals this whole process is a walk in the park, but ransom_man knew that most of his victims would find it daunting. Clearly, he wanted to make it as easy as possible for people like Tiina to pay up so he went to the trouble of including detailed instructions.

He also wanted Tiina to know this was real, so he included her personal details and social security number in the email. The realisation of what she was reading hit Tiina like a wave. Quickly she did a mental audit of what this anonymous blackmailer now had in his or her possession. Once a week for the last two years Tiina had visited her Vastaamo therapist to talk through her challenges in intimate detail. She had developed a strong relationship with her therapist and had spoken candidly about the divorce that had ended her first marriage. She had described the sometimes unbearable stress and work involved in caring for her four children, two of whom have severe disabilities. She had outlined the difficulties of her demanding job and her troubles with anxiety and panic attacks. Tiina thought of the psychotherapist's pen scribbling away while she had talked through the darkest moments in her life. 'I've never been raped, but it felt like a kind of psychological rape in a way. Somebody had invaded my really private world and said: "I'm going to make money with your feelings and all the trauma you've had."' She had an immediate and physical reaction. Her heart began beating uncomfortably fast as the familiar, but almost forgotten, feeling of a panic attack began to overwhelm her. Her husband came to help and stayed with her while she called the police but to their surprise the officers said they couldn't help as the case was not urgent and they had to keep the line open for victims of other crimes. Tiina felt completely alone.

But as a victim, Tiina wasn't alone. Far from it. Ransom_man had in fact sent out personalised extortion emails to every one of the 27,966 victims who had an email address registered with Vastaamo.

#

Anyone who has had therapy knows that the keystone of successful treatment is the trust between the therapist and the client. According to Finnish psychologist Dr Heidi Toivonen, this trust has two main components: a feeling that the therapist is genuinely here to help and a belief that whatever is said is confidential. Without these building blocks, there is no therapy in any real meaning of the word. 'You cannot access and formulate your innermost feelings and the most sensitive, shame-inducing, sad, crazy, angry and difficult thoughts and feelings without knowing that the therapist is holding a secure base for you and is ultimately on your side, like the mother or father figure that many therapy clients never had,' she says.

So, as a therapist herself, Heidi had a unique perspective when she too received an email from ransom_man. It was late on that same Saturday night when she opened up her laptop while watching TV with her partner Francesco. Heidi is an expert communicator thanks to her job and is usually a cheerful woman with busy and expressive features. As she read the email she at first froze in silence. She felt threatened, scared, vulnerable and exposed. But after a while, her fear turned to rage.

Heidi had only been to Vastaamo once. She had gone a few years earlier to talk through her anxiety about being single and not being able to find love. She had poured her heart out hoping to create a connection with the therapist but sadly they hadn't clicked. Heidi had moved on and thought nothing more of the session until she received the email. Reading ransom_man's message felt like being burgled. Like discovering that her home had been ransacked by an anonymous thief. Her partner instantly started trying to help her and they both frantically searched the internet for information about the hack. They soon discovered just how widespread the extortion was. As an IT expert himself, Francesco advised her not to pay the ransom but to cancel all her bank cards and call the police. After a stressful night of fear-fuelled admin, she wrote a blog post under the title:

'I Was Hacked – My Vastaamo Data Breach Story'. The rage behind her words is palpable: 'What I would like to say to this pathetic slime lurking somewhere in his musty garage and hoping he would have a girlfriend and a job: Go fuck yourself.' She then continued:

> Dear Hacker and Dear Extortionist, it is completely against my nature to hope anything bad to anyone, but I do hope that you get to seed what you sow and that both the earthly justice and the unearthly logic of karma do us all a favor. In my imagination, karma setting the records straight is you having a taste of your own medicine: Having your most embarrassing fantasies and fears ripped out of your subconscious and exposed publicly, visible for all of us. Feeling in your bones the terror of such a prospect, laying awake in the night thinking what could be your worst secret you don't want to go public and then seeing a sweaty, tormented nightmare where you are running around the city completely naked.

Heidi had no expectation that ransom_man would read it. Her post was about opening up and encouraging other victims not to feel any shame or stigma during this initial period when news of the hack was provoking a sense of national shock. As Heidi described it – 'a wave of disbelief, rage and disdain washed over Finland'. If you hadn't already heard about the Vastaamo hack, ransom_man's decision to reach directly into the inboxes of victims lit the touchpaper on the story. The cyber incident quickly went from shocking to unimaginable.

Data breaches and extortion were obviously nothing new in 2020. A cyber attack that targeted the field of medical care, however, was quite rare. There had been cases of hospitals being impacted – as in the 2017 WannaCry hack which knocked hundreds of computers offline across the UK health service. That incident remains one of the most serious ever. But the hackers in that case (thought to be from

North Korea) didn't deliberately target hospitals and it was doctors and nurses who bore the brunt of the mayhem, not patients.

There aren't many rules in the callous cybercrime underworld but some of the biggest gangs made a point of stating on their websites that they wouldn't target medical facilities, especially during the coronavirus pandemic. Yes, you could see this as a hint of some underlying humanity, but it was also a pragmatic approach aimed at protecting themselves. Hacking a hospital could genuinely lead to deaths, and law enforcement is far more likely to come after you if you have something like that on your rap sheet. A month before the Vaastamo hack, for example, there had been an attack on a hospital in the German city of Düsseldorf that shows just how serious such an incident can be. A ransomware gang had heavily disrupted all the computers and internet-connected devices in the hospital, forcing it to stop providing emergency care. Incoming patients, including a seventy-eight-year-old woman, were redirected to the nearest hospital, which lay some 30 kilometres away. The chaos delayed her care and she died from an aortic aneurysm.[2] There was intense speculation that this might prove to be the first ever case of a death being directly caused by a cyber attack but local prosecutors were eventually unable to prove causality. But it's notable that even this rare case of an attack on a hospital was a mistake. The hackers had meant to target a nearby university instead. As soon as the hospital contacted the hackers, the criminals apologised and sent the software needed to reverse the attack.

So the Vastaamo hack was seen as a new nadir in cybercrime. Not only did it cut to the core of a sensitive area – mental health – it was also one of the first cases of a hacker blackmailing patients directly with their stolen records. The only case that came close to this had occurred a few months earlier in January 2020 when a couple of dozen patients at a US cosmetic surgery clinic had been contacted by hackers who had stolen their notes.[3] Vastaamo was on another level in terms of scale, sensitivity and cruelty. 'Never have we seen outrage about a cybercrime at such a level,' wrote cybersecurity company Malwarebytes of the blackmailing.

News of the personal emails sent by ransom_man spread rapidly on social media that Saturday night. Some people were panicking and looking for advice, while others were expressing their shock at this latest twist. Former Member of Parliament Kirsi Piha was one of the first to share that she had received the blackmail letter. At around 9 p.m. she posted about it on Twitter with a defiant comment to the hacker: 'Fuck you! There is never any shame in asking for help.'[4] The post quickly spread with other users on the site cheering on her bravery.

At 11 p.m. a sympathetic Twitter user called Anttï Vesala sent a tweet in Finnish that translates as:

> A challenge for everyone! If I somewhere come across material from the #vastaamo data breach, I promise I won't read it. I don't want to know what someone I know or don't know has said in therapy or that they've been in therapy in general.[5]

In an immediate reply another user coined the hashtag '#lukemattomuushaaste', which is Finnish for '#donotread'. It quickly caught on and overnight morphed into '#enlue' and '#enjaa' which mean much the same thing – 'I do not read' and 'I do not share'. Hundreds of people – influencers, charities, politicians and brands – posted the message in sympathy on Twitter, Instagram and elsewhere. The charity 'Protect Children' tweeted a picture of a child's hand holding a green heart with the message: 'When private information is spreading online, it's important to remember that you haven't done anything wrong and the shame belongs to the perpetrator, not the victim. #vastaamo #enlue #enjaa.'

UNICEF Finland warned on Instagram that the hack could be spreading fear in children and young people who had received help from therapy. They emphasised that seeking help is always to be encouraged, and that 'being blackmailed with private information is pathetic – Let's not let this crisis break trust in important mental health work. #EnLue #EnJaa.' A picture of two people hugging with the hashtags superimposed on the wall behind them was posted by a university student service, with a message urging people who come across any leaked patient notes to report it to the police. But for every defiant and caring post there were thousands of desperate people suffering in silence.

#

Antti Laulajainen has been in cybersecurity for twenty years. A softly spoken and shy man with a big wiry grey beard, a bald crown and grey hair around his temples, he has always been extremely careful to protect his personal data. He insists on talking to his family on the ultra-private app Signal, has separate phones for work and home, and actively opts out of having his address listed on public records. So, when he saw the blackmail email, he initially thought it was just the work of a spammer. Perhaps someone trying to capitalise on the data breach story that had been on the news with a well-timed 'phishing' email. (Phishing is a common technique designed to trick or scare people into clicking on a dodgy website link or downloading a booby-trapped attachment.) But then Antti recognised his own private details in the text and slowly it dawned on him that this must be real. An anonymous cyber criminal – the kind that Antti had worked hard to protect himself and others from – now had a huge amount of power over him. He was in total disbelief. He had found it stressful enough in the past to have his credit cards stolen, but his mental health records were an entirely different thing. 'I'm a professional and it is my job to tell everybody how they should protect their privacy, but now this has happened to me,' he thought with an unnecessary bout of shame.

Antti immediately started the arduous process of trying to protect his bank accounts and apply for credit checks. It's an infuriating task for most people but all the more painful for someone who had always been so careful about such matters. However much he tried to calm down, distracting himself by watching a documentary with his wife, the anger grew inside him. Vastaamo and this hacker had destroyed his right to privacy. He had no intention of paying up, but he knew the hard truth – his data had been taken and was probably all over the internet already. There was a party in the apartment next door and as the night went on and the *thud thud* of the music filled his ears he became further enraged. He stormed out of his apartment and hammered on his neighbour's front door with his fist, accidentally punching a small nail left in the door after the previous year's Christmas decorations had been taken down. His hand started bleeding, snapping him out of his rage. He went to bed mortified, vowing to apologise to his neighbours in the morning.

Antti has had depression on and off for years and therapy has been a vital part of his life. He struggles in crowded places and with strangers, opting to stay in his house as much as he can. He had been to Vastaamo only twice to get treatment for work-related stress while on sick leave with depression. He had bared all to his therapist, telling her about the internal politics of the parliamentary IT team he worked for, the blazing rows people had had in the office and how his mental health breakdown had affected his marriage. It was the fact that he had mentioned his wife that upset him the most. She too was now a victim of this. The intimate details of their private lives were in the hands of an anonymous hacker and who knows who else. The genie was out of the bottle and there was nothing he could do.

By mid-morning on Sunday 25 October Finland's politicians had been spurred into action. Public statements of disgust came thick and fast. Interior minister Maria Ohisalo said she was summoning key Cabinet members into an emergency meeting and described the situation as 'shocking and very serious', vowing to provide speedy crisis help to victims. The president of Finland, Sauli Niinistö, called the blackmailing cruel and repulsive.

In the next forty-eight hours Sanna Marin, then the world's youngest prime minister, assembled a late-night roundtable with police and cyber experts to discuss the government's response. Pictures of the meeting posted online show the prime minister and her officials in medical masks practising social distancing (a reminder that all of this was taking place in the pandemic-stricken year of 2020). They are sitting around a large table in the circular government chamber under a giant screen showing digital folders and evidence of the hack. 'Everyone has the right to privacy,' she posted on Twitter in a message with the pictures, adding the hashtags '#enlue #enjaa'. The government reiterated its promise to provide victims with all the support they needed.

But as the days passed it became clear it wasn't enough.

#

'We were completely on our own,' says Salla (not her real name).

Salla was a shop assistant from Vantaa and the mum of two young teens. She had been having therapy for nearly three years at Vastaamo to help her come to terms with a difficult childhood beset with alcoholism and physical abuse. She first heard about the hack on Wednesday 21 October when it came up as a bulletin on the staff-room radio while she was on her lunchbreak. Falling back on her usual defence mechanism, Salla made a joke of it all to her colleagues: 'I feel sorry for anyone who reads my therapy notes – they'll need to have therapy after that!' But once the laughter died down her internal dread began to grow, as she wondered what would happen next. She tried to ignore the emails from Vastaamo warning her that she might be one of the patients affected, but became increasingly anxious the following Saturday afternoon when she saw some of the early reports of people receiving direct ransom emails. Then, after her Saturday night sauna, she checked her laptop and there it was – ransom_man's blackmail message.

'I wanted to throw the laptop across the room,' she says. 'I felt that if I could get rid of the laptop then it would all just go away.' She was shaking and too scared to read the email so her husband had to come in and help. Her mind went into defence mode. This is not real, this is not happening, she thought. And for a while at least, denial worked for her. The initial admin of dealing with the practicalities meant she had a long list of things to fix as quickly as possible to try to protect herself. She had to get a credit ban on her bank accounts in case someone used her details to take out a loan. She had to put in place change-of-address protection and switch up all her passwords. There was an endless list of things the internet was telling her to do that kept her too busy to really let it all sink in. But once the list was all ticked off, she broke down. 'I just couldn't stop crying,' she says. It triggered a bout of post-traumatic stress disorder that she is still dealing with to this day.

As the wave of sadness and shock swept over her, Salla realised it wasn't herself that she was most worried about. Like Antti, it was the potential impact on her family that cut deepest. She didn't know what kinds of details were contained in the many pages of session notes that Vastaamo had, and she was terrified that there might be something in there that would upset her children or other members of her family. Thankfully, her employer was very compassionate and gave her a week of sick leave. Her doctor was less sympathetic, unable to understand what the fuss was about. 'I wouldn't really mind if my data leaked as I've got nothing to hide,' he told her. She was prescribed some beta blockers and sent home. The police told her to call helplines that had been set up for victims. But getting through was difficult.

Vastaamo put out daily information bulletins but by Sunday evening the company admitted that its helplines had become overwhelmed and its staff were under a huge amount of pressure. To ease the congestion, the company announced that it had opened a separate crisis telephone number and thrown more staff into the fold.

At one stage, the firm said the crisis hotline was being manned by the 'strength of all of our employees'.

The police too were inundated and put up a notice in which Marko Leponen advised people not to pay the ransom and urged victims not to call the police emergency number. 'The emergency centre cannot help in this matter, and related calls burden the emergency centre,' the notice read.

'I don't think the national health system had ever even thought about having to handle cybercrime victims, especially this number,' Salla says. 'These aren't seen as normal crimes because they do not happen in the real world and you are not left with physical wounds to tend to.'

While the wheels of the establishment struggled to get into gear, other sections of society revved up and proved extremely valuable to victims. Cybersecurity experts and journalists led the efforts to get information and advice to people. One reporter in particular has been named by some victims as offering a vital lifeline during this time.

#

Laura Halminen was in the aisles of a military leftover store in Hämeenlinna, about an hour's drive out of Helsinki, when she first saw the news on Wednesday 21 October. Her fiancé was helping his eighteen-year-old son do some shopping, and as Laura wasn't busy that day she had tagged along. After watching them debate the pros and cons of various camouflage outfits for a while, she got her phone out to pass the time and saw that Vastaamo had been breached and the hacker had begun releasing data on the forums. Finnish-speaking social media was lighting up as people panicked and experts and journalists scrambled to find out more. Halminen was a reporter for *Helsingin Sanomat* (known as *HS*), the largest subscription newspaper in Finland and the Nordic countries. But her brief was to cover foreign news, so she decided to stay out of the story and put her phone away to get back to the shopping. But on the journey home she kept reading about it and found herself increasingly drawn in. Halminen had covered lots of stories about hackers and cyber espionage, so she was particularly interested in the topic. When she got home, she dived into the case, spending the next few days digging up as much as she could from her contacts in the cyber world and tweeting her findings out to grateful victims desperate for information. But she held off filing any official news stories at first, conscious that it was a mainly domestic story and so not her beat. But when ransom_man began releasing batches of records on his darknet server, the more she felt awful for the victims who were struggling to find out whether their records were among them.

'Customers weren't able to reach Vastaamo and get answers from them. People were growing more worried, and many didn't have the skills or knowledge of using the darknet,' she says. People started asking her on Twitter and by email how they could find out if their details had been shared, so Laura offered to search for their names in ransom_man's leaks. She asked for people to send their full names by private direct message on Twitter. Once she had a name she did a simple CTRL+F search and was able to provide people with a yes or a no without opening the actual files that contained the patient information. With ethics front and centre of her mind Laura spoke to her boss and followed a strict protocol of doing the search only, never clicking in to read the notes: 'All I could do was tell them that I will not study their information apart from the name they provide.' She helped dozens of victims in this way. She put each name in the search box, pressed enter and held her breath. The hardest part was when a result came back as positive. She would then have to break it to the victim as gently as possible. 'I tried my best to comfort them but I kept asking myself "What now? What can these poor people do?"' Although she never looked into their notes, some people openly volunteered information about themselves so she had an idea of how much they were struggling and how vulnerable they were. Childhood sexual abuse, divorce and depression were all mentioned.

Laura became increasingly frustrated that the victims weren't being given real and practical advice, so she made a to-do list and shared it on Twitter and Facebook. It consisted of twelve topics like filing a criminal complaint, increasing the cybersecurity of your online accounts, protecting your telephone and address information and even how to check if your home insurance would cover any costs relating to identity theft. She also spent a while thinking about mental resilience. For that she urged victims to 'perform a psychological practice in which they would argue to themselves why they could not be hurt by the hack'. Her posts were very popular and shared widely on Finnish social media. Within hours news organisations published their own versions.

By the fourth day – the Saturday when ransom_man sent his email message directly to patients – Laura had been called in by her newsdesk to work on the Vastaamo story full time. That was the day she decided to write a commentary piece as a way to channel the anger of the victims – and herself – at the lack of help being offered. As one of her friends said to her: 'If this was a "real-life" national catastrophe with even a tenth of this number of victims, we'd have all churches running extra services and crisis workers working overtime and providing their services free 24/7, but when it's a digital national-level catastrophe there's hardly any help.'

That friend was a 'white-hat' hacker – a term used to describe someone who hacks things in an ethical way and works to thwart the criminal 'black-hat' hackers. White hats are usually hackers who could have used their skills to go down a dark path but steered clear thanks to their strong moral compasses. They are typically extremely online people with strong and loud opinions about the good and evils of life on the internet. They were also some of the first people to hear about the attack and the shock of it immediately galvanised them as a community. Sometimes white hats quietly and begrudgingly tip their caps to black-hat activity if a cyber attack is highly technical or creative. The Vastaamo hack was neither. It was a horrible and cruel example of the worst type of abuse of the power that hackers can wield over society. The white hats of Finland and beyond came out in their droves. 'Everyone was working towards two mutual goals: catching the extortionist and protecting the victims,' Laura says.

For her it was a frantic time, but seeing the efforts of volunteers was also heartwarming, even beautiful. That was until she tried to call a government official. Wanting to write an opinion piece about the disparity between the response to a mass digital crime versus a mass physical one, she wanted to get a comment from Finland's Minister of Health and Social Affairs. But when she called the minister's assistant on his work mobile, she found that he had switched it off. Laura was enraged. 'I'd just spent my free days drowning in direct messages from victims and white hats who were chasing that sleazebag of a hacker and wanted to help people understand what was happening. There were tens of thousands of victims and the minister's assistant didn't even take a call to pass on to his boss,' she says. Even now, years later, Laura is still angry and disappointed by the authorities' actions.

Laura published her article later in the day on Saturday 24 October, under a headline that ran: 'Vastaamo breach is a national-level catastrophe event from the digital world, but where are all the comforting church services and crisis workers now?' About an hour or two later, she saw that ransom_man had begun his email extortion campaign. Things had taken a steep turn for the worse. Perhaps it was a coincidence of timing but her article, plus this new twist, led to a dramatic change in the way the hack was treated. Ministers suddenly seemed to swing into action with more than just words. Laura also received a private message on Twitter from a priest who had been touched by her article and had opened up his church as a 24/7 crisis centre.

But for some people the horror and personal tragedy was too great to bear.

Jenni Raiskio is a lawyer who represents almost 4,000 of the Vastaamo victims. When I asked her how bad the hack had been for the most vulnerable of them she replied with one word: 'Suicide'. Relatives of some victims have reported that their loved ones killed themselves when all of the records were published, and at least two suicides have been loosely linked to Vastaamo by Jenni and her team although no further details have been given. 'Of course these individuals had problems before, but was the hack the thing that forced them to do it? Was this the breaking point?' she said.

Raiskio has a unique insight into the breadth of the hack's impact and how it affected people in completely different ways. Some Vastaamo patients had records that only contained a few lines or just vague notes and so were able to shrug off the breach. Others had binders' worth of detailed therapy summaries. Everything was discussed in Vastaamo sessions. Conflicts at work, sexual problems, extramarital affairs, family secrets. Some notes also covered rape, rape fantasies, paedophilia and confessions of crime. All the notes contained the client's full names and contact details. One victim had to go into hiding to protect their family as they had discussed details of organised crime. According to Raiskio, there are people who now feel as if they are stuck in their jobs because they are afraid of what a potential new employer might find if they search for their name on the internet. 'Every day they go to the coffee room and wonder, "Who knows about my secrets?"' Raiskio said.

Salla has not been able to work since everything collapsed for her. She has developed an understandable fear of giving companies her information over the internet. All modern life is online but she struggles to share even basic details, worrying where the data might end up. She is hypersensitive to the threat of hackers and is now obsessively learning about cybersecurity to help protect herself, even enrolling to study IT at university as a mature student. But even that has come with difficulty. The first time her class was taught about tar files she had a panic attack and had to excuse herself from the room.

I GOT THE EMAIL

#

A total of 27,966 victims received ransom_man's email. If all of them had paid the 200 euros he demanded, it would have amounted to a major pay day of well over half a million euros. And that doesn't take into account the fact that he increased the ransom to 500 euros for anyone who failed to pay up within twenty-four hours – a form of social engineering common to cybercrime that is designed to increase the pressure on victims. Of course ransom_man knew that getting everyone, or even most people, to bend to his will was unlikely. But he didn't need everyone to pay. All mass extortions are a numbers game. You just need to scare a decent chunk of people to get a substantial amount.

Cybersecurity expert Mikko Hypponen has more insight than most into how many people paid the ransom. The morning after the blackmail emails were sent, he had already started collecting the emails that victims had forwarded him to ask for advice. One of them asked what the quickest way would be to pay the ransom. He explained that the data was already on the internet and likely impossible to contain, but the young man was so desperate that he wanted to pay anyway. Mikko talked him through the process and the young man converted his 200 euros into bitcoin on an exchange website. According to Bitbo calculator – an online tool for identifying the value of this volatile form of digital currency at any given point in the past – 200 euros would have bought him around 0.018 bitcoin in October 2020 (one bitcoin was worth around 10,000 euros back then).

The young man sent the money to ransom_man's digital wallet and hoped it would be the end of his nightmare. Mikko checked the public blockchain records using the wallet address ransom_man had given the victim and sure enough – the bitcoin had arrived.

Mikko had a few other people contact him with their ransom emails and he noticed that each one had been given a unique bitcoin wallet address. 'This hacker knows what they're doing with crypto,' he thought. Setting up slightly tweaked emails for tens of thousands of people is not that difficult, but creating more than 27,966 brand new bitcoin wallet addresses requires good knowledge of cryptocurrencies.

Creating one bitcoin wallet is pretty straightforward. Most exchanges do it for you when you first buy bitcoin. It's almost as simple as starting up an account with a social network. You end up with a long jumble of numbers and letters which is your unique wallet address. For example: bc1qtxhwythmu654vek57x4ehdkr7d7d5nv99ftc7r

It looks like a meaningless code but if you enter it into a website that tracks the blockchain it can tell you exactly how much is inside the wallet and where the money has come from. Making one for every victim was a smart move by ransom_man as it meant he could easily identify each person who paid. It also made it much harder, nearly impossible in fact, for cyber investigators to track the money. They would need to get hold of every single unique wallet address to see if the money had been sent and then find out where those funds had been transferred on to – a huge task that would require all victims to cooperate.

But Mikko was determined to try to trace as much of the money as he could. So on 28 October – four days after the blackmail emails had been sent – he took to his 230,000 Twitter followers and asked for help. 'Message to #Vastaamo data breach victims,' he wrote in English, then switched to Finnish to ask anyone who had paid the ransom to send him the email they had received so that he could collect wallet addresses. 'We are trying to trace where the money went,' he explained. His tweet went viral with more than 1,200 retweets and the project made national news in Finland and was shared worldwide by the cybersecurity community.

Based on all the bitcoin wallet addresses that were shared with him, Mikko knows of eighteen victims who paid the ransom. Court papers would later put this figure at twenty but Mikko believes the true number is higher, since both he and the police were reliant on people self-reporting that they had gone against official advice. One nineteen-year-old girl contacted him, ashamed and scared to tell him that she had paid despite seeing him counsel against it in a TV interview. Mikko says he would never judge someone for paying in that horrendous situation.

However, overall, the number of people who paid is still thought to be low. Dozens not hundreds. As well as the ethical reasons not to pay a blackmailing criminal, there were other more practical reasons that so few people paid. Firstly, the police asked the Finnish cryptocurrency exchange Bittiraha – the exchange that ransom_man himself had told victims to use – to block payments. In an unprecedented and controversial move the exchange apparently agreed.[6] But staff at the company had a quandary. They couldn't stop people from sending money to ransom_man's wallet addresses as they didn't know all of them. Instead they took the blunt but effective approach of banning anyone from sending sums of either 200 or 500 euros of bitcoin to any address for that period of time. If someone tried to do so, they would get a pop-up message saying: 'You've asked to send this specific amount of money which is exactly the same amount of money requested by the Vastaamo attacker. According to the police we don't recommend paying. We are not going to send the money unless you get in touch and tell us you really want to send the money. We don't recommend that you pay.'

It sounds sensible and no doubt some victims were ultimately grateful for this intervention. But it remains a controversial decision. The whole ethos of cryptocurrency is that it's peer to peer – anyone should be free to send money across the internet without the interference of financial institutions. Stopping one person from sending crypto to another is tantamount to treason to die-hard crypto believers.

Mikko told reporters that he knew of around fifty people in total who tried to pay the ransom but had their transfers blocked by the crypto exchange. He doesn't know if they found another way to get the money to ransom_man.

Mikko thinks the second reason so few people paid is that many victims would have known it was too late – anyone who searched online for what to do would have seen that ransom_man had already accidentally released the data. As Mikko says, 'the worst part is that these people who were so desperate and paid the ransom did it for nothing.' In fact, their records had already been copied, shared and published to multiple websites on the darknet amongst hackers and criminals who wanted to boast, score points or pick through the notes for salacious gossip.

One white-hat hacker called Jesse Rasimus had been watching the whole tragedy unfold from his home computer, staying up late into the night from day one to track ransom_man's activity. He was actually on the darknet site Torilauta when the first post popped up about the hack. He watched the database get thrown around and picked apart by other hackers who seemed to compete as to who could be the nastiest. 'It felt like they were trying to be as mean as possible. There were some police who were Vastaamo customers and obviously, these people aren't the biggest fans of police so they tried to make their life as difficult as possible,' Jesse says. One of the worst moments for him came when someone built a website on the mainstream internet which allowed people to search by names. Within a few clicks, and with no knowledge of the darknet, anyone could search for their friends, family, colleagues, teachers or any public figure to see if their notes had been hacked. Jesse investigated the site to try to find out who had built it and get it taken down, but discovered that someone else had managed to do so already.

But the Vastaamo database itself is still very much online. It's surprisingly easy to find without the need to venture into the darknet. I found it on one easily accessible hacker forum on the mainstream internet and had professional cybersecurity investigator Amir Hadžipašić verify that the data was definitely from the 2020 hack. He also found the data being discussed and potentially shared on two other hacker spaces. 'It's pretty normal for leaked databases to be recycled and rehosted on data-leak sharing forums. If a data leak has any level of interest or curiosity factor then it may have value,' he says. Amir said the database is being given away for a small fee linked to credits that cyber criminals can earn or buy on these websites. None of the money is going back to ransom_man.

So, despite inflicting untold suffering with his blackmail emails, ransom_man didn't make much in the end. Around 4,000 euros worth of bitcoin is a rough estimate. One imagines he was hoping for a lot more. While some people celebrated his misfortune, others became even more determined to track this callous criminal down. Not just the police but white hats like Jesse, Mikko and many others were collecting and sharing information on forums and handing over anything they found to the police. 'Everyone wanted to catch the bastard,' Mikko says.

And one name that kept coming up time and again in the cyber community's email threads and message groups was Julius Kivimäki. Mikko too pondered if it could be him. But he didn't want to get carried away with what were, at that stage, just half-baked theories. He had followed Kivimäki's rise through the hacking scene and his run-ins with the police for years. But he also had a history with the hacker that dated all the way back to 2010, when Mikko had received a phone call out of the blue from the teenager's worried parents . . .

//4
The rise of Zeekill
2010

The headquarters of well-known cybersecurity company F-Secure has a bold and unforgettable design, like a series of blue shipping containers stacked on top of each other. Half of the building starts six storeys up, supported by a criss-cross of giant orange struts, and a statement staircase weaves up into the building. On the roof a large rectangular box juts out precariously at a jaunty angle to offer stunning views of Helsinki's sprawling harbour. On a crisp and clear day you can see Estonia over the freezing waters of the Gulf of Finland.

It was here, in 2010, thirteen years before Kivimäki would be arrested in Paris, that Mikko Hypponen tried to turn Julius Kivimäki's life around.

It started when Mikko got an unexpected phone call from the thirteen-year-old's father. He was concerned his son was spending too much time on his computer and had fallen in with the wrong crowd online. The boy had already attracted the interest of law enforcement for some low-level hacking and his family were trying everything they could to get him onto the straight and narrow. As Mikko was a successful and famous cybersecurity professional, the worried father asked for his help. Mikko came up with a plan to woo Julius over to the good side of hacking. There is a crossroads moment in every hacker's life and although Julius was starting out on the path to mischief, or even crime, Mikko thought there might still be time to reverse that.

Every hacker, whether a white hat or black hat, seems to have a similar origin story – one of curiosity and experimentation online. Unlike most physical crimes, the lines between right and wrong can be fuzzy. Many talented cybersecurity professionals have stories from their early days of accidentally accessing places and information they shouldn't before noticing their mistake. Sometimes you don't realise you've crossed a line until the police come knocking. But sometimes, even at a young age, you know what you're doing is wrong and that people are being impacted by your actions.

Mikko hoped it was the former with Julius and that if he came and spent a day at F-Secure it might set him straight. F-Secure was one of the most trusted brands in cybersecurity and one of Finland's biggest technology success stories. (F-Secure and WithSecure used to be a single company but split in 2023.) Mikko gave Julius a tour around the building, introducing him to the company's white-hat hackers and showing him the state-of-the-art facilities and products that teams were working on. They had lunch and chatted about computers and programming as Mikko tried to win him over. 'What I was really trying to do is impress him,' he says. 'I was basically saying: "Look at all these really cool things we're doing and look at all these machines and data centres and all this cool stuff."'

The thirteen-year-old was shy and didn't ask many questions. Mikko wasn't sure if he really wanted to be there. But he was struck by how good the boy's English was and amazed at how fluently he talked to the international research teams in the building. This was perhaps a clue as to how much time the boy was spending talking to people in other countries online. He left it until the very end of the visit to give Julius 'The Talk'. He told him that talented people can have a good life in cybersecurity and get to use all these impressive tools and do important and worthwhile things. But he warned Julius that none of that would be possible if he 'messed up his future by doing stupid stuff on the internet'.

Even as Mikko waved Julius off, he was worried it had all been a waste of time. 'I knew right away that he wasn't really registering what I was saying. He didn't really care. I was speaking into a void.' But Julius was still young so maybe that would change, Mikko hoped.

A few months later Julius got back in touch and asked about his school-mandated work experience. Most work placements are pretty dull and not that aligned to a student's interests, so Julius wanted to come back and do his time with F-Secure. He asked Mikko if he could spend a week in the labs with the researchers who were studying how viruses and other malicious software work and figuring out how to improve their protection products.

The request left Mikko with a horrible decision to make. Did he let the kid come in, hoping that this would be the catalyst that pushed him onto the path of the good guys? Would he be risking the company and his reputation by letting a known hacker into sensitive parts of the operation?

'How do you bring someone you don't trust into your own sphere of trust where everyone has been vetted and checked? The answer is, you can't. So I refused,' Mikko says. He admits he thinks about that decision often and still agonises over that moment. He wonders what might have been – maybe Julius would have changed his ways and gone on to have a great career in cybersecurity. He too could now be touring the world giving conference speeches and spreading the virtues of cybersecurity. But Mikko also thinks about the more likely scenario – one where the headlines would have been screaming that this notorious cyber criminal used to be an employee of F-Secure.

That was the last time Mikko had contact with Julius. But ever since then he's watched his rise and fall with disappointment and regret.

Even at thirteen years old, then, it seemed Kivimäki was already on a path towards the dark side. This was in spite of having an outwardly normal childhood. He was born on 22 August 1997 and grew up with two younger siblings – a brother and a sister. They lived in a suburban home in Espoo not far from Helsinki. Very little else is certain about his family life. Finland's press is not like that of the UK or the US; despite Kivimäki's infamy, reporters have published very few details about his family or upbringing. There are no interviews with upset, ashamed or defensive parents, for example, or shocked school teachers and classmates. But we can gather some details from his interviews and online activity to help flesh out the person behind all the fake names and online aliases. He's not exactly a trustworthy source so we have to take each claim about his childhood with a large pinch of salt. But here's what he has said.

In a police interview he described his father as working in construction. On his own website,[1] which he seemingly went on to set up himself at some point in 2021, he goes further, asserting that his father is 'the founder of the world-renowned construction company YIT Corporation'. But there's no evidence of this online and the company was founded in 1912 which would make his father about 130 years old. He told police that his mother worked as an engineer focusing on uranium enrichment. His website, though, says that his mother 'has worked as a business consultant since 1996'. Both things may be true, of course. The bio says he spent his childhood summers at his grandfather's farm in Savonlinna in the east of the country, where 'he learned to appreciate nature and its beauty while taking care of animals such as cows and chickens on the farm'. We know that he did indeed spend time at his grandfather's lakeside cabin (a detail that would later become a part of the criminal case against him). The rest of the bio is dubious.

Some key information about his childhood comes instead from the very boastful Kivimäki who emerges from later police interview tapes. On these, he says his love of computers began at the age of ten when he claims to have 'taught himself how to write code in the Python and C programming languages', learning everything from the internet. He also told a reporter at Finnish magazine *LongPlay* that going to school interested him for the first six or seven years, after which he realised that he could 'make more money online than people who graduated from school'.[2] He dropped out. He also insists that he did have friends at school and didn't hang out with them online. We now know of course that his true friends were other hackers and delinquents who he spent most of his waking time with.

It's not known how he fell in with this crowd but his hacking origins may have been similar to so many others I have encountered in my reporting over the years. Almost every hacker I've ever interviewed started their journey in gaming. The PC games platform Steam shows that someone matching Kivimäki's details registered a profile in August 2008 when he was ten years old. Digital badges awarded to his profile for activity show him as a 'Power Player', and he had 158 games in his game library collection, so we can assume that he was a prolific gamer who spent a lot of money on his hobby. He posted screenshots from sessions on *Portal* – a shooting game where solving puzzles is key to winning. He is also known to have been a keen *Minecraft* player. The Steam profile showed he joined discussion groups, including one called 'Yololads'. It's not possible to read the chats in the group any more but the description gives us an insight into its youthful energy: 'welcome to the sikkest group :)' it reads. One can only imagine the sort of discussions that took place far from the prying eyes of parents. It's not too much of a leap to speculate that some of the boys or young men struck up a rapport that took them into other forums and chat rooms where the conversation drifted away from gaming and into other thrilling ways to have fun on the internet. The Steam records show that Kivimäki called himself 'MemeSquad' amongst other player names. But the permanent web address[3] for his profile was set up with the now infamous username: 'Zeekill'.

So how did he go from playing innocent games and chatting nonsense online with strangers, to a Most Wanted cyber criminal?

Well, Zeekill wasn't created in a vacuum.

He was both a product of his time, and one of the chief architects of a particular period in youth cybercrime. The online communities that he grew up in were testosterone-filled vipers' nests where friends turned on one another on a dime desperate to win approval. They didn't give a damn who they hurt on their path to online fame, fortune and folly. It was all a big competition where we – the public – were collateral damage.

But teenage hacking culture wasn't always like this.

//5
Hacking for retweets

In 2002, nearly a decade before Kivimäki made his first steps towards criminality, a bald portly man in his late thirties wearing a scruffy orange T-shirt and sporting a goatee is standing behind the podium in front of an auditorium full of hackers. To the side of the stage there is some distracting chatter as the previous speakers and hosts file off to let him speak. He leans on the podium and waits. Hundreds of pairs of eyes are on him, as well as a recording camera. But he waits for silence with the confidence of a person who knows they deserve their time on that stage. Then, without introducing himself, or his talk, he starts reading:

Another one got caught today, it's all over the papers. 'Teenager Arrested in Computer Crime Scandal', 'Hacker Arrested after Bank Tampering'...
Damn kids. They're all alike.

But did you, in your three-piece psychology and 1950s technobrain, ever take a look behind the eyes of the hacker? Did you ever wonder what made him tick, what forces shaped him, what may have moulded him?
I am a hacker, enter my world...

Mine is a world that begins with school... I'm smarter than most of the other kids, this crap they teach us bores me...
Damn underachiever. They're all alike.

I'm in junior high or high school. I've listened to teachers explain for the fifteenth time how to reduce a fraction. I understand it. 'No, Ms. Smith, I didn't show my work. I did it in my head...'
Damn kid. Probably copied it. They're all alike.

I made a discovery today. I found a computer. Wait a second, this is cool. It does what I want it to. If it makes a mistake, it's because I screwed it up. Not because it doesn't like me...
Or feels threatened by me...
Or thinks I'm a smart ass...
Or doesn't like teaching and shouldn't be here...
Damn kid. All he does is play games. They're all alike.

And then it happened... a door opened to a world... rushing through the phone line like heroin through an addict's veins, an electronic pulse is sent out, a refuge from the day-to-day incompetencies is sought... a board is found.
'This is it... this is where I belong...'
I know everyone here... even if I've never met them, never talked to them, may never hear from them again... I know you all...
Damn kid. Tying up the phone line again. They're all alike...

The essay goes on much longer – it takes him three and a half minutes. When he stops talking, he's given a standing ovation that lasts thirty seconds. The man, seemingly embarrassed by the adulation, smiles as the camera zooms out to reveal the room filled with people clapping, whistling and whooping. 'I'm Loyd, by the way,' he says, remembering that he's not yet introduced himself.[1] He doesn't need to, of course. Loyd Blankenship will always be known to hackers and cybersecurity experts as 'The Mentor'. The mini essay was his. He had written it in 1986, just after he had been arrested for hacking. It was published in online hacker magazine *Phrack* and instantly became known as the 'Hacker Manifesto'.[2] It was (and in some quarters remains) a foundational document of hacker culture.

In his talk Blankenship comes across as a true believer that hackers are a largely innocent group who do more good than bad in the world.[3] Enraged that his friends had been getting rounded up and prosecuted for their largely minor crimes of trespassing into online places they shouldn't have, he had written his essay to argue that hackers are misunderstood and should be celebrated, not arrested.

As a teenager Blankenship had joined various hacking groups – most notably 'Legion of Doom'. They were one of the earliest hacking groups that arose as the personal computing and online network revolutions were taking off in the mid 1980s. The group became synonymous with elite hacking and pushing limits. But despite the arrests of various members, they outwardly had a do-no-harm approach. As *Phrack* magazine later wrote in a sort of obit: 'The Legion of Doom will long be remembered in the computer underground as an innovative and pioneering force, that consistently raised the collective level of knowledge, and provided many answers to questions ranging from the workings of the telephone system to the structure of computer operating systems.'[4]

Yes, there were bad apples. Yes, there were individuals out to make money from credit card spoofing and other basic enterprises that were just coming to the fore. But Legion of Doom and the hacker groups of those days seemed uninterested in personal gain, other than perhaps winning kudos amongst their peers on the bulletin boards they communicated on. Around the same time that Blankenship was hacking, thousands of miles away another group of young men were also testing the limits of early internet security. In Germany, Chaos Computer Club became well known for highly technical but ethical hacking. They performed edgy stunts like hacking into the German federal post office system and stealing 135,000 Deutsche Marks (about £60,000). But the whole thing was carried out in front of the press and they returned the money straight away. It was all designed to highlight the security flaws that the group had already tried to warn the post office about. In the days before Blankenship's Hacker Manifesto, these amateur young hacking groups were operating within a largely benevolent culture.

Afterwards, other groups took the baton and ran with it in the same direction. One of them was called 'L0pht' (pronounced 'loft'). A US group made up of a close-knit gaggle of young men and boys who hung out together in literal lofts, they developed protocols for warning organisations that their computers were at risk from hackers. 'Responsible disclosure' is the term now used for this, and the rag-tag lads of L0pht were pioneers. They even famously appeared in front of the US Senate in 1998 to warn lawmakers about the potential risks of cyber attacks disrupting internet communications.

In his book about L0pht and its larger collective Cult of the Dead Cow, Joseph Menn relays a story that epitomises the culture of these early hacking groups. One of the youngest members of L0pht – a teenager called Joe Grand – was brought into the group deliberately to keep him away from criminality. Grand had been applying for credit cards with stolen identity documents and had then found himself in even more serious trouble in 1992. As Menn writes: 'He broke into a Michigan AT&T office, avoiding jail only because he was a juvenile. Grand's parents let him keep hanging out at the loft realising the older guys there could help redirect him. And they did.'[5]

Now, decades later, Grand is one of the most famous and successful cybersecurity experts around. In fact, I interviewed this passionate hacker and life-long tinkerer in 2023 for a brilliant story about how he rescued a fortune in cryptocurrency from a super-secure crypto device by hacking it on behalf of a customer who'd lost their passwords.

If you search online for 'famous hacking groups' you'll find L0pht, Chaos Computer Club and Legion of Doom on many lists. They populate the hall of fame, alongside hacking groups of a very different stripe including professionally run organised crime groups and covert government hacking teams. Looking in detail at these latter types of group is for a different book; our focus is on what can loosely be referred to as amateur hacking groups.

But among these amateur groups something has gone horribly wrong since the days of the Hacker Manifesto. In some ways the individual hackers within the groups still share the same characteristics as their predecessors of the 1980s and 1990s, but the mentality of the groups has shifted dramatically. This is perhaps best captured by a method of categorisation invented by former hacking gang member turned cyber CEO Dug Song. According to Song, hacking groups can be placed on a four-quadrant matrix divided by one axis that runs from good to evil and another that runs from lawful to chaotic. If Darth Vader of *Star Wars* fame was a hacking group, for example, he could be placed somewhere in the Lawful–Evil quadrant – he was following the laws of the Empire, but for evil purposes. L0pht, on the other hand, would best fit in the Lawful–Neutral zone. And, as Joseph Menn writes in his book, Cult of the Dead Cow would be Chaotic–Good. But fast forward to the 2010s and while the hacker gangs of Kivimäki's teenage era are most definitely Chaotic, you would struggle to place them anywhere near Good.

So how did this shift take place? One factor that's hard to ignore is the rise of social media. More specifically – Twitter, or X as it has been known since July 2023.

#

Hackers love to boast.

As the Hacker Manifesto describes, these kids are the smartest guys in the room and they like to let others know it. Often this confidence is well-placed. Learning computer skills and doing new and interesting things with them is hard and often impressive. Just as a teenage boy loves to show off his football trophies and talk about the goal he scored for his local team on Saturday, so young hackers like to brag about the cool things they have built or broken. Before social media, teenage hacking gangs had no real outlet for their boasting. Yes, there were bulletin boards, chat channels and niche sites – but there's a good argument to say that Twitter was the real gamechanger. Before Twitter, social networks were places to meet your friends and be . . . social. Facebook, MySpace, Bebo, MSM Messenger – these were mostly about sharing your life with a close circle and chatting to people you knew. Twitter, on the other hand, was a place where you could build followers and fans. It wasn't really about socialising at all. In fact, being anti-social or edgy was the way to get noticed. Followers, retweets and likes quickly became currency. The bigger the stir you made, the more online clout you would have. Arguably, Twitter gave birth to a new generation of fame-hungry hackers.

The first ever tweet was sent by the platform's co-founder Jack Dorsey in 2006. The site grew quickly as a place where people could share real-time short updates about their lives, but it really popped off between 2009 and 2011 when it became the place for discussing (and arguing) about the news. An average of 2 million tweets a day were sent in 2009. That jumped to 65 million in 2010 and then to 200 million in 2011. And in 2011 tens of thousands of those tweets were about, and from, a notorious teenage hacking gang called 'LulzSec'.

LulzSec announced its arrival on 7 May 2011 with a tweet from its newly minted Twitter account. It was like the sounding of a starting pistol for what would become a period of teen cyber mayhem. LulzSec was like no other previous group. It took its name from a combination of the text abbreviation 'Lol' (laugh out loud) and 'Security'. They emerged as a splinter group from 'Anonymous' – a collective of loosely linked activist hackers (or 'hacktivists') who had already become widely known thanks to some high-profile attacks, for example against the Church of Scientology and in support of

WikiLeaks. And it helped that they created a brand for themselves by wearing Guy Fawkes masks whenever they appeared on screen.

Although Anonymous operates according to a diverse, and at times bewildering, set of principles, it was, and still is, a serious hacking group hell bent on punishing corporate greed, scandal and corruption. It has no leader and anyone can digitally don the mask and carry out hacks (known as 'ops') under its name. On the hacker matrix you could make a strong case for putting it in the Chaotic–Good or Chaotic–Neutral quadrants depending on your viewpoint and its latest stunt. Crucially, what helped the group take the decades-old idea of hacktivism to new heights was its masterful ability to harness the power of Twitter to marshal throngs of hackers around the world towards a common hacking purpose and to publicise its operations.

By 2011, through a combination of its eye-catching activities, masked imagery and self-promotion, Anonymous had succeeded in etching its earnest motto onto the public psyche: 'We are Legion. We do not forgive. We do not forget. Expect us.' The LulzSec lads chose a very different tagline: 'This is the Internet, where we screw each other over for a jolt of satisfaction.'

LulzSec's logo also spoke volumes about the ethos of the group. Gone was the sinister illustration of an Anonymous hacker looming over a globe. In its stead LulzSec chose a monocle-wearing, wine-swilling cartoon man with a moustache and top hat – an image that suggested a sense of amused, detached, self-congratulatory arrogance.

The group's first headline-grabbing hack in 2011 laid out their stall perfectly. They hacked into the databases of Fox – the makers of the hit TV show *The X-Factor* – releasing the personal information of 73,000 contestants and hijacking the company's LinkedIn and Twitter accounts to publicise their successful breach. The gang claimed it was all done in retaliation for one of Fox's presenters saying on air that the rapper Common was 'vile'. 'We don't like you very much. As such, we cordially invite you to kiss our hand-crafted crescent fresh asses,' wrote LulzSec in a post-attack tweet.

As well as these attention-grabbing antics, the gang released a more serious tranche of the stolen data a few days later: the email addresses and passwords for 363 Fox employees. They also used those credentials to take over and deface the LinkedIn profiles of staff members. The hack was a shock, but the motive and the way it was publicised was equally troubling. As author Geoff White wrote in his book *Crime Dot Com*, this kind of group was something not yet seen in the world of hacking gangs:

> They were breaking in, stealing personal and sensitive information and then smearing snippets (and sometimes swathes) of it online for all to see. And unlike many hacking groups of the past, LulzSec's members . . . were on Twitter to answer questions. Hacking had always happened in the shadows, but LulzSec were conducting their affairs in the full glare of publicity.'[6]

LulzSec didn't seem to have any of the lofty moralistic ideals of Anonymous. And another difference between the two was their size. Anonymous could swell at times of heightened activity to encompass thousands of hackers (not to mention plenty of glory hunters and hangers-on too). But LulzSec had a core membership of only six, with a few others on the periphery. They organised themselves in private chat rooms, predominantly on the Internet Relay Chat (IRC) system. IRC was a once popular text-based chat system for instant messaging. It was a revelation for these communities, allowing them to find like-minded people. Anyone could host a chat room – called a channel – and invite others to join. If a group got too big, members could splinter off and talk more privately. Thanks to a leak to the *Guardian*,[7] the world was given an insight into the conversations the members of LulzSec were having amongst themselves on IRC. The logs showed a disorganised group obsessed with its media coverage and Twitter clout. They shared pictures of articles written about themselves in newspapers like the *Wall Street Journal*. They also managed their public image meticulously, with a dedicated hacker named 'Topiary' tasked with sending antagonistic and provocative tweets to further anger and amuse people.

They chose their targets to get as much attention as possible, like the US TV network PBS where they managed to get into the news website's back-end system and successfully publish a fake article headlined: 'Tupac still alive in New Zealand'. This was apparently because the network aired a documentary unfavourable to WikiLeaks. LulzSec played a similar trick on the website of the *Sun* – the UK's most-read newspaper – redirecting visitors to a fake story about the company's chairman Rupert Murdoch committing suicide.[8] There was no apparent motive for this and notably the gang redirected visitors of the site to their own Twitter feed. Other hacks saw customer data stolen and published from Sony – multiple times. The group also drew the ire of law enforcement by temporarily disrupting the websites of the American Central Intelligence Agency and the UK's Serious Organised Crime Agency with what are known as Distributed Denial of Service (DDoS) attacks.

DDoS attacks are a low-skilled hacker's favourite method of annoyance. They flood a company's web servers with too many hits, forcing it offline, normally for short periods of time. The analogy I always give is the moment when tickets for the Glastonbury festival go on sale and so many people land on the website at the same time that it fails to load. These days most websites have enough DDoS protection to ward off all but the most severe of these attacks. But back when Anonymous and LulzSec were sending waves of junk traffic, websites were less well defended, and these attacks took down services for minutes or even hours. This could lead to a minor inconvenience, embarrassment or a full-on crisis depending on how much the targeted organisation relied on its online connection.

So, with a mix of low-level DDoS attacks, news website hijacks, data breaches and plenty of juvenile tweets, LulzSec made a name for itself quickly. By 10 June 2011, just over a month after launching, the group had gathered more than 100,000 followers on Twitter according to *The Next Web* reporting at the time.[9] Their every move was newsworthy and the gang lapped up the attention – as their chat logs and subsequent interviews make clear. One of the hackers would go on to brag that LulzSec was once trending more online than the massively successful pop group One Direction.

But LulzSec didn't last long. One of their last hacks was less about causing annoyance to large institutions and more about causing real harm to individuals. On 16 June 2011 they published a list of 62,000 people's email addresses and passwords and invited other people to use these credentials to break into the victims' private accounts themselves. 'Be creative instead of being a potato. Try PayPal combinations, Twitter, Facebook, eBay, Runescape. Pick a target from the list.'

It's not known where the data came from or how much of it was real but there were reports on social media of people noticing strange Amazon purchases being made on their accounts – presumably by hackers taking up LulzSec's invitation. According to LulzSec, the list of targets was downloaded thousands of times. It represented a shift in the culture of the teen hacking world – a deliberately cruel act designed to harm thousands of randomly targeted people. And it wasn't just carried out in public – it was carried out in the hope of creating a public scare.

On 26 June 2011, LulzSec posted a retirement message online stating that their '50 days of Lulz' were over. The truth was that behind the scenes, the group was being quietly dismantled. Its ultra-paranoid leader, known as 'Sabu', had been arrested in New York, and turned out to be twenty-seven-year-old Hector Xavier Monsegur – a Puerto Rican freelance programmer. He agreed to help police catch the other members in a deal to get a more lenient sentence and avoid jail so that he could look after his young family. One by one, LulzSec's main players, plus some on the periphery, were arrested. All except one – the elusive hacker called 'Avunit' who remains unknown and at large, apparently somewhere in the US.[10]

Two men were arrested in Ireland and four others were found in the UK. They were a diverse bunch, only brought together after bumping into each other in an IRC channel and speaking the same languages – English and Hacking. Three of them were teenagers. The first time they met each other in person was in court in London for their trial which was widely covered. The press and public struggled to get their heads around the case, finding it hard to believe the damage these teenagers could cause from behind their keyboards without even knowing each other's name or location.

LulzSec's youngest hacker was just sixteen years old. Mustafa Al-Bassam, known as 'tflow', was one of the founders. He was arrested in his bedroom in London on 19 July. Years later, he gave an interview with *LadBible* that racked up more than 5 million views on YouTube.[11] In it the confident but awkward and fidgeting young man explains that he was held for three hours in his room while a team of cyber detectives searched for hard drives and computers. In the end he pleaded guilty to computer misuse and received a twenty-month suspended sentence with 320 hours of unpaid community service work and a two-year internet ban. He was also barred from using any encryption on his communications for five years – a wise move given that encryption, especially 'end-to-end encryption', makes it impossible to read messages sent between people online unless you get hold of their phone or computer.

After serving his sentence, Al-Bassam went straight and is now a successful businessman who runs a blockchain security company and speaks at conferences. In one talk he said he had been drawn to hacking after experimenting on the internet from the age of nine or ten.[12] He spoke fondly of his time in LulzSec, saying he hadn't been scared at all of the consequences back then. As a juvenile hacker, he knew he was protected by the law. Herein lies a pattern we see in many young hackers: being a teenager already gives you a sense of immortality and power – knowing that the law will protect you from the worst punishment if you break it adds a whole extra snug layer of comfort.

When the police went after LulzSec's 'Kayla' they were expecting to find a seventeen-year-old girl. That was how she described herself and acted to the rest of the crew. She was so convincing that Sabu had become quite smitten with her, according to one of his FBI handlers. But Kayla turned out to be a twenty-four-year-old former army infantryman in Yorkshire in the north of England. He was jailed for thirty months. Quite the contrast to Al-Bassam's juvenile sentence.

Also in court for the LulzSec trial was eighteen-year-old Ryan Cleary, who was arrested at the end of June 2011. The court was told he had autism and agoraphobia. He was jailed for two years and eight months for providing the infrastructure to carry out LulzSec's DDoS attacks. At one stage he was also found to be in possession of child abuse images, which were discovered by police on his hard drive. He was released after time served but barred from using the internet to talk to anyone under the age of sixteen and given severe online restrictions. He was also placed on the sex offenders register for five years.

Cleary was only a bit-part player in LulzSec but somehow made a big impression on the other young hackers of that time – particularly Julius Kivimäki. Around the time that LulzSec was being rounded up by police, Kivimäki started using 'RyanC' or 'Ryan' or even 'Ryan Cleary' as another of his aliases. (There are a ridiculous number of 'Ryans' in this story, partly out of bizarre coincidence, but the repetition is made worse by Kivimäki taking Cleary's name at many different points.) One hacker from the time said the two teenagers may have been mates at one point, playing online games or chatting in IRC channels. But whether or not they were friends, Kivimäki started to use his name, either as a joke or as a way to embarrass, annoy or frame him after he was arrested.

The fourth British LulzSec hacker to be tried was eighteen-year-old Jake Davis AKA Topiary. Topiary was the chief tweeter of the group and had managed to throw people so far off his scent that reporters at the time were convinced he was a Swedish-born citizen living in the Netherlands.[13] But the cops tracked him down to a static caravan on Yell – an island of fewer than a thousand inhabitants that forms part of the remote Shetland Islands in Scotland. He was living alone. This softly spoken and polite hermit had been LulzSec's antagonistic, funny and cocky mouthpiece, posting wry and sarcastic celebrations and taunts to make the group go viral. He had done a good job too. By the end he'd helped the group achieve celebrity status with more than 340,000 followers on Twitter. In the final days of LulzSec, Davis deleted his entire tweet history except a single one: 'You cannot arrest an idea.'

He was arrested shortly after and watched as police confiscated every piece of electronics he had. They even prised open the fish fingers in his freezer to search for hidden USBs. There weren't any. Davis and all his electronics were flown to London on the private jet that Metropolitan Police officers had arranged. He commented later that it was surreal to watch the police perform frantic computer forensics on his laptop mid-flight before the battery ran out. He was given a two-year sentence and served a short thirty-seven-day stint after taking into account the months he spent wearing an electronic tag. It was a short stretch but it was spent inside a notoriously rough institute for young offenders – Feltham Prison. He came out full of regret and remorse. He was interviewed by the BBC's *Newsnight* programme and was unusually honest in a world where bravado and nihilism rules.[14] He described the hacking culture as a very cynical world and admitted that he had become a very cynical person. He warned other young people at the time about the perils of falling down the rabbit hole of cybercrime: 'I would say if you have a passion and an outlet for creativity, try and do something beyond the front door. Because if you get sucked into that computer world, you get dependent on it, and if you're dependent on it, it's very hard to say no to things that you may later come to regret.'

It's clear from listening to these young men talking about their hacking past that they had been completely wrapped up in the excitement of it all. Their Twitter followers had skyrocketed, and they couldn't get enough of the attention. The thrill of going viral must have been intoxicating. They were hooked and wanted to go further each time. Unlike low-level criminals in the physical world, they had the cloak of anonymity that the internet gifts you. And though they don't admit it in interviews, it appears that they were all also lonely and isolated (Davis geographically so). The chat logs show a feeling of camaraderie and kinship.

Davis's heartfelt warning to other online delinquents was of course ignored. Not only would it have been hard for an interview on *Newsnight* to cut through the noise and fun, it also came in spring 2013, by which time LulzSec had been replaced by other gangs. LulzSec's demise in summer 2011 had started the ball rolling and there was no stopping it. On IRC and its successors like Team Speak and Skype, new groups started forming as boys and young men found their way into the community and attempted to show off and try to win approval.

Although the leaked LulzSec chat logs gave us a hint of what was going on in these channels, we would soon be given an even better insight. A huge amount of audio recordings exist from subsequent

HACKING FOR RETWEETS

groups that further fleshes out how these hackers worked, played and often argued online. Most of the archive comes from another hacker called Ryan who went by the name 'urharmless' online (we'll use that for clarity). Urharmless recorded literally days and days' worth of material and still has it all on an enormous stack of hard drives. He used to upload some of the best bits to a popular YouTube account called 'Hardchats'. He says the channel had millions of hits and people enjoyed featuring. But he admits that some people now aren't happy with the unwanted attention. 'It's not that I was intentionally trying to log my friends but rather that it was more about recording funny moments,' he insists. Looking at his mountains of material now, he sees the recordings as part of an 'insurance plan' in case other hackers tried to snitch on him. Though Urharmless insists he would never snitch or share incriminating audio with police.

As with many of the hackers I've spoken to, I was introduced to Urharmless through a series of other chats with various people who were in the scene at the time. He remains under the radar, perpetually fearful of being caught for his hacking offences. Most of these were carried out in the 2010s but he hinted at other fresher offences too. He's never spoken to a journalist and now lives a solitary life. He suffers from a long-term serious throat illness – when we first had a voice call late one night on Discord nearly every one of his sentences ended with a painful-sounding coughing fit. As well as Urharmless he was also known as 'virtualrapist' or '120FPS' during the hacking days of the 2010s. He claims to have carried out cyber attacks with two of the other gangs that we'll hear about. He also has an encyclopaedic knowledge not just of the groups he was involved with, but the others that rose and fell during this time.

Some of the audio chats record him in group calls with Zeekill himself – he says he helped Kivimäki on various attacks and stunts. I don't know much about Urharmless for certain but I think that Ryan is indeed his real name. It's the only real name he's operated under since his hacking days and he is very protective of it. It still annoys him when he gets confused with other real and not-real Ryans.

He is also apparently rich, thanks to ill-gotten gains: 'If you're wondering, yes, crime does pay, haha.' He is now in his mid-thirties. And he's not very popular with some of the other hackers who accuse him of overstating his involvement in the gangs. He refutes this vociferously and has spent weeks sending me evidence to back up his claims. He says most of the vitriol is a result of him trying to expose one of the gang members as a sexual predator.

He shared with me dozens of long and sprawling group calls, recorded between 2011 and 2016. They are chaotic, inane, juvenile and sometimes offensive. Homophobia, sexism and racism are rife as the teenagers work hard to shock each other or make each other laugh. Hackers would log in to the chat rooms from their bedrooms and keep their microphones open for hours, striking up conversations but also going about their days and nights in between. The longest continuous Skype recording is apparently eighty hours long, with dozens of people drifting in and out of the channel to hang out. The calls give us an insight into how these boys and men lived. Nearly all of them were teenagers and there are very few girls present in the recordings.

One short exchange gives a good snapshot of the type of conversations they were having. In it, one hacker stays on the Skype chat while urinating. The boys all find it hilarious and bait him into sending them a picture of his penis: 'I'll give you $500 to send us a pic,' one of them urges to much laughter in the group. But as soon as the laughter dies down another boy begins talking about a new technique he has found to do a deep clean of your internet history to cover any criminal tracks. They flit from nonsense to hacking and back again in seconds without skipping a beat. It must have been exhausting to keep up with, and new people would join and find themselves on the receiving end of brutal hazings for the others' amusement.

The chats show teenage boys at their worst in many respects. Tucked away in their bedrooms, they were away from the prying ears of parents and free to flex their muscles and show off like school kids behind the bike shed. Quite often the chats would descend into shouting matches, making it hard to understand what's going on. But then there would be moments of pure silly fun like rap battles. And other moments of calm during which the boys would ramble on in smaller groups while high on marijuana. In one recording a stoned Zeekill slowly explains his technique for setting up an all-night smoking session. 'The trick is – you need to pre-rolllll,' he says, apparently off his head.

These Skype group chats were the source of many impromptu hacks as the bored teens egged each other on. And sometimes a hack or a chat would lead to the evolution of a brand new crew determined to go bigger and be bolder than the one before.

//6
Hacking for power – and bitcoins
August 2011

The 1995 film *Hackers* is both of its time and ahead of its time. It's also so bad that it's brilliant.

The film stars a young Angelina Jolie as a schoolgirl hacker known as 'Acid Burn' who joins a hacking team led by another high schooler calling himself 'Crash Override' – played by Jonny Lee Miller. The film is frenetic, visually impressive (in a cheesy 1990s kind of way) and accidentally hilarious. The hacking sequences show computer code floating around the actors' heads as they tap impossibly quickly on their keyboards. Rays of light zoom around the inside of computer chips made to look like cityscapes. The gang escape police by rollerblading through traffic with a thumping Prodigy soundtrack in the background.

The film was largely panned by audiences and critics and did not set the box office alight. But amongst a certain internet clique it was instantly beloved and has since grown to hold cult-like status. Anniversary articles and online events celebrate its release date. Aside from the 'so bad it's good' appeal, it also touched a nerve with some young minds when it came out. Inspired by the hacking subculture of the 1980s and 1990s it visualised and glamorised the amateur cyber elite. The characters save the day and overcome evil corporate cheats while being framed themselves. One scene has a confused cop reading passages from the Hacker Manifesto. As the narrator for its dramatic trailer puts it: 'Hidden beneath the world we know, is the world THEY inhabit. They're hackers. It's not just something they do – it's who they are. They can crack any code. Get inside any system.'[1]

The film is full of moments where hackers look powerful and cool. Crash Override hacks his school sprinkler system to get revenge on another hacker. And the team repeatedly humiliate a cop who's trying to catch them – at one point registering the hapless detective as officially deceased. But the most famous moment of the whole film comes towards the end when Crash Override is arrested. He hangs his head out of the patrol car window and screams out the rallying cry 'Hack the Planet!' That phrase is now so famous that it's a popular meme, GIF and T-shirt slogan. Either ironically, or out of true fandom, the next teen hacking gang to rise after LulzSec chose this phrase as their name.

Hack The Planet, or HTP for short, emerged the month after LulzSec unravelled in summer 2011. Like LulzSec, the group was a dispersed team of mostly teenage hackers, all coordinating in online messaging platforms, predominantly IRC. HTP was made up of hackers from the US, UK, Ireland and . . . Finland. Yes, Kivimäki was a key member of HTP. He joined, like many of its members, after hanging out in the IRC room for the gang which anyone could join initially. The channel was, according to police, called '#thegibson' – another reference to the film *Hackers*. The Gibson was the name of the supercomputer that one of the hackers breaks into in the film. The movie makers had in turn named the supercomputer as a homage to cyberpunk author William Gibson who coined the term 'cyberspace'. References wrapped in references.

At first Kivimäki, who had recently turned fourteen, just hung out and chipped into conversations from the sidelines, but slowly he grew to become a major player. HTP became Kivimäki's first proper hacking crew but there are clues that he was also involved with an Anonymous-linked gang shortly before this. At one point an unconfirmed IRC log (along with plenty of his private details) was leaked online by one of the many people he pissed off. In hacker parlance this publishing of stolen or discovered details is called a 'doxxing' – think 'documents'. It's the kind of thing hackers do to get revenge on one another and intimidate each other. 'We know who you really are and where you live,' is the message a thorough doxxing sends.

Kivimäki got doxxed many times and in this one, the chat records apparently show that he had been busy before he joined HTP. In the text chat from May 2011 he's asked by a user called 'Kottizen' why he's attacking a community discussion group linked to Anonymous called 'AnonOps'. AnonOps was a group of hackers described at the time by *Forbes* as 'the elite and rather more organised arm of Anonymous' responsible for DDoS attacks on Visa and PayPal in protest against their treatment of the controversial website WikiLeaks.[2] In the published chat record Zeekill, in his now customary short and nonchalant style, explains that he's angry with how AnonOps is being run – a community he says he started. Here's a snapshot:

> Zeekill: I regret ever starting the chain of events that created anonops
> Kottizen: and that's why you're ddosing them?
> Zeekill: Yes
> Zeekill: Pretty much
> Zeekill: They don't deserve to exist

Tech website ZDNet published a story in May 2011 about users of AnonOps being warned to stay away from the community IRC channels because of the attacks from Kivimäki (who was at that time calling himself 'Ryan'): 'a former member and IRC operator known as "Ryan" turned against the group due to an apparent falling out over how the organisation is run.' The reporter describes how Ryan launched a DDoS attack against the AnonOps network.

Interestingly, in that same leaked chat conversation, we see a side to Kivimäki which suggests that, at this stage, he still had a moral compass of sorts. Kottizen tries to tempt him into helping carry out a cyber attack against a large number of people. Kivimäki repeatedly refuses to join in the attack, saying: 'I don't care about harming masses of people. That's why I rather take down routers of ISPs [Internet Service Provider companies] rather than targeting single users.' Harming masses of innocent people, or attacking single users, is not something that troubles him later but at this stage there was evidently some level of restraint to his criminality. Kivimäki was nearly fourteen at the time so it's likely that Kottizen was an older hacker who tried to coax the boy into more serious cybercrime. It makes you wonder whether or not some element of grooming was taking place on these IRC chats where younger novice hackers were mingling unsupervised with older and more serious cyber criminals. Kottizen would have known Zeekill was a young boy because in that same chat he talks about dropping out of school. I couldn't find out any information about Kottizen but who knows how old, skilled or criminal this anonymous person was.

It's not unheard of for younger hackers to be taken under the wing of older more experienced criminals. In fact, in a report published in 2015 (as a direct response to the chaos that unfolds in the next few chapters) the UK's National Crime Agency (NCA) points to this exact pathway as being a problem: 'As young people become involved with other online coding or hacking forums they may be identified by individuals or groups involved in cybercrime who start to "groom" them to encourage them to participate in illegal online activities.'[3]

Based on interviews with experts and former hackers, the NCA research paper describes the typical pathway for young hackers:

Computer gaming >
Online gaming >
Computer gaming cheats >
Computer gaming modifications >
Hacking forum participation >
Minor cybercrime to beat the system >
Minor cybercrime for financial gain >
Serious cybercrime.

The research also describes the types of people drawn into this online subculture. In an eerie echo of the Hacker Manifesto written nearly thirty years earlier, it speaks of how young hackers are often 'academically gifted and start to investigate the intellectual challenges coding and hacking present' in part because they are 'not adequately challenged by school or university technology subjects'. Some have been diagnosed with forms of autism or with Asperger's Syndrome. The participants that the cops interviewed said that hacking allowed them to 'acquire power' where the rest of their lives were perhaps devoid of it, as well as providing a technical challenge. Some said they were bullied at school or had a tough home life. Hacking forums and chat rooms gave these boys a 'sense of belonging'. The desire to prove themselves within these communities was cited as a huge driver that could lead to more serious illegal activity – carrying out a so-called 'righteous hack'. The term is another quote from *Hackers*, again demonstrating its long-lasting influence: 'If you want to be elite, you've got to do a righteous hack!' It means to carry out a hack that has not been performed before. And just breaking in isn't the point – it's about breaking in with finesse.

There wasn't much finesse in Kivimäki's vengeful actions against AnonOps but they certainly helped put him on the map. He was fast building a reputation as a bold, young up-and-coming hacker with a lot of spare time. But soon that spare time would be eaten up by HTP. The gang launched in summer 2011 in an old-fashioned way in keeping with their throwback hacker culture. They published a 'zine' – a fan-made online magazine about a specialist topic. In this case the topic was hacking into websites, embarrassing rivals and stealing from private companies. HTP's zines were painstakingly produced and must have taken hours to put together. Each one contained bespoke pieces of art made in the ASCII style, which uses characters from the ASCII (American Standard Code for Information Interchange) character set to create a picture made up of carefully arranged letters, numbers, punctuation marks and special symbols. At the top of each zine was the HTP logo – a globe with HTP written in giant letters underneath. The zines were published to websites like PasteBin – a simple site that allows people to anonymously post anything on a permanent webpage. The group also had a Twitter account, though it was quickly suspended, but all of their zines were shared far and wide on Twitter, with each one making the intended splash.

In what appears to be their first zine,[4] HTP made it clear why they were in business – they wanted to outdo LulzSec and prove that they were the most powerful and feared hacking group in the world: 'You may have read about the various attention-whoring skid injections of LulzSec in the news lately, who hasn't?' (By 'skid injections' they mean low-level and unskilled cyber attacks.) But the zine also accuses LulzSec of betraying the 'anti-sec' movement – an anti-cybersecurity ethos that believes hackers should not tell the world what they have stolen and how they did it. It's about keeping things to yourself. Or making money, as HTP evangelised: 'The more skilled among us know not to broadcast our various ownages. ['Ownages' is a hacker term for when something is 'owned' and stolen or taken over.] We silently slip in and sift through large networks. Releases are private. Obviously, when you have a group that comes along such as Lulzsec [sic], the question is not what they will get into, but how long they will last.'

We don't know if Kivimäki was involved in this zine, but you can feel that same arrogant and defiant tone here – this is a group who are obviously jealous of LulzSec but also want the community to know that they are superior. It's amusing to think that these are kids or very young men, trying to give themselves the elite and professional air of elder statesmen hackers. This entire group and their actions seemed to be aimed at embarrassing or showing up LulzSec – who were largely already in custody around this time.

I did find a snippet of LulzSec's (unconfirmed) chatlogs where they talked about an annoying kid called 'Zeekill' causing them some grief. 'We have our target,' they said. The trail went cold at that point, so it's still not clear how such animosity built between the groups. But HTP seems to have been formed in revenge for something. Hacking groups waging war on one another is part and parcel of this interwoven and claustrophobic culture. Even back in the days of Legion of Doom and the Hacker Manifesto there had been beef between groups, with one rivalry even exaggeratedly dubbed 'The Great Hacker War'. This seems to have been overblown by media commentary, amounting only to pranks played against each other that never spilled out of the community. HTP's campaign to show up LulzSec would impact the general public a great deal more.

It started off much like those early days of hacker vs hacker tit for tat. In spite of HTP's high-minded chat about not broadcasting their ownages, they leaked hundreds of lines of chats, usernames and login details for people from an IRC chat service called Mibbit that they felt was popular with too many LulzSec fans.

HTP stamped their authority as the next top dog of the teen cybercrime world and nudged the culture into a different direction. Publicly they were less funny and more spiteful. Privately they were more greedy and cynical. They dedicated zines to doxxing rivals or people who tried to stand up to them. One of their releases, likely led or inspired by Kivimäki, went after AnonOps with a spiteful and homophobic rant: 'AnonOps no longer stands with Anonymous, but rather against us as an agent of censorship, unlulzy pseudo-activism and immense faggotry, and thus must be eliminated.'

One zine went into a huge amount of detail about a Microsoft engineer and his family who had apparently criticised the group online. In another, the gang published a conversation log stolen from another hacking gang to embarrass them. In the chat logs the rivals are seen talking about Zeekill and worrying about what he was capable of. No doubt this particular snippet of conversation would have been an ego-inflating piece of gold for him, showing him to be a powerful player in the scene.

Overall, HTP *were* more careful than LulzSec. They managed to stay quiet until they were ready to pop back up online with another bombshell zine. One of their biggest moments came around a year after they had formed, with the announcement that they had stolen a huge amount of data from the popular and respected cybersecurity company Symantec. For some unexplained reason the company had pissed HTP off so the group dumped thousands of lines of data, apparently taken from internal databases, plus employee details into the zine. It is still online now.

That same zine from November 2012 also contained data stolen from the once popular picture-sharing site ImageShack. 'ImageShack has been completely owned,' HTP declared, dumping a huge amount of data stolen from the company's servers. The incident was another example of HTP's devil-may-care attitude and scattergun approach to hacking – attacking whatever organisations they could and concocting a motive afterwards. A far cry from Anonymous' moralistic actions. Even LulzSec had some logic to their actions. But the ImageShack hack is significant for another reason: it was the first documented moment that Kivimäki got paid for one of his attacks.

#

The HTP boys thought they were on to a winner when they digitally snuck into ImageShack. It's not known how they did it, but it wasn't actually the first time that the company had had a security breach – it had already been broken into in 2009 by a group that called themselves 'AntiSec', which may or may not have had links to Kivimäki. As ever, it's all very murky – the timelines of these groups and the way they mix and merge make it hard to pin things down. But if Kivimäki had been part of the previous hack, that may have given the HTP guys an in. It's not uncommon for hackers to go back to the scene of previous crimes and try their luck again. Some even plant pieces of computer code that allow them to have continued access.

Once HTP had connected to ImageShack's powerful computers they had full remote access to them, and they used the processing power to run a piece of software that could syphon through passwords to crack into other private accounts from different companies. This kind of computer-power hijacking can be big business, especially in recent years when it's been done to carry out a 'cryptojacking' attack. The hacker will sneakily use a company's computer power to run bitcoin mining software. The software quietly crunches through complex mathematical problems 24/7 and the perps will be rewarded every so often with new bitcoin. While the criminals cash in, the victims get nothing other than overheated hardware and a monster electricity bill. Sometimes IT technicians can smell a rat when they notice things are running a bit slower on their computers, which is likely what happened at ImageShack. The HTP boys weren't mining for crypto but the hacking tools they were running had obviously made enough of a noise on the company network for engineers to look into it.

The first the hackers knew they had been rumbled was when their IRC chat was interrupted by a message from a stranger who had suddenly joined their channel. 'I'm the CEO of ImageShack – we need to talk,' it read. You can only guess the shock the hackers must have felt; they'd been caught red-handed and had now had their inner sanctum invaded themselves by their victim – a man who was clearly a force to be reckoned with.

Jack Levin is not a typical CEO. He is a highly technical computer engineer who proudly boasts of being an early employee at Google in 1999. On his LinkedIn profile he says he designed and deployed Google's first networks and 'crawled under the floor with Larry Page' – the co-founder of the internet behemoth. He founded ImageShack in his last year at Google, and it was a rapid success. The business quickly made enough money to hire hundreds of servers handling mountains of data a day. So the HTP hack probably took a while to find amongst all that activity on all those busy machines. But find it the IT team did, and they contacted their boss to let him know what was happening. Rather impressively, Levin followed the trail back to the hidden IRC channel that the hackers were on. 'They were all shocked and quite impressed that I had the skill to do it!' he laughs.

It was Kivimäki, calling himself Ryan, who decided to handle the conversation, opening a private channel with the CEO. Instead of getting mad, Levin wanted to understand how the boys had broken in, so he did a deal with Kivimäki. The leaked conversation shows the boy flexing his muscles as a negotiator and striking up an arrangement in exchange for some bitcoin. Bear in mind at this point the Finn is still only fourteen years old.

Jack: how do you want to do this?
Ryan: I guess I'd prefer being paid in bitcoins
Ryan: Giving you my real name still puts me in a situation where I could be risking my job
Jack: yes, bitcoins will be appropriate
Ryan: good
Jack: as I said I am not at all vengeful...
Ryan: I am quite sure we didn't cause any real damage
Jack: yes, so no fault no foul... I think we can work this out.

Levin sent Kivimäki ten bitcoins, together worth about $120 at the time, although if Kivimäki still has them today they would be worth nearly a million dollars. He seems more than happy with that payday. Not bad really, considering he and his gang were caught doing something illegal on illegally accessed computers.

Jack Levin these days is a successful cryptocurrency entrepreneur who calls himself 'Cyphereus Prime' and has a large following on X. I asked him if he had spoken to the police about the security breach and his secret arrangement with Ryan. He felt that there was no real harm done, so he didn't report the hack. He doesn't consider it to be extortion, harbouring no hard feelings against Kivimäki. As for the potential victims whose accounts were cracked open by the hacking tools being run by HTP on his servers, he says now that he didn't consider that then – 'these were just kids causing havoc online'.

Interestingly, he says he didn't know about the ImageShack data that was stolen and published by the gang weeks later, in spite of the hack being covered at the time by specialist news outlets including *Computerworld* and *DarkReading*. But he did say that someone from the IRC chat contacted him shortly afterwards looking to 'dish the dirt' on Ryan. Someone in the gang was clearly annoyed with his secret side deal.

The incident gives us an insight into how Zeekill was already learning how to manipulate and extort his victims for money. It also perhaps points to the corrupting power of bitcoin. Making money from hacks is not something that the Hacker Manifesto talks about. Yes, in those early days hackers were costing companies money by using their skills to avoid paying for services like long-distance phone calls. The more criminally minded might even have found a buyer for some stolen data or carried out credit card fraud and the like. But the rise of bitcoin no doubt opened up a world of opportunity for these gangs. It was launched in 2009 by an anonymous forum person or group of people called Satoshi Nakamoto and by 2012 cyber criminals had started latching onto it as a way to get paid anonymously. Could the advent of this new form of money have spurred on these boys in their bedrooms? In the NCA research report, the hackers interviewed refer to financial gain as only a secondary motivation. Clearly, in the ImageShack hack, money was not the main motivation. It was a bonus for Kivimäki. But who knows what other hacks the gang was carrying out with the accounts that their software tool cracked open? It is also worth bearing in mind that HTP were operating in 2011 and 2012 while the hackers in the NCA report were interviewed in 2014 and 2015. Things have shifted a monumental amount since then as bitcoin is worth so much more. Money is much more important to the teen gangs of 2024 than of 2012. But Kivimäki's extortion marks a significant shift in his mentality and perhaps that of the boys around him.

It was around this time that Zeekill was also making some side hustle bitcoin by scamming users on HackForums – a website for hackers to share tips, discuss cybersecurity and buy and sell hacking tools. With the help of another hacker from HTP he attacked other less experienced users who were advertising DDoS tools. After rendering the tools useless through attacks, Kivimäki would extort their makers for bitcoin in return for leaving them alone. The hackers would relent and pay up, only to have Kivimäki and his friend attack them again anyway. They would do it over and over again, extracting more and more bitcoin from gullible and helpless hackers.

In spite of this shady activity, Kivimäki, who called himself 'RyanC' on HackForums, quickly became a big name there. There's even an entry about him still on the site's wiki, which is like an online museum for notable activity and users.[5] The flattering biography (written by an unknown user) says he joined the site on 2 September 2012 to 'teach people about the different ways to properly perform website hacks'. He was a prolific poster, chipping in and chiding other hackers for not knowing as much as him. As the bio puts it, his posts were 'seemingly rude and offensive to some'. Regardless of his reputation he was given a Black Hat award for hacking into a website and was made leader of a forum group. For the next seven months as leader, he posted 'very informative threads in the Website & Forum hacking section, detailing methods to gain access to servers which had not been looked at yet on Hack Forums,' according to the bio. It didn't last. Once again he got into a row with other hackers on the forum and got revenge by messing up the forum groups he controlled. He even spread a rumour that one rival member had died. Getting into arguments and picking personal fights with people is something that Kivimäki was getting good at by now. At fifteen years old he had built up a name as a powerful hacker with tonnes of free time and a growing source of income. It was a potent mix. And the next person unlucky enough to find himself in his crosshairs felt the force not just online but in the physical world too.

#

It started with a ring on the doorbell.

A delivery driver had arrived unexpectedly at the Strater household in Oswego, Illinois with a handful of pizzas. Mr and Mrs Strater laughed it off as a mistake until the driver explained whose name was on the order – Julius Kivimäki. Immediately their son Blair knew what was happening. Apologising to the driver, he explained that he had recently gotten into a silly row with someone online and that this must have been a little payback prank.

Blair, who was about seventeen at the time, wasn't really a proper member of HTP – just one of the few dozen people who hung out in the chat channel for the group and sometimes helped out with publishing and publicising their zines. 'I was more of a friend of the show,' he says. He claims that Zeekill wasn't a core member either, saying 'he was not skilled enough', though events, and eventual police evidence, suggest otherwise. According to Blair, the row had started when he and Zeekill couldn't decide on who would have the honour of posting the next HTP zine online.

Kivimäki's pizza prank was just the start. Blair still has the Domino's pizza receipt with the name Julius Kivimäki on it, plus slips for three more that arrived at his door. Then there was Chinese food. Then pies from local restaurants. At all hours of the day and night. Within a few weeks the family had learned to expect the deliveries and became experts at waving the irritated drivers away. But the deliveries weren't just annoying. They were also a message. They meant that Zeekill knew where Blair lived in real life. He had taken the dispute off the text or voice chat rooms and into the real world.

The deliveries got worse and more imaginative – at one stage a truck with tonnes of sand and gravel arrived. Luckily the driver was stopped before he tipped it all onto the family driveway. Things escalated in November 2012, with an email sent from an account that looked like Blair's email address to the local police station. It was a bomb threat to the station that read: 'Man you ruined my life, and you are fucking going to get to pay for it. I hope you enjoy the explosions.'

Blair was on court-ordered probation at the time, after hacking and defacing his school's website in 2010, so the police quickly arrested him. In total, he says they held him for fifteen days across two stints while they investigated. In the end Blair decided to say that he had sent it – but only so that the police would let him go. The judge in his case read him the riot act, warning him that if anything else like this occurred again he would be put away for a long time. Though he was freed, he was on edge, waiting for the next thing to happen. The harassment was relentless and whenever something happened that affected others Blair had to quickly call the cops and explain it wasn't him.

Blair sent me a zip folder with files of evidence of the stunts and attacks he faced. There are documents showing that he (or someone using his name) fraudulently applied for disability benefit 'on behalf of Blair' and child medical care insurance in an apparent attempt to get him in trouble. Some of the paperwork shows the Straters' home internet was cut off by someone pretending to be Mr Strater cancelling their contract. These tactics caused Blair and his family untold annoyance and unwanted admin, but the next form of attack that Kivimäki and some of the HTP kids chose was straight-up dangerous.

Swatting is a harassment technique used by online bullies who contact local police with a fake emergency at someone's home so that the police – preferably an armed SWAT team – arrive to handle the bogus situation. The aim is to trick the cops into thinking there is some sort of horrific domestic violence incident taking place at the victim's address so that they arrive and kick the door in. By this point swatting had become enough of a problem for US cops that the FBI had published a bulletin in 2008 about the 'new phenomenon'.[6]

Blair was asleep when the first swatting happened. The police arrived at 3 a.m., waking up his confused parents. The officers were deadly serious and didn't relax until Blair's father woke his wife up and she came downstairs to prove that all was well. When Blair found out about it from his furious parents in the morning he was understandably fuming. But it didn't stop. The Strater family was swatted countless times after that. It would come in fits and starts – nothing would happen for weeks, and then there would be a flurry of swatting calls that wasted police time and caused the family to be permanently on edge. Blair puts some of the blame on the police who just kept falling for it. 'It got to the point where I'd answer the door to the cops and it was just a joke. I'd be like "right – who'd I kill this time?" The cops would say "your mother" and I'd have to go off and bother her and bring her to the door.' The unwanted attention to the family home in their peaceful cul-de-sac took its toll on neighbourhood relations. 'Our neighbours have completely ostracised us,' Amy Strater told *Fusion* in an article in 2015 aptly titled 'Haunted by Hackers'.[7]

The worst moment of the harassment campaign, which continued on and off for three years, came when Blair's tormentors hijacked the Twitter accounts of Tesla and the car company's CEO Elon Musk. The gang posted a picture of a Tesla with Blair's head on the roof and a message declaring that the company had been 'raped by BLAiR STRATER'. They changed the name on Tesla's Twitter account to '#RIPPRGANG', and posted: 'THIS TWITTER IS NOW RAN BY HENRY BLAIR STRATER FROM OSWEGO ILLINOIS.' They posted Blair's real phone number, promising to give away a free car to whoever called it. Similar posts were published to Elon Musk's account which had nearly 2 million followers at the time. Blair received five calls a minute for hours with thousands more calls to his mum's phone from all over the world. Through tears, his mother told *Fusion* how unbearable the harassment was. She had her Twitter account hacked and abhorrent things were posted under her name. 'I think all jews and muslims should die they're subhuman filth,' ran one such message.

Another message from her email account was posted to 300 residents of a local community group she was part of. 'I Will Shoot Up Your School,' it threatened. Oswego police quickly debunked the message and told the group that Amy's account had been hacked, but the damage was done. Her LinkedIn account was also hacked, the profile name changed to a slur against her employer: '[Redacted] IS A TERRIBLE COMPANY RAN [sic] BY JEWS.' She was fired from her job as a biostatistician shortly afterwards. She has always blamed the harassment and says she struggled to get a job because of the search result history linked to her name. Briefly she signed up as an Uber driver to make ends meet and her marriage with Blair's father ended amid the chaos. She eventually restarted her career under a different name.

I asked Blair if he ever felt physically in danger during all this and he said no. But he did share with me a voicemail he received that was, to my ear, extremely intimidating and unhinged. The caller speaks with an American accent – Blair is convinced it's Kivimäki but I couldn't confirm it. Whoever it is threatens to kill Blair and his family. The caller is either an exceptional actor or is genuinely out for blood: 'We know exactly where you live mother fucker and when you walk the fucking streets you'd better look over your fucking back motherfucker. I don't give a fuck if we have to burn your fucking house down and track your fucking family down . . . I swear to god they'll never find your body.'

In just over a minute the caller screams 'fuck' thirty-six times into the phone. Two other prank calls that Blair has recorded sound a lot like Kivimäki. He also has a picture of the caller ID on his phone which is 'Ihateblackpeople' – apparently Kivimäki's Skype name at the time. Blair insists he wasn't scared by the harassment and that he and his dad actually *hoped* that someone – especially Julius Kivimäki – would be bold enough to turn up at the family home. 'By that point, my family and I really wanted him to show up on our property with violent intent, because Illinois has very strong stand-your-ground laws. If he showed up, he would have been shot dead. And that you can publish,' Blair says.

The anger that this family had – and still has – for this teenager thousands of miles away is palpable. Blair is still furious, vengeful and bitter. Even now, ten years later, he says he struggles to get hired because of the harassment and its indelible history online. Blair's professional website, which he uses to show off his work as a computer systems administrator and programmer, begins with a message in English and Finnish about Julius Kivimäki.

Blair admits that he didn't help himself. He blames his autism for some of the antagonistic things he said and did in the chat rooms back then. But none of this could have justified what happened to him and his family. He describes what happened to him as a phenomenon called 'lolcow culture'. A 'lolcow' is someone on the internet who can reliably be poked at for a reaction, and this attracts people who want to 'milk' the cow for 'lols'.

Kevin Roose, who wrote the piece about the harassment of the Strater family for *Fusion*, asked Kivimäki about it all in 2015 – years after the harassment started. Kivimäki denied doing any of the delivery orders but admitted that, yes, he'd trolled Blair in IRC channels, and had harassed him offline on occasion. He admitted to tricking Comcast into cutting the family internet 'a few times'. He also said that he'd pasted the passwords to Amy's social media and email accounts to an IRC chat room but denied hacking her online life himself. He blamed the harassment on Blair himself, arguing that he was 'not very well liked in the hacker scene' and had been 'a pain in the ass' in hacker chat rooms. There were many other members who were eager to mess up his and his family's lives offline, he said. 'I have hard time [sic] feeling sympathy for them,' he told the reporter.

Ryan (AKA Urharmless) corroborates what Kivimäki says. 'Blair was very annoying and I remember we spent a lot of time harassing him and his family. Everyone was fair game back then.' Urharmless claims that, at one stage, Zeekill and another hacker called 'Veri' handed him all the paperwork needed to foreclose on the Strater family home. He tried but didn't succeed in tricking the bank into taking possession of the property.

There was something of a feeding frenzy around the poor Straters – the equivalent to school playground bullies picking on a misunderstood kid. But in the culture of teenage hacking gangs it seems there are few things off limits. Harassing someone's physical home and family from hundreds or thousands of miles away comes with none of the risks usually associated with causing a fellow school pupil problems. Harass a school kid and the teachers might find out or you might get an angry parent knocking on your front door.

The Straters pleaded many times to get the police to take action against Kivimäki. Blair says the cops did take more of an interest when he received that threatening voicemail but aside from lodging reports, nothing was ever done – Kivimäki was safely behind his computer in Finland far from the jurisdiction of US investigators.

But that was about to change when Kivimäki took a trip to the Mecca of hacking in 2013.

#

Every summer, thousands of hackers, researchers and the occasional undercover police officer descend upon Las Vegas for the world's largest hacking conference – DEF CON. What started as a low-key party for one hacker and his mates in 1993 has become an iconic calendar event for hackers around the world. Like a cybersecurity festival, there are talks from top professionals, hacking contests and plenty of parties fuelled by energy drinks and overpriced beer. It's all perfectly legal and celebrated by the great and good in cyber, in spite of its edginess. DEF CON visitors are famously warned not to access the wi-fi – there's a good chance someone has messed with it to try to hack into delegates' devices to gain kudos.

The conference in 2013 had all the ingredients for a classic event. Around 12,000 people walked in from the sweltering Vegas strip to the air-conditioned conference halls where some gobsmacking hacking demos took place. On stage, one group of hackers showed how it was possible to take control of a cute wi-fi bunny toy called Karotz. With a few clicks, this popular home assistant toy was turned into a surveillance camera. Elsewhere hackers showed off a new technique they'd invented to control a car's steering wheel, brakes and fuel gauge from a laptop. Actor Will Smith even attended briefly to conduct research for an upcoming movie role. The conference was buzzing and attendees seemed to be having a ball.

But DEF CON 2013 had a different vibe to normal. Usually federal police are an expected part of the crowd. For years they've mingled and pressed the flesh with hackers to either recruit them or get ideas. There's even a playful game nicknamed 'Spot the Fed' which has become a delegate favourite as attendees joke that the Feds are everywhere, trying (and failing) to blend in. But weeks before the 2013 event had come the global scandal of the Edward Snowden leaks, revealing shocking details of the US government's Prism programme of extensive digital mass-surveillance. Privacy-loving hackers were pissed off. So much so that the founder of DEF CON – Jeff 'The Dark Tangent' Moss – sent out a message on his blog to any cops planning to come to the conference: 'When it comes to sharing and socializing with feds, recent revelations have made many in the community uncomfortable about this relationship. Therefore, I think it would be best for everyone involved if the feds call a 'time-out' and not attend DEF CON this year. This will give everybody time to think about how we got here, and what comes next.'

It was quite a shock as relations between the event and the authorities were, until then, at an all-time high. The head of the NSA had given a keynote speech only the year before. But Jeff Moss's warning was largely heeded apparently to help prevent relations souring even further. So there weren't many feds to spot during the 2013 event. However, there *were* two who couldn't stay away that year.

Software developer turned federal agent Ryan Brogan had been in the force for four years when he arrived in Vegas for DEF CON. The fresh-faced FBI man was a long way from his field office in New Jersey, but took the flight in the hope of making a major breakthrough on a case he'd been toiling over for months. He and his partner Special Agent Nathan Burrows had got a tip-off that there were two DEF CON attendees who could be of huge interest to their investigations. Among the throng of visitors, all using their online monikers instead of their real names (as per the culture of the conference), were Zeekill and a new character in our story: 'Starfall'. Zeekill had come from Finland for the event and was a month away from his sixteenth birthday. Starfall was a sixteen- or seventeen-year-old fellow HTP hacker from Kentucky whose real name was Ryan King (so we have two more Ryans to add to our list).

The day before the official start of DEF CON on 31 July, the FBI agents went to the iconic Bellagio Hotel on Las Vegas Boulevard (the one with the giant dancing fountains as seen at the end of the film *Ocean's Eleven*) and made their way up to room 20104 – Starfall's room. At 6 p.m. they let themselves in, arrested Starfall and took him away. Zeekill, who was also in the room, was told he was not being arrested and that he was free to leave at any time. Whatever evidence they might have had, the FBI could only treat Kivimäki as a witness in the case as he was a minor and a citizen of a foreign country. But he chose to sit and talk to the police. Agent Brogan's notes show that he needed very little persuasion to open up about HTP and its members. He told the agents everything he knew about the gang, explaining that it had been created by someone calling themselves 'XIX' who lived in Florida and whose real name was Nathan. He even told them which internet provider XIX used. Later the police would identify him as Nathan Nye.

According to Kivimäki, HTP had formed long before they became publicly active, but perhaps that only refers to the group, not the hacking activity. Kivimäki himself first hung out in the general HTP IRC channel that anyone could join but was invited to a private HTP group by Starfall. He said he joined at the start of 2012 but that the group had recently disbanded after a disagreement about which direction it should take. He told the FBI agents about the hacks they'd carried out and who had done what. He also confessed to helping out on some of their attacks and admitted that he 'liked to buy things with stolen credit cards as it was easy'. He was also asked about offline harassment – potentially a reference to the Blair Strater case – but denied he had done anything serious, saying only that he snapped at people 'for fun sometimes'. According to the notes, he claimed to suffer from memory problems when asked about his other suspected crimes. The whole interview, which lasted less than an hour, was bizarre. The fierce and feared hacker Zeekill had rolled over on his friends instantly and seemed to have no worries about admitting his involvement.

But he also seemed to like talking about himself and bragging about his skills. He said he became interested in computers at the age of ten and had taught himself three different programming languages before writing his own malicious software applications. The agents must have been shocked at his candour and demeanour. Bear in mind that this was a fifteen-year-old Finnish boy in Vegas whose only friend had just been arrested. The police notes give the impression he really didn't care about what trouble he might be in. Either that or he knew the police had no power to touch him.

The only time the teenager seemed to show any emotion was when he asked to speak to his parents back home. His phone didn't connect so Agent Brogan called Kivimäki senior on his police BlackBerry. The call was successfully connected and Agent Brogan began talking to the father. At that point, according to Agent Brogan's notes, the boy became agitated and made 'aggressive gestures'. He tried to grab the phone and demanded to speak to his father himself. When the phone was handed over, he spoke in Finnish so the agents couldn't understand what was said.

Aside from that moment, Zeekill comes across as a cocky and unbothered teenager. He even asked to stay in Starfall's room for the rest of his stay in Vegas as 'Starfall won't be needing it now and it's a nice room'. The agents had to remind him several times that the room was under FBI surveillance. Although it's not in the court papers, I was told that the agents confiscated Zeekill's laptop and sent him back to Finland on the next flight.

As for Starfall – Ryan King – there is no official record at all about the arrest or any charges being brought against him. The 'DEF CON Drama', as it was known, was a big talking point in the hacker community, but there seemed to be no verifiable information about what happened to Starfall. 'Ryan King' has no online presence and has never spoken to journalists. There are also no results for Starfall or any of the other monikers used by him such as 'Aurora' and 'Xero'.

But after months of scratching my head and searching online I found out why there is no public information about the arrest. It wasn't real. During my interviews with Blair Strater the truth came out. It turns out that Blair Strater and Starfall are now a couple. Blair told me that Ryan King – now Sarah King after transitioning – is his girlfriend and he says she was only 'fake arrested' by the police on that day. The whole DEF CON meet-up with Zeekill was a sting set up by the FBI. Starfall was in on it from the beginning. The cops wanted to speak to Kivimäki in connection to a whole host of cyber attacks and possibly because of his alleged harassment of Blair Strater and his family. In fact, they were so desperate to set up the interview that they apparently paid for Starfall's flights to DEF CON and the luxury Bellagio hotel room.

Speaking to me via Blair's webcam (although she stayed off screen), Starfall (now Sarah) said that she had got to know Zeekill through HackForums and on IRC channels. She was impressed not by his technical hacking skills, but by his methods of scamming and tricking people – including other hackers on the forum. It was with her that Kivimäki had hatched the plan to repeatedly extort bitcoin from more naïve hackers on the forum by attacking their tools. Kivimäki was fearless, enterprising and didn't give a damn, and Starfall enjoyed his company, at least at first. A year before the FBI sting, in September 2012, Zeekill had posted an advert on HackForums for a powerful DDoS tool that he had either built, acquired or stolen. Starfall was one of the people who backed him up when others accused him of lying about how powerful his tool was. Here's a snippet of the customarily toxic thread under his advert (I've edited it to make it easier to follow):

> Dorkslavz: I doubt you can have even 10% of what you claim to have.
> The Ice King: i think this guy here is trying to scam everyone
> rilWrruren: This kid is dreaming. Just another HackForums troll we should all ignore.
> Starfall: I've seen this guy in action and though I can't back up the 500G claim, he has taken down some massive servers, even Black Lotus and Awknet DDoS protected ones, with what seems to me like ease.
> The Ice King: lol you are kidding right ithink this guy here is multi accounting and trying to scam everyone . . .
> aivpot: This guy is legit. He's kept my home connection down for weeks. I can't vouch for power but he's damn persistent.
> Starfall: I'll say this again: I can't vouch for the 500G but I CAN vouch for it being ridiculously powerful. I have known this man for four years, and bought thousands of shells from him. He is as legit as they come in that respect. I AM NOT SAYING HE HAS sOOGBPS. I'M JUST SAYING HE'S REALLY DAMN GOOD.

Starfall's so-called 'vouch' for Kivimäki would have gone a long way. She was a well-known name on the forum and there is still a wiki page about her on the site. It says she 'often wrote tutorials on coding and hacking and was friends with RyanC [Kivimäki]'. The bio also describes Starfall as 'one of the best hackers to have come onto the site' and a regular name dropped by other hackers seemingly looking for clout online. Starfall now laughs at that description of her skills back then. 'We were just script kiddies really,' she says but she admits that she knew more than most on the site who were pretending to be hackers.

Starfall and Zeekill, then, were friends. Starfall eventually introduced him to the core HTP members and says that, for a while, he was a useful and important member of the group. But over time the others started to dislike him because of his cruelty and desire to make money. 'We were all teenagers and just wanted to have fun. We started to realise the type of person he was. The way he treated Blair was wrong,' Sarah says.

The side deal Kivimäki made with the ImageShack CEO was the final straw for Starfall and the others, and they began plotting how to take Zeekill down. Starfall says the FBI was already talking to another member of the group who had been informing them about HTP's activity. (This person is known as #CW1 in the court papers but Sarah says it was not her and their identity remains unclear.) Once the activities of HTP drew to a close, sometime before spring 2013, the FBI seemed to be more interested in Zeekill than the others, so Starfall secretly started talking to them about him. She was the one who told them he was coming to DEF CON, which prompted the FBI to use her to set up the sting. Records show they went as far as to bug the hotel room the night before the pair arrived.

On the afternoon of the sting, Starfall invited Kivimäki over to show him around. Kivimäki wanted to leave to go and buy a camera. Nervously, she persuaded him to stay, having agreed with the cops that the two of them would be in the room when the clock struck 6 p.m. She still isn't sure if he ever realised what was happening, though to her it felt horribly awkward and obvious. Just as he was about to leave the room the agents burst in. There were six of them, including Brogan and Burrows. Once Starfall was bundled out of the room she was told she could stay for the conference. Not only that, the cops said she could use the credit card linked to her room for whatever she wanted. She had a great time splashing the FBI's cash. 'I went to some of the talks at DEF CON and bought all my food and drinks and even went down to the casino floor and gambled away 500 bucks! I would have carried on but then they asked me for ID and I was of course underage.' She didn't speak to Kivimäki afterwards and assumed that he had flown home to Finland after his run-in with US police.

Back then she was reckless. 'I was an autistic teenager who didn't really know right from wrong,' she says. She regrets some of the attacks she carried out with HTP, but argues that most of it was 'really fun' and not that damaging to the companies affected. There can't have been much harm done, she says, given that the cops didn't do much to the other members of the group. After DEF CON, Starfall carried on hanging out in the group chats but says she never got involved in hacking again. Recordings of her in the sessions show her being regularly picked on and teased about transitioning but she never shied away from being herself and seemed to brush off the juvenile jibes.

The FBI haven't confirmed or denied the Bellagio set-up, but I have found no reason to doubt Sarah's version of events. She insists that she doesn't regret setting Kivimäki up at all, especially in light of what he would go on to do. But Starfall and HTP weren't the only hackers to have developed a hatred for him, as Zeekill was about to find out when Finnish police finally came knocking.

//7
Zeekill arrested
2013

By 2013 Kivimäki was known to Finnish police, but not by Nixu's Antti Kurittu who was a detective at the time. Other officers had visited the Kivimäki home and spoken to the boy at least once in previous years. But it had been a while since his name had been uttered around the police station. So when Antti was tipped off about a kid called Julius Kivimäki, AKA Zeekill, he was intrigued.

The tip came from another suspect who police were investigating for a cyber attack on a Finnish business. While in custody, the hacker named Kivimäki as a collaborator in one of the attacks under investigation. It was 23 September – less than two months after the Bellagio sting. Antti and his officers drove west across Helsinki to Espoo not knowing what to expect when they arrived at the grey, five-storey Soviet-style block of apartments where the Kivimäki family lived. The building itself is stark and unappealing – a giant rectangular box sat on top of fat concrete pillars with a car park at its feet. It's not much to look at, but the apartments inside are spacious and airy. Antti knocked on the Kivimäki door and found Julius and his brother were home.

Julius was tall and blond with a cherubic face, but he looked like he hadn't left his bedroom for a while. At first the teenager was compliant and docile, but when Antti and his officers searched his bedroom he became agitated. He managed to switch off the internet modem to the apartment by toeing a power switch on an extension cable, much to the annoyance of officers. They knew exactly why he'd done it and their suspicions against him sky-rocketed. Cutting the internet meant that any live connections to servers or websites on his computer were instantly severed. It was when they told him they were going to have to confiscate his computers that Julius got upset and started shouting at the police. He had only just turned sixteen but was over six feet tall and Antti felt the situation was edgy enough to force him to call for backup. The boy didn't seem like he could put up much of a fight, so Antti wasn't physically intimidated, but he judged it could get dangerous if he was 'forced into a wrestling match in a small bedroom'. When the uniformed patrol team arrived, Kivimäki was arrested and led out of the house in flip flops, then taken to the station in a police car. Antti carried on his house search and Mr and Mrs Kivimäki arrived amidst the mayhem.

All eyes were on Julius's computer. Luckily it was unlocked and unencrypted so the team was able to do some quick searches for evidence of criminal activity. Straight away they found signs that the kid had been involved in cybercrime. The officers had to be sure that the computer hadn't been booby-trapped to delete data once it was switched off. So, before they unplugged it, Antti ran tests to check. It wasn't – a mistake Kivimäki would obviously learn from. In total, they confiscated a computer, two laptops and some hard drives for more careful cyber forensics work.

Meanwhile, Kivimäki was put in a cell and fell asleep almost immediately. In fact he slept for eighteen hours straight. He had clearly been online for days, fuelled by energy drinks and adrenaline. Officers theorised this was the first time he'd had a sustained screen break in weeks. Once Antti and his cyber forensics team started digging into the seized devices, they unearthed a gold mine of criminal evidence. 'Right away we stumbled into credit card numbers, passwords, and databases. It was more than enough probable cause to have him in custody for at least a couple of weeks,' Antti says.

Funnily enough, they didn't find any evidence linking him to the original reason they had knocked on his door. Sometimes the digital evidence just isn't there. One thing was for sure though – the Kivimäki investigation now took priority over anything else. This was a lucky break for the suspect who had mentioned Kivimäki – a small-time hacker who very quickly got himself back on the straight and narrow after the incident. 'If you want to throw a wrench into a police investigation, just throw Julius Kivimäki into it. Then you'll be sure that cops are busy for a year,' Antti jokes.

In Kivimäki, the cops had stumbled upon 'a real hardcore hacker'. They were grudgingly impressed by the scale of the cybercrime this boy was involved in. The types of tools found on his computers weren't that sophisticated, but there were lots of them. His computer was a cyber armoury chock full of every hacking tool readily available on the open internet or for purchase in hidden hacker marketplaces and forums. Police also found custom-built software that could steal details from targeted computers. In other folders they discovered digital keys allowing high-level access to many places online that should not have been open to him. Yet others contained thousands of credit card numbers, most of which had not been reported stolen at that time. 'He had obviously spent a long time amassing that amount of illicit information,' Antti says.

There was so much illegal activity on Julius's computer that the police had to limit their investigations severely to just the bigger cybercrimes. They chose to file four criminal complaints based on their initial forensic analysis to ensure they had him under lock and key for as long as necessary to do a thorough investigation. He was held for nearly four weeks, and unlike most suspects, staying in police custody actually seemed to do him some good. His hacker lifestyle had clearly been taking a terrible toll on his body. IRC text logs stored on Kivimäki's computer showed him up till the early hours talking to other hackers in the US and beyond who were in different time zones. Initially the team had no idea of Kivimäki's extended involvement with HTP, but that would change with a visit from the FBI. The investigation report shows that FBI officers – probably Agents Brogan and Burrows – flew over from the US once they had heard about the arrest. They shared information with Finnish police on HTP and Kivimäki, handing over their notes from his confessions in the Bellagio. They also brought over the laptop that they had taken from him and analysed in Vegas. It was all good ammunition for the Finnish cops to get more out of him in their own interrogations. Not that it was needed. Just as in the hotel room, Kivimäki opened up to cops without much persuasion. He liked to talk about computers and enjoyed showing off his cyber knowledge. He also freely threw his hacker mates under the bus, for example telling cops that an American hacker called 'KMS' was a prolific participant in various credit card stealing schemes. Notes from his interrogations show him admitting to numerous offences too. Perhaps, once again, he felt that the police couldn't do much to him as a minor. Or he knew that denying everything was futile when there was so much evidence on his computers.

Like so many other hackers in this twisting and turning story, Kivimäki was a hoarder. Police had a field day sifting through all the digital evidence and requested more records from PayPal and his email provider. They found folders and files linked to multiple cyber attacks, often with the kinds of names that only immature teenagers could conjure up: 'jewwslayer.exe', 'cuntbag.exe', 'dicksinmyarse.exe' and 'niggersone.exe'. They found receipts for items for everything you can imagine a boy would buy if he had a near endless supply of stolen credit card numbers: PlayStation vouchers, Netflix subscriptions, top-of-the-range gaming headsets, an iPad, an iPhone, a MacBook laptop, a high-end computer graphics card, mail order drugs. He had also paid to own a tiny bit of land in Scotland through

Highlandtitles.com so that he could legally call himself a 'Lord'. Clearly he was having a blast spending vast amounts of other people's money on a whim. Some of the charges were blocked by banks but police estimated that the receipts they had collected totalled about 35,000 euros.

Kivimäki was called out of his prison cell almost every day for police interrogations. The lengthy interview transcripts show the officers asking him about every purchase receipt they could find in his emails and on his computer. Kivimäki admitted to carrying out most of the purchases with stolen cards but he denied some, claiming that they had been done for, or by, other members of HTP. He had made sure that nothing was delivered to his own home or under his real name. Many of the purchases were made under the name 'Ryan Cleary'.

Other times he bought items under random names, including some offensive ones like 'niggerslayerpro'. Physical items were shipped to an empty house in Ireland, and someone called 'Deathbolt', who Kivimäki knew from the community, would collect them for onward shipping. Kivimäki said in a police interview that he didn't know Deathbolt's real name but guessed that he or she must have lived near the empty property. Police found three pictures sent to Kivimäki by this unknown person in June 2013 as proof of delivery. The pictures are of a 300-euro case of champagne purchased by 'Ryan Wellman'. As well as the leisure goods, items that you could describe as 'operational equipment' were also purchased with the stolen cards. Hard drives, cloud storage space, subscriptions to privacy-enhancing services and website-name buying all featured. One particular URL address – ugnazi.com – was to become very significant. So too were two names that Kivimäki mentioned in police interviews as other hackers who used the stolen credit cards: 'Cosmo' and 'Mir'.

Mass credit card fraud is a serious crime on its own but the police also became very interested in an HTP attack on a large cloud computing company called Linode. Used by many website developers around the world, the company had been hacked by the group in April 2013. The gang had used a flaw in a popular piece of software called Adobe ColdFusion to burrow deep into the company's innards, gaining access to pretty much everything. Company source code, partial customer credit card numbers and weakly encrypted account passwords were all accessed. Kivimäki admitted to police that he had done it with XIX and others 'because Linode was a big company and it hosted interesting websites and it seemed like a fun idea at the time'. They had also done it as part of an elaborate multi-pronged attempt to get revenge on a rival hacker or hackers but Kivimäki doesn't mention that in his police interviews. The hack caused mayhem, worry and a whole lot of admin for Linode and its hundreds of thousands of customers. Here's the notice the firm put out on their website apologising for the hack: 'We take your trust and confidence in us very seriously, and we truly apologize for the inconvenience that these individuals caused. Our entire team has been affected by this, leaving all of us, like you, feeling violated.'[1]

Yes, they were only words. And probably words that had been run through twenty-five corporate lawyers. And yes, the company had made the mistake of not fixing the known bug in ColdFusion. But this notice reminds us of the human impact on the people caught up in the schemes of these carefree boys fuelled by energy drinks, inflated egos and pubescent hormones.

Of all the things Kivimäki and HTP did though, it was the creation of a powerful botnet that police considered most serious. It was also probably the thing that had most piqued the interest of the FBI in the first place. A botnet (short for robot network) is a network of hijacked computers that can be controlled by one person or group. Like a digital army, these computers can be manipulated like puppets by the malicious hand of the hacker, who is often referred to in such cases as a 'bot herder'. With a few clicks the bot herder can command all their bots to carry out simultaneous actions such as, for example, 'connect to this website every three seconds'.

ZEEKILL ARRESTED

This particular command is the type we see in DDoS attacks – a teenage hacker's favourite form of cyber vandalism. DDoS attacks don't really require much technical skill, but when the botnet being deployed is large enough they can be immensely powerful and damaging. Even now DDoS attacks are still being used to great effect by vigilante hackers in cyber wars between, for example, Russia and Ukraine. The incredible thing about botnets used in this way is that all of this happens without the owner of the infected device having a clue that their computer is part of the bot army. Your own computer might be part of a botnet right now, quietly being herded around the internet to cause mischief to an individual or company thousands of miles away without you even realising. And it's not just laptops and desktops – almost any internet-connected device can be enslaved into the zombie army, including CCTV cameras, wi-fi routers and digital video recorders. Even smart fridges have been proven to be susceptible. Often, these so-called 'internet of things' gadgets are poorly secured with default passwords, so it's child's play to log into them and secretly take them over.

Regardless of all the illegal things that a botnet can do, even the creation of one is of course against the law as it involves infecting and enslaving computers with a piece of malicious software. HTP was responsible for creating a huge botnet. When the Helsinki police went public with their main charge against Kivimäki it was blockbuster stuff and became the largest cybercrime case in Finland's history. On 18 October 2013 they put out the notice: 'The Helsinki police have revealed an extensive series of data breaches in which a young Finnish man had access to a total of more than 60,000 hacked internet servers around the world. The suspect has worked as part of an international hacker group. The suspect has been captured.'

The notice cited aggravated data breach, aggravated payment instrument fraud and interference with telecommunications. It emerged that Julius also had the details of more than 3,000 credit cards on his home computer.

Kivimäki was released shortly after that on bail while police continued to build evidence against him. Most of all they wanted to find out how on earth this sixteen-year-old and his gang could have hacked into 60,000 computers to amass what at that time was one of the most powerful botnets around.

Kivimäki didn't build the botnet – it looks like that was the work of other members of HTP – but he admitted to police that he had helped tweak it to make it faster and more efficient. He denies spreading the malicious software around to infect more servers and grow the size of the bot army. But evidence proved otherwise and that appears to be exactly what his role was. His computers had passwords to some of the hacked servers and chat logs showing him and the others celebrating how fast it was growing.

In March 2013, for example, a cybersecurity researcher called Joe Giron had discovered that his company's computers were part of the HTP botnet. Giron proceeded to write a blog post about it: 'The other day at work, I encountered a number of machines all attacking other hosts. Normally it's just one machine, but this [time] there were several.'[2] Kivimäki shared the post with the other members of HTP in their chat channel 'Operation Dildos'. HTP had a good laugh about Giron's blog, mocking his analysis as a 'horrible job', but they also got offended by some of it. 'I like how he said it's amateur. Apparently he's never heard of "I don't give a fuck,"' said one. 'Amateurs don't make thousands of bots,' said another. 'Yea, amateurs don't infect servers,' Kivimäki replied. They then congratulated themselves on how they had managed to grow the botnet from 900 bots to 2,000 overnight.

There were other money-making schemes and damaging cyber attacks that Antti and his investigators looked at: a complicated and sprawling web of cybercrime involving dozens of anonymous and faceless hackers all over the world. For example, police were puzzled as to why a convicted cyber criminal from the UK called Edward Pearson had sent the fifteen-year-old 6,588 euros. Somehow Pearson had entered Zeekill's orbit (or vice versa) and done some sort of deal. Kivimäki claimed to have forgotten what the money transfer was about. It shows us just how deeply embedded Kivimäki was in this interconnected subculture where there is no knowing where the next chat room encounter might lead.

Despite – or perhaps because of – the wealth of evidence, it took Antti and his team months to compile their 315-page investigation report. And it would take the Finnish court system even longer to decide on Kivimäki's fate.

In the meantime, he was free again, albeit with no computer. It took a while, but he then resurfaced online apparently undeterred by his month in prison. News of his raid, arrest and release had spread fast through the teen hacking world. But instead of putting others off, the fact that Kivimäki had emerged from his time offline unharmed and unhindered seemed to encourage other groups to rise up out of the chat rooms to try to get attention and cause chaos. For some cybersecurity professionals, it was clear that teenage hacking culture was shifting towards a much darker place.

//8
Addicted to hacking
2012

Allison Nixon is a professional lurker. For more than a decade she has snuck her way onto hacking forums and into group chats to sit, wait, watch and learn. Hackers hate her. You can see why – from inside their groups she has exposed individuals and unearthed their tactics. She has a tough time online with regular threats to her safety from cowardly hackers who hope to deter her. They've never succeeded and likely never will. She is probably the world's foremost expert on teen cyber gangs and her earnest youthful face – with its thin-rimmed glasses and framed by long black hair – has appeared on dozens of documentaries and news channels to talk about the topic.

It was in June 2013 on Rhode Island, USA, that she planted her flag in this otherwise overlooked area of teen cybercrime.[1] Allison and her colleague Brandon Levene provided a thorough breakdown of how these teenagers worked and why they should be taken seriously. They also introduced a new term to describe these types of hackers: 'Noob Persistent Threats' (NPTs). The term is a tongue-in-cheek play on a universally used term for describing the top tier of hackers – 'Advanced Persistent Threats' (APTs). APTs are the cream of the cyber crop. They are groups made up of the most technically skilled hackers in the world and are well funded, patient and, as the descriptor suggests, persistent. Almost all the known APTs in the world are organised and paid for by governments. They are cyber spies or cyber military tasked with gathering intelligence, stealing secrets or carrying out disruptive (and sometimes even destructive) cyber attacks. Although they operate in the shadows, these groups are given names or numbers to make it easier to share information about them. Perhaps the most famous is the Russian government hacking unit known as 'Fancy Bear'.

So Allison's new term was created to poke fun at teen hacking groups for being 'noobs' or 'newbies', meaning that they were new to the scene and not experienced or knowledgeable. But they *were* definitely persistent and, as Allison convincingly argued, they *were* a threat. She characterised NPTs as script kiddies – the lowest tier of the cybercrime underground. They had very basic technical skills compared to APTs and were hacking and learning at the same time. According to her research, they mostly did it out of curiosity, to get attention and earn respect with their peers. But lately, they had been experimenting with ways to get paid too. Most of them were American or European and nearly all of them had terrible OpSec – operational security – which as Allison and Brandon joked 'is great for us researchers!'

Allison's interest in NPTs started when she noticed the emergence of LulzSec copycats like HTP and others. She wanted to know how these kids with low levels of skill were able to cause such chaos and make it look easy. So she started seeking out hacker IRC channels and logging them to see how these gangs organised themselves. 'People were looking at the attacks from these groups like Black Swan events – unpredictable and abnormal. But quickly I realised that by lurking and learning about the community you could correlate their chatter with their targets and find out who, and what, was next.'

Allison was working for a cybersecurity company that started offering her insight and research as part of their services to clients.

She found herself more and more drawn into this underground network and discovered she was exceedingly good at the patient and crafty style needed to extract gold from the frenetic and toxic chat rooms and forums. She credits her lurking skills to playing hundreds of hours of the computer game *Eve Online*, a sprawling space game that allows players to explore an enormous galaxy collecting resources and fighting off rival factions. The game encourages theft and double crossing. One way to sabotage enemies is to sneakily infiltrate their social guilds under false names to sow confusion or steal secrets. 'It's kind of remarkable how similar what I do now is to what I used to do back during my *Eve Online* days,' Allison laughs.

Like so many of the hackers we've heard about in this world, gaming was Allison's gateway into learning about computers. Her fascination was sparked when playing another game called *Sim Park* when she was thirteen years old. She realised it was possible to use a glitch to break the game and give herself unlimited in-game money to buy new things for the simulated park she was controlling.

But her career was no game and she was taking her research – known in the business as 'threat intelligence' – very seriously. Her team built profiles of the active groups so that they could warn customers about how this new type of cyber criminal might try to hack them. Although you never really know who is behind an online moniker, Allison was able to identify certain patterns of behaviour. There are no leaders as such, but there are normally one or two hackers who are the 'centre of gravity' – usually the most skilled or the most reckless. You can make up for a lack of technical skill by being the loudest and most anarchistic. The kids are often from stable, middle-income families who can afford decent computers and internet connections. It stands to reason that they are largely unsupervised by parents as they are able to spend hours at a time online. Most come from English-speaking countries like the US, Canada, UK or Ireland. Other nations that seem to have a disproportionate number of young hackers are ones that have good English language teaching, like the Netherlands and of course Finland. There hasn't been much mingling between Western hacking communities and those in Russia or China which also have a strong foundation of cyber talent – but that is changing.

Back in 2013 when Allison made her presentation, the cyber industry was more interested in the risks posed by the far more glamorous APTs, or the imagined threat of terrorist hackers. Not a bunch of kids. But US cybersecurity journalist Brian Krebs agreed with Allison that there was a tendency to dismiss the activities of these script kiddies. Known for investigating and uncovering the real-world identities of hackers on his website 'Krebs on Security', he too began to look into their activity.

Krebs, as he is affectionately known in the cyber world, had been on the receiving end of an NPT attack so had first-hand knowledge of their capabilities. In 2013 he was already busy looking into teenage hackers who were making money creating and selling services for DDoS attacks called 'booters' or 'stressers'. There were a lot of booters being launched at this time with dramatic names like 'Asylumstresser', 'RageBooter' or 'PedoBooter'. They weren't all botnets built by enslaving people's computers. Most were just lazily piggy-backing on the computing power of cloud service providers. The criminals would hire a lot of computing power from a large company and then sell access to it for DDoS attacks. Some sellers were making thousands of dollars flogging their services to other kids who wanted to annoy their mates by knocking them offline in the middle of an online game. Or take their school's website out for a bit. Or get revenge on a shop for bad customer service. The only limit to who the tools could be aimed at was the imagination of the customers. The services were cheap and easy to access. All you needed to do was pay some money – maybe $20 via a PayPal account – enter the IP address of the site or server you wanted to take out and press 'go'. No skill needed at all. If you're wondering why nothing was done to stop this burgeoning industry (which still exists today) it's because booters/stressers *can* have legitimate purposes. They're needed by web service developers to stress-test the robustness of their sites and apps. Developers need to have a way to know what kind of level of traffic they can sustain before they have problems or outages. These booter kids got away with selling their cybercrime services by having vague disclaimers – like 'We bear no responsibility for how you use it' – on their sites that feigned ignorance about what people were really doing with their stresser services. Thankfully, they have become rarer and less easily accessible nowadays.

Krebs' work on this area struck a nerve, and in March 2013 he was hit by a multi-pronged harassment campaign by a mystery hacker group. A swatting attack saw a large armed police team arrive at his home in Virginia – an experience that Krebs described on his website at the time:

> When I opened the door . . . I heard someone yell, 'Don't move! Put your hands in the air.' Glancing up from my squat, I saw a Fairfax County Police officer leaning over the trunk of a squad car, both arms extended and pointing a handgun at me. As I very slowly turned my head to the left, I observed about a half-dozen other squad cars, lights flashing, and more officers pointing firearms in my direction, including a shotgun and a semi-automatic rifle. I was instructed to face the house, back down my front steps and walk backwards into the adjoining parking area, after which point I was handcuffed and walked up to the top of the street.[2]

Krebs had warned the cops six months earlier that he might be a target of swatting and had instructed them to call him before they sent out the cavalry. But he was vacuuming when they called and didn't hear his phone ringing. So the cops rolled up, guns cocked and ready. Once Krebs had explained everything again they all stood down. The supervising officer told him that someone had called 911 pretending to be him and saying that Russians had broken into his home and shot his wife.

The attack had been well orchestrated. At the same time that he was being swatted, his website provider received a fake letter from the FBI about illegal content being hosted on his website. Luckily they ignored it, but they couldn't ignore the DDoS attack that followed and briefly took his site offline. It was a wild twenty-four hours. Not only that, but when the tech website Ars Technica published a story about his ordeal, they too were hit by an identical and powerful DDoS attack that took the site offline for a short time and stopped them publishing or editing any stories for two hours.

Allison was called in to investigate. It was a 'huge pivot moment' in her career that set her firmly on the path to specialising in this area of cybersecurity research. She was one of a team of experts who rallied around Krebs to help him find out who had harassed him. 'Many parties jumped in all at once,' she says. It took them a while but they eventually zeroed in on one gang calling themselves 'UG Nazi' (pronounced 'You-Gee' Nazi). It stood for 'Underground Nazi Hacktivist Group'.

These teenagers, mainly from the US, were seemingly inspired by LulzSec and wanted to be as provocative as possible. Their logo was a cartoon of Adolf Hitler with his eyes made to look like those of an innocent baby. The name and logo showed a level of immature attention seeking not yet reached by previous groups. These kids wanted to show that they didn't give a damn who they offended. It's an example of 'edge lord' culture – a desire to be more provocative and extreme than the next person. As Dictionary.com describes it, an 'edge lord' is a person (usually male) who affects a provocative or extreme persona, especially online.[3] An edge lord, for instance, 'might say positive things about Hitler, or they might aggrandize mass shootings, hoping their edginess makes them seem unique or especially intellectual'.

It's also notable that the *Oxford English Dictionary* recorded the first mainstream use of the term in 2013. Something was happening online at this time that empowered or encouraged young men and boys to do outrageous and antisocial things. It's hard to know if LulzSec, HTP and now UG Nazi were part of that swell of sentiment or just another mirror to the online culture. Either way, UG took the baton from HTP. Being arrested as a teenage hacker became something to be shrugged off, even encouraged.

At first UG Nazi feigned a political bent stemming from the ethos of Anonymous. For example, they defaced the website of the UFC (Ultimate Fighting Championship) in response to its support of the Stop Online Privacy Act. (This was a bill considered in 2011 that aimed at cracking down on online piracy by granting authorities broader powers to combat copyright infringement and counterfeit goods.) UG Nazi also performed DDoS attacks on the websites of the CIA, which they managed to keep offline for hours. That was coordinated with a DDoS attack on the US Department of Justice (DoJ) in protest of the Cyber Intelligence Sharing and Protection Act – a proposed law that would allow for the sharing of internet traffic information between the US government and technology and manufacturing companies. But in spite of these semi-noble motives, one of UG Nazi's core members, Eric Taylor, known as 'CosmoTheGod' (who we mentioned previously as someone Kivimäki claimed to have collaborated with on credit card fraud) admits now that 'if there was any strategy to our attacks – it was mayhem'.

Eric Taylor is now in his late twenties living in Florida. He is a good-looking slim man with a chiselled jaw, short-cropped hair and a penchant for colourful and eye-catching clothing (he's done some modelling too). In many ways his story echoes that of Kivimäki, albeit with a happier ending. Eventually, Eric is now a proud member of the white-hat hacking world. While he is quick to say he regrets his time as CosmoTheGod, he admits with a smile that as a fifteen-year-old, hacking into websites and making global headlines made him feel 'like a god'. His time as Cosmo was an intoxicating and wild ride that he couldn't get off even when things got way out of control. A lonely but largely happy teenage boy, he had got into hacking at the age of thirteen through gaming. Back then he and his mother lived at his grandmother's house. His single mother worked twelve hours a day, six days a week, so he was left alone on his computer in the evenings. His obsession with winning the player-versus-player shooting game *Call of Duty* led him to online forums about hacking that taught him how to cheat to win. He claims he was a talented player but admits lots of his tournament wins came after he'd knocked his opponents offline through hacking them mid-game. It didn't take long for the fourteen-year-old's love for gaming to be overtaken by his interest in hacking.

Eric's gamer tag, CosmoTheGod, became his hacking alias. He was quick to learn – apparently through group chats with the likes of Ryan Cleary – how to take over Xbox accounts and sell the ones that had cool names. It sounds insane but people were (and still are) willing to part with real cash to buy a rare or intriguing Xbox username. Eric was able to get hundreds of dollars for some of the more desirable Xbox accounts. He also had his own booter service which he says could bring in $5,000 a month. All of this at the age of only fifteen and under the nose of his grandma and mother. The only time his mum started asking questions was when she noticed the stack of twenty discarded Xboxes in his bedroom. Every time Eric got banned from Microsoft for stealing an account or cheating in a game he would have to buy a new console. He somehow managed to explain away the mountain of expensive and discarded hardware and carry on.

But when Eric was expelled from school due to apparently making multiple bomb threats there could be no doubt in the minds of his mum and grandma that he was involved in something bad. The teenager had somehow pissed off some other boys online, and they had decided to call in a bomb threat in his name every day for two weeks. The police walked into the classroom to take him out of school and interview him.

'When they walked into class one part of me thought it was funny and the other part was like "Fuck, what am I going to do now?"' he says. He spent a day at the police station until his mum came to bail him out. Meanwhile the police had turned their house upside down. He was charged with data theft and impersonation. They confiscated his computer, which was particularly galling for him as it had the keys to his digital bitcoin wallet that would now be worth hundreds of thousands of dollars.

The police told him to stay off the internet and stop stealing usernames. They tried to scare him out of the hacking gangs. But it didn't work at all. 'I really wasn't fazed about it, so I just played it smart. I waited a couple of months then I got new laptops and hardware and started again,' he remembers. That was at the end of 2011. LulzSec was down and out. HTP was flying high.

At the start of 2012 Eric was invited to a group chat on a messaging service called Jabber by a friend he used to steal Xbox accounts with. The name of the group was UG Nazi and they wanted him to join. His acceptance marked the beginning of a turbo-charged period of mayhem in his life. 'Before UG Nazi I was just having fun and games and seeing how far I could take my computer skills. But once I joined that Jabber group I just started hacking things all day directing my attacks at people that I thought deserved it,' he says. With UG Nazi, Cosmo 2.0 was born.

Eric says the core of UG Nazi was made up of just three teens who were all from the US – CosmoTheGod (Eric), 'JoshTheGod' (Mir Islam – who Kivimäki would later mention in his interviews with cops) and 'OsamaTheGod' (Troy Woody Jr). Another hacker called 'Cyberzeist' was sometimes involved too. And so was Kivimäki. Eric says Kivimäki was an occasional player in the group at the same time as he was hacking with HTP. We also know from court records that one of Kivimäki's purchases with those stolen credit cards was for the website address 'www.ugnazi.com'. But there's no trace of the site being launched. Once again the incestuous nature of the teen hacking community is evident. And Kivimäki was a common denominator.

In UG Nazi, Cosmo was the social engineering specialist. He had honed his skills with Xbox account takeovers and he had a plethora of methods to use. For example, let's say he wanted to steal the Xbox account '@GreatestGamerEver'. He would find out what email address was linked to that account: greatestgamerever@gmail.com for example. Then it might be as simple as guessing their password ('password123' is a classic) to log in and take it over. Sometimes the password might be harder to guess and a bit more work was required: for example he might have to search through previous data breach lists for non-Xbox-related accounts to see if the email address greatestgamerever@gmail.com appeared along with a password. Given that a lot of people use the same password across multiple services, this leaked password might then also work for the Xbox account.

Sometimes yet more trickery was required. Cosmo developed a knack for sending cleverly presented emails or making plausible conman-like phone calls to service providers. He was an expert sweet talker and would fool helpdesks into thinking he was the rightful owner of accounts to persuade staff to give him passwords or other forms of access. He also developed ingenious ways to string together bits of information about people to break into their accounts. With these skills he soon branched out from Xbox accounts to Amazon, Gmail and Netflix profiles.

It was a hack of this kind, which involved all these methods and more, that really put UG Nazi on the map. In summer 2012 Cosmo and the lads attacked the infamous website 4chan, on the feeble basis of their claim that 'everyone on 4chan is a child molester'. It took weeks to pull it off. The gang realised that in order to get to 4chan they had to go through its cloud service provider Cloudflare. So, incredibly, Cosmo hacked into the personal Gmail account of Cloudflare's CEO, Matthew Prince, to get access to his company's back-end admin area. The amount of work he and UG Nazi put in to pull this off was mind boggling. I've read about how they did it[4] dozens of times and I still find it confusing but here's my attempt to explain it:

1. Find Matthew Prince's personal details, including phone number, personal email account and social security number from previous data breach marketplaces.
2. Call telecom company AT&T pretending to be Matthew Prince and convince them to forward any new messages to a Google Voice voicemail number that UG Nazi controlled.
3. Call Google pretending to be Matthew Prince and ask to set a new password for his email account, so prompting them to send a password reset code to his voicemail.
4. Use this code to set a new password for Prince's personal email account.
5. Log in to Prince's email account.
6. Try to log in to Prince's corporate Google account and request that a password reset code be sent to his personal email account.

7. Use this password reset code to gain access to Prince's corporate Google account.

Bingo.

After all that work, fuelled by adrenaline and junk food (Cosmo was very overweight at this time) they finally had access to the internal control panel of Cloudflare. This allowed them to redirect anyone trying to access 4chan to UG Nazi's own Twitter account. Cosmo tweeted that the crew had 'gained full access into Cloudflare's server and obtained the database – 4chan defaced'. But the redirect was only active for less than an hour before it was fixed. You could argue it was all a bit pointless. But the teenagers were happy – they had humiliated the owners of 4chan, annoyed its users, and shocked the cyber world once more. They also got a monstrous surge of serotonin as they saw the number of their Twitter followers skyrocket and tens of thousands of people celebrating them online. UG Nazi were in the headlines and Cosmo – still only fifteen years old – was over the moon. In a surprisingly honest post he announced on PasteBin: 'We will not tell lies and pretend that it was all to fight an injustice. This was for the lulz. This was for the fame. This was done because only we have the skill to do it. This was done, so that we can laugh at your butthurt. We did it because we can.'

None of the elaborate and time-consuming steps that they took are the sort of hacking we see in the movies, where cybercrime masterminds are depicted hunched over their computers furiously typing complex codes to gain access into systems (yes, like *Hackers*). Some will argue UG Nazi's methods don't even count as hacking as they didn't involve technical expertise. But these kids were hacking *the system* to get what they wanted.

There is often a snobbery from cybersecurity experts and hackers about this kind of thing. These types of attacks and attackers are sneered at because their methods are low-skilled and unsexy. But for researchers like Allison Nixon, this UG Nazi hack in particular was a

ADDICTED TO HACKING

watershed moment in the NPT story, a gobsmacking example of what these kids were capable of. 'It was a really troubling development as you can see the persistence and the creativity in these boys which I just knew could, and probably would, be used to cause a lot more harm,' Allison says.

Hacking into the back-end of Cloudflare could have had worse consequences if UG Nazi had been an APT or a well-run criminal gang with an actual plan to make or steal money. Although some teen hackers had started dabbling in extorting bitcoin from people, UG Nazi seemed far less interested – perhaps because Cosmo was already making money from his other criminal endeavours. They didn't make a penny from the 4chan hack but it was a wake-up call for all the parties involved in their long attack chain. AT&T, Cloudflare and Google all instigated changes to security after the incident to prevent the methods from working again.

Interestingly, even at such a young age Eric knew that what he was doing was wrong, and out of guilt he says he tried to warn Matthew Prince the night before the hack. Underneath the bravado, Eric knew this hack was going to be a major criminal one and he had second thoughts. He couldn't pull the plug directly as it would lose him a great deal of respect with his gang mates and wider community. But he could secretly warn Matthew Prince and therefore get it stopped that way. He called Prince, but the CEO hung up on him before he could warn him about the incoming attack. UG Nazi instigated the takeover the next day.

It didn't take long for the cops to come knocking, though Eric thinks it wasn't the 4chan hack that prompted them – there wasn't much sympathy for 4chan and its users. It was more likely UG Nazi's hack of a British web-hosting and billing agency called WHMCS.[5] They used the same social engineering tricks to get into and steal a huge amount of private customer data. Around 500,000 customer usernames, passwords, IP addresses and in some instances credit card details were unceremoniously dumped onto the site PasteBin for all to see, download and use for whatever nefarious purposes they could dream up. The boys also deleted tonnes of company data, briefly took its site offline, and hijacked its Twitter feed. Again, there's no suggestion this was financially motivated – they did it because they could.

The police response was swift. In June 2012 the FBI arrived at Cosmo's house in Long Beach, California and arrested him again. And turned his grandma's house upside down. Again. They confiscated his electronics and put him in a cell for two days this time. He left the house in the shorts and T-shirt he was sleeping in when police arrived and he says they made him stay in those clothes until he was let out on bail. He didn't know it at the time, but his arrest was part of a larger multinational bust that the FBI called Operation Card Shop. Police forces in thirteen different countries arrested twenty-four hackers and fraudsters of varying levels of criminality. UG Nazi had been bundled into a larger group of people wanted for making money from carding – the type of credit card fraud we saw with Kivimäki and co. that involves stealing card information to make purchases. Although carding wasn't something UG Nazi bragged about on their Twitter feeds, they were experts at it and some members apparently stole a considerable amount of money (they would never say how much).

This time Eric fessed up to the police about most of his crimes and began the long wait for them to sentence him. Cosmo 2.0 had been cut down in his prime – a once successful thief, vandal and anarchist now adrift and separated from his hacking community without any devices to get online with. Maybe he was bored or badly advised but shortly before his sentencing the fifteen-year-old invited *Wired* magazine to his house for an in-depth interview about his life.[6] He showed little remorse and seemed to enjoy bragging about the social engineering methods he had perfected. His compulsion for, even addiction to, hacking comes across in the pages.

It's fascinating that in spite of everything, his grandma describes Eric in the article as a good boy. She seems pleased he's not out on the streets getting in trouble. 'Eric is always, always home. He don't go anywhere. He's a good kid. He's a very good kid,' she told the reporter Matt Hanon. No criticism of Eric's grandma but here we see another potential issue with teen hackers – the perception is that they are shy, nerdy and harmless because their criminal actions are largely invisible. If Eric was out late at night hanging out in parks or on street corners as a small-time drug dealer or violent gang member then his grandma might have thought differently. Teen cyber criminals are unseen despite their crimes happening under the noses of their parents and guardians. The irony is that this good, homely kid was upstairs causing disruption, financial loss and distress to victims that went far beyond his neighbourhood.

Weeks later, in November 2012, Eric was sentenced to six years' probation, which meant no internet without permission and supervision until his twenty-first birthday. He was only allowed online for school work and not allowed to speak or communicate with any of his hacking buddies. At this point UG Nazi was pretty much over – JoshTheGod (Mir Islam), who was now eighteen years old, had also been arrested in the big carding bust. Troy Woody Jr told Eric that he had been raided too. But there is no public record of that.

At first, Eric complied with his probation order. Sort of. He soon returned to the chat rooms but started off innocently enough – sitting silently and anonymously watching other hacking gangs and individuals in action. He sat on his hands whenever hacking operations were announced. But then a horrific event drew him back into the fray.

#

On 14 December 2012, twenty-year-old Adam Lanza shot his mother, then drove across town with an AR-15 semi-automatic rifle, two semi-automatic pistols and a shotgun to Sandy Hook Elementary School in Newtown, Connecticut. He opened fire and killed twenty children under the age of seven and six teachers before committing suicide. It was one of the deadliest school shootings in US history. But it was what happened in the days after that prompted Cosmo to act. Claiming that the shooting was divine retribution for Connecticut's legislation in favour of same-sex marriage, the extremist pressure group the Westboro Baptist Church announced they were going to picket the funerals of the Sandy Hook victims to draw attention to their anti-gay campaign. Cosmo was furious. Even talking about it now, years later, he remains angry. He fired up his computer in earnest and proceeded to hack into the church leader's Twitter account. He took control and tweeted offensive things about the church under her name for eleven hours. The attention was once again like a drug to him and he outed himself with a declaration that 'the account is being run by CosmoTheGod'. Tech reporters straight away picked up on it. Surely this was a breach of his probation? Surely this was legal suicide? Why did this kid not care about getting arrested? But there were no notable consequences. Maybe the police didn't put two and two together or were too busy with his ongoing case. Either way – Cosmo 3.0 was born. More experienced and even less bothered about what was going to happen to him. The probation officers turned up regularly during this period to check up on him. They would sometimes come at 7.30 a.m. when Eric was still asleep. But their impromptu visits and searches never uncovered anything. Eric was tall – he's six foot seven now – and whenever police arrived at his house he would hide his laptop on the top of a tall wardrobe. 'They never looked there, and it took them so many visits to actually find it,' he laughs. Eric admits that he was addicted to being Cosmo and enjoyed coming up with new ways to cause mayhem. But his next – and last idea – was the darkest yet.

    Exposed.su was the type of website that a lazy thriller writer would come up with.

    It was sinister and cheesy, with a giant picture of a ghostly looking girl staring into the camera with her finger on her lips. At the top of the jet-black web page it had a foreboding line in quote marks: 'If you believe that God makes miracles, you have to wonder if Satan has a few up his sleeve.' With its '.su' web address the site looked like it came from Russia (formerly the Soviet Union). But all was not what it seemed. The quote was actually from a popular Showtime TV series called *Dexter*. And the site wasn't run from Russia – but from Cosmo's mum's house. But it was what the site did that really put shivers down the spines of the public. The site was for public doxing – publishing the personal contact details of the biggest celebrities Cosmo could find details for. Kim Kardashian, Tom Cruise, Donald Trump, Michelle Obama, Bill Gates, Beyoncé Knowles, Jay-Z and Ashton Kutcher were among his victims. They had their physical addresses, social security numbers and in some cases financial details published on Exposed.su.

It was Cosmo's site but he had help, including from former UG Nazi buddy Mir Islam. He claims other hackers like Kivimäki were also involved in choosing targets and carrying out attacks using the leaked details. The group apparently got the information by breaking into the database of a Russian hacking forum that had gathered data on millions of US citizens. The Russian criminal site had been selling this database and Cosmo says he pretended to be the owner of the website on a call to its hosting company. Once again, he convinced them to hand over control of the website and therefore the database. Once a new victim's details were posted, Cosmo would encourage other hackers in the chat channels to do their worst. That often meant swatting victims or calling in bomb threats. Eric says Kivimäki was one of the most prolific at this, making swat calls multiple times a day. 'He would attack anything – celebrities, FBI agents, whoever. I remember, he used to do the swatting calls, probably like 5 to 7 swats a day for a long time.' They also doxxed the then FBI director Robert Mueller and CIA director John Brennan.

By this time swatting had become a key tool in the NPT's arsenal of mayhem. When I challenged Eric on why they swatted the celebrities after already destroying their privacy he seemed embarrassed and ashamed about it. 'It was our way of saying fuck you to the police,' Eric says with regret, knowing now what was to come.

It was the push the cops needed to really come down on the teenaged Cosmo like a tonne of bricks. They gave him a real-life swatting that shook the sixteen-year-old to the core. Eric was at his computer in his bedroom up to no good when it happened. He was attempting to mount a DDoS attack on the home internet service for the Los Angeles police chief when he got a call from his grandma downstairs. There were men in the house and they were coming upstairs, she said. He quickly hid his laptop in the usual spot and then waited, becoming increasingly confused as he couldn't hear any sign of people outside. Then there was an explosion as they threw a flash bang grenade into his bedroom. 'FBI! Get down!' they shouted and six officers stood over Eric with assault rifles. There was smoke everywhere as he was dragged outside by the officers who smashed the glass door off his mum's apartment as they went. 'It was terrifying,' he admits. Outside Eric saw thirty other officers with guns and the whole street blocked off from traffic, with his confused neighbours lined up watching the spectacle. Eric was told by the police that they'd come from Washington DC and he was in deep trouble. To add to the trauma, he developed a condition called Bell's Palsy, brought on by accidentally rubbing the orange flash bang chemicals into his eyes. He couldn't move his face for three weeks. 'The experience taught me a lesson, and I never went back to cybercrime after that.'

That was 23 July 2013, but it wasn't until 15 February 2017, when he was nineteen, that Eric was finally sentenced. Thirty-six months on probation. So even after all his crimes there was no prison time. But by the time his sentence was delivered, Eric had already turned his life around. He'd started modelling, then managed a modelling agency before moving back to computers and into cybersecurity. He started hunting for vulnerabilities (known as 'bugs') in software for companies to help them defend themselves from hackers. This so-called 'bug hunting' is a potentially lucrative path for white hats using their skills for the good. One Argentinian hacker I interviewed for the BBC in 2019 called Santiago Lopez was the first to earn $1 million through a dedicated 'bug bounty' platform called Hacker One. By 2021 nine hackers had crossed the $1 million earnings mark.

Eric now runs his own cybersecurity company, and another that creates new crypto coins for clients. Computers and hacking are still a passion for him but he's matured. He uses his skills and knowledge to make a living, and it seems a good one. Just as we saw with Mustafa Al-Bassam from LulzSec, there's still a sense of pride when he talks about the technical complexity of his teenage black-hat hacking. He smiles in interviews when talking about the success and the headlines he made with UG Nazi. But the smiles fade when he is asked about the damage he caused.

It's notable that for the LulzSec guys their brush with the law was final and immediately stopped them all in their tracks. Four of them met up for a panel discussion a few years after their arrests, and they all seemed to love the memories, but admitted that the police action had stunned and scared them. It probably helped that LulzSec's leader Sabu was taken out first and the tight-knit group was comprehensively dismantled. For many teenagers, a stern talk is often enough to set fledgling criminals right. But for people like Eric, Kivimäki and some others, this just doesn't seem to cut it. It took a huge amount of police time, effort and resources to get Eric onto a good path. And many people suffered along the way, including his victims, his family and the public purse. Society is ultimately now benefiting from Eric's skills as he tries to make amends. But the story of his UG Nazi accomplices Mir Islam and Troy Woody Jr is not one of redemption. In fact it provides a strange, confusing and sinister twist.

Woody Jr seems to have been largely left alone by the cops as he was still a minor and, unlike Eric, was less implicated. But Mir Islam spent the years after his arrest in and out of court and was re-arrested for breaking his bail conditions. News camera footage of him appearing at court showed the chubby, scruffy-looking teenager posing for photographs and seemingly enjoying himself. In 2016 he was sentenced for various offences carried out with UG Nazi including swatting Krebs and his involvement in Exposed.su but also for a nasty campaign of personal cyberstalking directed at a cheerleader in Arizona. She had stopped responding to him so he phoned local police saying that there was a crazed gunman on the loose at her university. A total of fifty-four officers responded to the threat and painstakingly searched the campus before giving the all clear. Islam was sentenced to two years but only served one after convincing the judge that he had learned his lesson and was desperate to use his skills for good. He also used a diagnosis of obsessive compulsive disorder (OCD) and bipolar to explain his actions. 'I didn't expect to go as far as I did, but because of these disorders I felt I was invincible,' he told the court. The judge's low-ball sentence was well under the sentencing guidelines and proved very controversial.

Cyber expert Gary Warner from DarkTower Threat Intelligence wrote a scathing and detailed blog post describing the sentence as a 'travesty of the American criminal justice system that takes mentally ill hackers, ignores all of the minimum sentencing guidelines, gives them a slap on the wrist and lets them run along.'[7] Cyber reporter Brian Krebs agreed, writing that Islam expressed 'exactly zero remorse for his crimes' and that if the judge hoped to deter other teens from cybercrime, 'today's sentence sent the wrong message'.[8] Many commentators were worried that Islam would reoffend. But no one could have predicted how.

Shortly after he was released from prison, he bought a one-way ticket to the Philippines. Islam was prohibited from flying but according to Buzzfeed he travelled on his younger brother's passport. Within a few months he convinced Troy Woody Jr to join him, and he in turn brought along his long-term girlfriend Tomi Masters who was twenty-three years old.

In December 2018 she was murdered in their apartment. Woody Jr and Islam were arrested after being caught dumping a box containing her dead body into the Pasig River. CCTV footage shows the two men loading the box into a taxi – at one stage helped by the unwitting taxi driver. The men asked the driver to stop while they dumped the box on their way to a shopping mall. The taxi driver thought it was all very suspicious and called the police. The next day the authorities recovered the box and identified the victim. The police spoke to Buzzfeed about what they found: 'Covered in shattered glass and mummy-wrapped in duct tape and black plastic was the unmistakable shape of a body. Police peeled back the tape to reveal a young white woman, small and pale, flat on her back. Her hands rested on her hips. Her hair, dyed reddish blond, made a bright halo around her head. She was naked.'[9]

Both men were jailed the next day. But in spite of blaming each other for the murder, police told Buzzfeed that they heard chatter and frequent laughter coming from their cell. Before their trial both men told contradictory and nonsensical stories. Tragically, what exactly happened still remains a mystery, other than the fact that Tomi died of suffocation. Her relationship with Woody Jr had been fraught and explosive towards the end, and as her father and friends became increasingly worried she had nearly flown home on more than one occasion. The Philippine authorities have not answered my requests for information about the case and the US will only say that they have no record of the men being back in the country. So it seems they are still there, potentially serving a lengthy prison sentence.

Eric was just as shocked as everyone else to hear about this. He had met and hung out with Woody Jr and on one occasion with Tomi too. He had never met Islam but could not imagine that either man would be capable of murder. But when everyone is hiding behind aliases, you never really know who people are. Or what they are capable of.

By the end of 2013 some people believed that the tumultuous era of teen cyber gangs might have come to an end. LulzSec were gone. HTP and UG Nazi were disbanded. Yes, other copycat groups had arisen but they had fallen fast and disappeared with a whimper. Hackers were in prison, in hiding or, most likely, on long probation sentences. But there were still enough talented, bored and immature boys like Kivimäki knocking about to unleash yet more mayhem. Indeed, the next group to emerge is the most infamous of all. And with good reason. Combining all the bravado, stupidity, nihilism and cruelty that had characterised the previous three years of chaos. They called themselves 'Lizard Squad'.

//9
Hacking to harm
2014

Of all the screenshots, images, videos and audio clips I've gathered during the research for this book, there is one that shocked me the most.

Ryan ('Urharmless') shared it with me. It's what's known as a 'fansign': a photograph of a person with writing – usually on their body or a piece of paper – shared online as a mark of devotion for a celebrity or group. In the context of teenage hacking gangs, however, a fansign is a trophy of power. The 'fan' in this case had been blackmailed into making the image by hackers. The image, probably taken at some point in 2014, is of someone who has cut themselves dozens of times along their forearm. Long thin red lines, some weeping with blood, are clearly visible running from the wrist up to the elbow. Next to the arm is a piece of paper with the handwritten words: 'Lizard Squad made me do it.'

The fansign – or more accurately in this case 'cutsign' – was made after a thorough life-ruining campaign had been directed at a young wannabe hacker for mouthing off online about the new Lizard Squad crew. He had had his online accounts hijacked and was coerced into making the fansign to get his online life back.

The image highlights a pattern with these teenage gangs: one of escalation. As Allison Nixon put it: 'every year since 2011 it's like these crime groups have gotten more extreme than the last.' Lizard Squad was no exception. These kids seemed to enjoy hurting people. They used all the tools in the NPT armoury to inflict pain, humiliation and distress on their victims. The high-minded ethos of the Hacker Manifesto was long gone, and Lizard Squad epitomised this descent into chaos and darkness.

The group's logo became so recognisable it was almost like a brand. Once again the inspiration seems to have been LulzSec – the wine-swilling man in a top hat replaced with a pipe-smoking lizard in a top hat. It seems to be aiming – however spuriously – for that same gentlemanly comedic irreverent aesthetic. It's fascinating to me that years after LulzSec had been rounded up and put in prison, hackers were still creating new groups in their image. None of these boys seemed to have learned any of the lessons of recent hacking history. The IRC channels and now Skype Group calls were still frothing with hormonal boys and young men desperate to prove themselves in any way they could. Things were already out of hand but, as one of the members of Lizard Squad put it to me: 'There was a major turnaround at that time where things were no longer for fun, for comedic value, it was pure sadism.'

HACKING TO HARM

'Satan', as he was known, claims that he was part of Lizard Squad from the beginning. I've not been able to verify this. In fact it's been hard to verify a lot of the Lizard Squad stories. All of those involved – or who claim to have been involved – are now grown men, but they continue to argue over who should take credit for doing what and when. Unlike previous gangs that were tightly knit, Lizard Squad was a much larger community with people wafting in and out of chat channels to take part in attacks or claim some of the glory for stuff others did. Absolutely everything is contested and nearly everyone I spoke to insisted that they were there at the beginning and were a core member. 'Everyone else was useless or a liar' was the most common thing I was told while interviewing around a dozen people who claimed to be members of the crew.

Time and again it struck me that some of these now grown men were still trying to get a thrill from their past adventures online (even if they hadn't been involved) and some are still trying to profit from their association with the hacker gang whose notoriety endures to this day. There are regular viral videos on YouTube about Lizard Squad, featuring interviews with former members. Even in the final stages of writing this book, men came out of the woodwork claiming to be 'the real deal' and to say all others are fakes. I was spoiled rotten when writing about LulzSec, HTP and UG Nazi thanks to the wealth of trustworthy information from court records and mature and reliable sources to fall back on. With Lizard Squad, reliable sources of this kind are few and far between. Satan sympathised with my frustration: 'I was involved in it all and even I don't have a clear picture. You've interviewed more than a dozen people and still don't know for sure who was who and what was what. I think it's beautiful.'

Even the group's inception is a point of contention. Some say the name came from a change of branding from another mostly insignificant group called 'Catsquad'. Others say the group was formed after some of the gang were called 'lizard people' online. Some say

133

it was because one of the founders had a pet lizard. And others say Lizard Squad started as 'ISIS Gang' which was itself a relaunch of another crew.

At this point it is worth taking a look at ISIS Gang, because their deplorable activities mark a shift away from hacking and towards hoaxing and swatting at scale. They displayed little hacking skill, creativity or humour and seemed to be on a mission to upset and scare as many people as possible on their path to infamy and, eventually, prison. Even their name was an attempt to get attention and troll the press into thinking that these delinquents were part of a terrorist group. This was 2014 and the world was watching with horror as the Islamic State of Iraq and Syria (ISIS) was gaining infamy in the Middle East for subjecting its enemies to horrific beheadings and crucifixions. As well as physical attacks, some feared that cyber attacks could also be launched by ISIS sympathisers. So, the ISIS Gang knew exactly what they were doing when they named themselves.

With no evident strategy or motive other than getting noticed, this small group – mostly made up of teenagers from the UK and the US – were prolific swatters and bomb hoaxers. They threatened mass murder, hostage taking and the release of poisonous gas. Their victim organisations were mostly in the US and included Hebron High School in Carrollton, Texas, two New Jersey high schools, Boston University, the Boston Convention and Exhibition Center and the University of Connecticut, which was hoaxed with a bomb threat call backed up by Twitter posting. Bomb disposal teams and heavily armed police came to search the buildings. It took hours for things to return to normal. At the Boston Convention and Exhibition Center a gaming exhibition was interrupted by a call from someone saying they were 'working for Allah' and had planted plastic explosives around the building the night before. It's estimated that responding to the hoax calls made by the gang, which were all delivered anonymously through Skype, cost police and local authorities around $1 million in total over the months they were active.[1] We'll never be able to quantify how much emotional distress was caused for people evacuated from the buildings in fear of their safety. Or for the responders searching buildings for deadly explosives or armed and dangerous terrorists.

ISIS Gang prided themselves on pulling off a good hoax call. Urharmless, who says he was a member of the group, shared one of the calls that he recorded at the time. It was of a swatting by his fellow ISIS Gang mate Tommy, who is British but put on a passable American accent for the call. Even though it's all fake, the audio is still shocking and dramatic. You can hear the concern in the call handler's voice. Here's the transcript:

> Responder: 'Hello this is dispatch.'
> Tommy: 'Hello ma'am? Can you hear me ma'am?'
> Responder: 'I can hear you. What do you need help with?'
> Tommy: 'I need help actually. I'm at 849 Broad Street.'
> Responder: 'Okay, what's going on?'
> Tommy [sniffling and crying]: 'I shot. I shot my mom. Can you please help me?'
> Responder: 'Yes, I can. Where's the gun now?'
> Tommy: 'The gun is in my hand.'
> Responder: 'Can you put the gun down for me? And walk away from it?'
> Responder [on dispatch radio to officers]: '741, we have a shooting on 849 Broad Street. I'll advise further.'
> Tommy [crying]: 'Ma'am I don't wanna get hurt here. I don't want anyone to get hurt.'
> Responder: 'I understand. I want you to put the gun down and go outside for me. So that you're not near the gun, okay?'
> Tommy: 'I'm scared. I'm scared I might get shot. I don't want to get shot. My name is John, ma'am.'

> Responder: 'We're not going to let that happen as long as you don't have that gun, okay?'
> Responder [on dispatch radio to officers]: 'Suspect's name is John. I have him on the line. I'm trying to get him to leave the gun inside and go outside.'
> Tommy [crying]: 'Ma'am I might just kill myself. I don't feel good here.'
> Responder: 'We don't want you to do that. That's not the answer here. Don't do that John. Walk away from the gun okay? Nobody wants that. Don't hurt yourself John.'
> Tommy [crying]: 'My mum is bleeding. I think she's dead.'
> Responder [on dispatch radio to officers]: 'K3789 to Station 1. Standby for a shooting at 849 Broad Street.'
> CALL ENDS

But of course there was no shooting and no one was in danger. That is until the armed police turned up on edge with guns cocked and ready for violence.

Urharmless insists that there is an element of skill involved in these hoax calls. They used hacking techniques to get extra information about their targets' houses and families. They also developed scripts to make sure that their calls were believable and escalated by the cops to a serious threat level. One exhaustively compiled document shared with me is called 'FBI Buzzword List'. It's a detailed sheet, 800 lines long, of all the types of guns, ammunition and bombs that they would reference to convince responders that they were armed and dangerous. Categories like submachine guns and sniper rifles helped the hoaxers quote to police what weapons they had in a believable way.

But for all the planning and process, these attacks from ISIS Gang were a far cry from some of the resourcefulness we've heard about from other groups. They were also random and seemingly without purpose. At least Anonymous justified its illegal activity with a reason. But ISIS Gang didn't seem to have any real motive. At one stage the gang targeted Sandy Hook – the same school that Eric had tried to protect from protesters just six months before. According to reports, a man claiming to be 'Mohammed Jamile' called the school saying he was on his way to 'kill all your asses'.[2] It was a miracle that no one got shot or killed during this time of heightened tension. But these hoaxes set in motion a trend that would lead to tragedy within a few years.

#

On 28 December 2017, Xbox gamer Casey Viner in Ohio had just played a heated online match of *Call of Duty* with a player called Shane Gaskill in Kansas. Viner was eighteen years old, Gaskill nineteen. Apparently, they had made some sort of bet. It was very low stakes but somehow the pair ended up having a blazing row about it over voice chat. Viner was so angry that he called up a twenty-five-year-old called Tyler Barriss, who was known for being good at swatting calls and apparently enjoyed making them. He called himself 'SWAuTistic' online.

In a vengeful rage Viner gave Gaskill's address to Barriss and asked him to swat the teenager. Barriss called the local cops, disguising his phone number to make it appear as if he was calling from the Wichita area code. He pretended to be Gaskill and said that he had shot his dad in the head and was holding his mum and little brother hostage. In the recording of the call later released by police, you can hear Barriss threatening to attack the cops if they arrived. 'Are you sending someone over here because then I'm definitely not going to put [the gun] away . . . I poured gasoline all over the house, I might just set it on fire.'

Armed police arrived late at night and called out to the house. On the body-cam video that was also released you see the house with reflected red and blue lights flashing from the patrol cars lined up on the other side of the street. Police are leaning over the roofs of their cars, guns trained on the house. 'Show your hands!' one of them shouts at a man as he stands in his doorway. 'Walk this way!' the officer hollers, and the man starts walking out of his front door with his hands in the air. But something in his movement spooks the police and they open fire. He dies there on his porch. But it wasn't Gaskill – it was an innocent father of two called Andrew Finch, who died having no idea why armed police had arrived at his family home that night. It turned out that Gaskill had given Viner his old house address to thwart the swatting threat.

Tyler Barriss had been convicted the year before for making hoax calls against two Los Angeles schools and a TV station. But he had been released early in January 2017 and carried on making calls – sometimes being paid for them. The tragic swatting shocked the world. It was the first time someone had died from a hoax call of this kind. Dozens more cases of swatting and bomb hoaxes were added to Barriss's charges and he admitted to nearly all of them in court.[3] He was sentenced to twenty years in prison in 2019. Viner, who ordered the swat, was sentenced to fifteen months[4] in prison and Gaskill, who gave the false address, received an eighteen month sentence.[5]

The way Barriss was handled by police has been criticised. If they had come down on him harder in 2016 he might not have carried out the fatal call in 2017. There were other horrible incidents that should have acted as warning signs about the dangers of swatting. In 2015, a twenty-year-old man in Maryland in the US was shot with rubber bullets in the torso and face.[6] He suffered significant injuries including bruised lungs, a fractured rib, and numerous broken bones to the left side of his face. He was transported to hospital where he underwent multiple facial reconstructive surgeries. Forty officers had to respond to the call and remained there for over two and a half hours at an estimated cost of $10,000 to the local police. The person who ordered the call was sentenced to two years in prison. Robert Walker-McDaid from Coventry in the UK, who faked the call, became the first person sentenced by the British courts for offences associated with swatting – for some reason nine years after the event, in April 2024.[7]

One of the most prolific ever swatters was called 'Veri' or 'Verified'. His real name is Robert Barr, a teenager from a small Scottish town called Kilbirnie near Glasgow. At one point during the summer of 2014 Urharmless says he and Veri had a competition with the other members of ISIS Gang to see who could perform the most swat or hoax calls. Ryan says he stopped counting at 450 swatting calls and Veri was pushing 700 total calls made: 'Veri was a sociopath and he never showed remorse for his actions. He could often be heard cackling in laughter and excitement as his acts unfolded right before our eyes. It was scary and made me never want to cross him.'

In July 2014, in the middle of the ISIS Gang period, Veri got into an online spat with his hacker mate Jamie Sales AKA 'Declaws'. Barr called local police at 2.30 a.m. and, according to reporting from local news outlet *The Courier*, pretended to be Sales. He claimed that his father had assaulted his mother, that she wasn't breathing and that his dad was trying to attack him with a knife.[8] As soon as he ended the call Barr tweeted on his account 'SWAT coming' and said: 'I wanted the cops to kill his rabbit . . . I'm going to prison.' Clearly the teenager thought it was funny, but he also knew how serious the swatting was. He was caught and admitted to making the call. He was released on bail and told not to go online. Within a year he was found to have broken that order. So the police sentenced him in 2016 to a community payback order of 120 hours of unpaid work, and a year's supervision, including the task of 'consequential thinking' – encouraging the offender to take responsibility for his actions.

The punishment did not deter him. Barr went on to reoffend in progressively more serious ways. In that same year he was convicted for football violence during a pitch invasion at the Scottish Cup Final between Hibs and Rangers. After the final whistle he and many others ran onto the pitch and assaulted a rival fan. He was given another 150 hours of community service. Fast forward to 2022 and he was once again arrested for hacking into people's cryptocurrency wallets to steal money. In 2024 he was jailed for twenty-one months.[9] Detective Chief Inspector Andy Maclean from Police Scotland said at the time: 'Barr's sentence sends a clear message to those acting in such a manner that this type of behaviour will not be tolerated.' But the police failed to mention at the time that, incredibly, Barr had committed this hack while already on bail for an even larger US scam. He's accused of working with two other hackers in 2017 to steal an estimated £7 million in cryptocurrency from New York-based financier Reggie Middleton. The cryptocurrency dealer told reporters that the theft set off a chain of events which led to his financial ruin and effectively put his firm out of business.[10] Barr is accused of using a so-called 'SIM swap' attack to syphon off the fortune with two other accomplices. But he is currently fighting a lengthy extradition case as the US wants him to be tried and jailed for the crime in Georgia. If he loses his extradition fight he could be jailed for twenty years. Mugshots show a pale, blond young man – the press has dubbed the now twenty-seven-year-old the 'Baby-faced hacker'.

So, for Veri, the swatting and bomb hoax calls were just the start of what became a near ten-year cybercrime spree, during which he seems not to have been at all deterred by the punishments he received. It's hard to know whether or not the online culture he experienced in these chat rooms made Barr the criminal he is or just enabled him. Barr has also been accused of ordering and arranging physical attacks too, which is another escalation that we will come to. Either way, Barr is an example, like Eric Taylor and Kivimäki, of a kid who didn't seem to take much notice of police action against him. But his arrest back in 2014 did at least bring the activities of ISIS Gang to an end.

Urharmless shared a recording of the moment that he and Tommy saw the news online. 'Oh my god Veri's been arrested! What the fuck! Look at this from eleven minutes ago, oh my god!' Tommy shouts. He breathlessly reads the article out loud: 'It's on the *Daily*

Mail! "A team of British computer hackers as young as sixteen that call themselves ISIS" – oh my god we're on the news what the fuck!' he laughs nervously. You can hear him smiling as he rattles through the article but you can also hear his voice shaking as the adrenaline surges in him. This is what the lads have always wanted. Attention. Clout. Notoriety. But then it hits Tommy. 'Oh shit. I might get raided, dude. I'm running DBAN now.' (DBAN is the acronym for Darik's Boot and Nuke – a free program that wipes your entire hard drive so that it's no longer readable. In other words, it destroys all evidence of criminal activity.)

Tommy clatters away from the microphone and starts clicking on his computer. You can hear him swearing, his voice shaking. He comes back to the microphone and continues a stream of frantic rambling as he half-reads articles and swears and laughs nervously. 'If they snitch on me I'm going to be fucking mad pissed,' he screams, adding 'I'm mega paranoid about this because my mum will fuck me up man.' After seven minutes of the Skype call Tommy logs off. Urharmless was never in direct contact with the Scot again but heard that he went straight and now has a wife and two children.

The recording highlights how things should be – police take down a couple of guys from a group and the rest scarper and get on the straight and narrow. But for at least some of the members of ISIS Gang this wasn't to be. Instead they appear to have regrouped as Lizard Squad, together with a new recruit – Julius Kivimäki.

#

It was late at night in February 2014 and Kevin and Judith Brogan had just got into bed when they were disturbed by a frantic knock at the door. When they opened it, they found a team of highly alert and heavily armed police officers outside who warned them to get out. There was a powerful bomb planted in the house and they were in danger, they said. The cops told the couple they had been threatened as a result of an FBI investigation. As they waited anxiously, the police searched the whole house and found nothing. Mr and Mrs Brogan were confused, until they spoke to their son. Special Agent Ryan Brogan knew exactly what this was and who was responsible. Only a few months earlier he had sat in front of the defiant and cocky Julius Kivimäki and tried to scare him into stopping his online activity. Clearly that hadn't worked. Now Zeekill had been released from prison in Finland and was out for revenge. But he didn't attempt to get Agent Brogan directly – he found the contact details for his parents in Langhorne, Pennsylvania. And not just his parents. The boys had also found the address of his uncle: earlier that day another hoax call had been made to police by someone called 'Vypor' who said they were Ryan King (Starfall) and that they were holding Agent Brogan hostage at the uncle's address. Vypor told the local police call handler that he wanted $50,000 in bitcoins or else he'd blow the house up with napalm bombs. Police say that some calls were made by Kivimäki himself. But they were ignored by the Middletown Township Police Department. So he and his mates tried to harass Agent Brogan again by going after his parents.

Court records showed Kivimäki and the others planning the calls in a chat room. They were all made in frenzied succession, likely as a result of the gang getting excited after Kivimäki apparently shared the personal details of the Brogans. He can be seen in the chat logs egging Vypor on. It was also he who came up with the idea about blowing up the house. He suggests that Vypor tell them that they are being killed 'because of an FBI investigation'. Police records show it caused a huge amount of distress to Mr and Mrs Brogan. Agent Brogan's blood must have boiled when he got their call.

Kivimäki was sixteen years old at this point, and according to Allison Nixon the incident was part of a sustained campaign against the agent, all led or spurred on by Kivimäki. Agent Brogan didn't reply to my requests for an interview about this difficult period. But it seems he was also being subjected to another form of attack. After viewing a leaked database listing all those who paid to make use of one of Lizard Squad's DDoS tools, reporters at Ars Technica noticed that one of its most prolific users was someone calling himself 'ryanbrogan'.[11] Someone was using the agent's name as a joke or to implicate him in the attacks. Whoever it was carried out a fifth of all the attacks launched by the hacking weapon. Not only was this person prolific, they were also vindictive. Records show that 'ryanbrogan' attacked one single computer server 1,468 times. Similarly, in one of the Skype call recordings, an unknown delinquent repeatedly tells a frustrated 911 call handler that his name is Ryan Brogan. In fact, many of the hackers from the time were surprised when I told them that Ryan Brogan was a real person. His name got thrown around so much by people like Kivimäki that everyone thought it was a made-up name.

During her lurking, Allison Nixon saw the name mentioned all the time. So often in fact that she also didn't think he was real. But then – like a cyber phantom come to life – Agent Brogan walked into her office out of the blue. 'He worked out of the Newark Field Office at the time, which was really close to my office and he just walked in off the street one day to ask about script kiddies as he'd heard we were collecting intel,' she says. 'I was shocked. I thought he didn't exist!' she laughs. Allison gave the agent everything she had gathered on the NPT gangs and kept talking to him afterwards. They are still in touch.

But Agent Brogan wasn't the only target Zeekill and his friends went after in new and ever more elaborate ways.

Lizard Squad first started getting noticed after launching DDoS attacks on gaming services like League of Legends, Twitch, Blizzard and Sony PlayStation Network in summer 2014. In some cases, as with Blizzard, they were also able to access some private employee data. But it was the minor and annoying DDoS attacks that Lizard Squad were most known for. The resulting disruptions were so commonplace that they became routine stories for gaming websites including eTeknix, which implored the industry to do something about them.

One man who tried was gaming executive John Smedley, the outspoken head of Sony Online Entertainment. When Lizard Squad targeted his company with a DDoS attack on 24 August 2014, Smedley received a torrent of complaints and abuse from users furious about not being able to play their games. Dozens of people blamed him personally on Twitter. Smedley, who was a prolific tweeter, acted like a patient customer service rep for the company. He responded to dozens of angry tweets with updates and sympathy. He also tried to explain that this was not his or his company's fault and that DDoS attacks are extremely hard to protect against. He replied to one user: 'Yeah this is unfortunate. The guys who do this will do jail time if caught. The FBI is exceptional at catching them.'[12] It's not clear if it was this tweet or another that put a target on his back, but this was the start of a horribly personal, dark and dangerous harassment campaign from Kivimäki and Lizard Squad. Later that day they carried out their most audacious prank yet.

#

F-16 fighter jets can go from hangar to airborne in less than five minutes during an emergency. Videos released by the US Air Force on YouTube show how the process works. Pilots, often in a pair, race across the tarmac in full flying gear as a siren whoops in the background and a recorded voice says 'scramble, scramble, scramble' over the intercom. The well-oiled ground team quickly attaches a ladder up to the cockpit, removes the engine coverings and directs the jet out onto the runway with exaggerated hand gestures. The slowest bit – which must be painful to watch when the clock is ticking – comes as the jet taxies its way out to the strip. But once in the air these aircraft can reach a top speed of 1,500 mph when they need to. And on 24 August they needed to. A call had come in about a potential bomb on board American Airlines-362, flying from Dallas to San Diego with 179 passengers and six crew onboard. Two F-16 jets were scrambled at speed to get up close to the Boeing 757-200 and escort it to safety.

The flight was about two hours into its three-hour journey, just outside Phoenix, when the pilot made the decision to land the plane as quickly as possible. A call went out to the passengers that they were diverting due to 'a safety issue'. After landing in Phoenix, the plane taxied to a remote area of the airport, where passengers exited and their bags were lined up on the tarmac for a sniffer dog to search. But one man was singled out and taken for questioning by police at gunpoint. By that time, John Smedley knew what it was all about – Lizard Squad.

As soon as they had landed, he started tweeting what was happening, telling his 40,000 followers that he was sitting on the tarmac because of 'something about security and our cargo'. Quickly he received a flood of messages from users pointing him to tweets from Lizard Squad, including this one directed at the airline shortly after the plane took off:

> @AmericanAir We have been receiving reports that @j_smedley's plane #362 from DFW to SAN has explosives on-board, please look into this.
>
> — Lizard Squad (@LizardSquad)

Smedley, who was apparently travelling back from dropping his son at college, was questioned for an hour by police before being released. It didn't take long for the authorities to confirm the Lizard Squad connection – in true NPT style the boys had not given a thought to protecting their identity. The reporting at the time credited the Lizard Squad tweets with bringing down the plane, but what actually prompted flight controllers to take the threat seriously had been two related phone calls. And it was Kivimäki on the end of the phone, making no attempt to even disguise his voice.

Noticing that John Smedley had tweeted that he was flying back to San Diego, Kivimäki had called the American Airlines customer service line posing as the executive and pretending to have mislaid his flight details. After that, one of Lizard Squad sent the tweet about a bomb on the plane. To further the panic Kivimäki called customer services back, once again posing as Smedley and saying that there was an imposter on the flight pretending to be him. Here's part of the transcript:

> Kivimäki: My name is John Smedley. I was supposed to board the flight 362 in Dallas, but at the airport I had a call telling me that a family member had been in a car accident and I left. In my car I noticed that my passport and plane ticket are missing.
> Customer service: Your passport, your plane ticket are missing? And you left them at Dallas airport?
> Kivimäki: I think somebody stole them and boarded the plane . . . something says on my Twitter some tweeter says there is a bomb in the plane.
> Customer service: Don't leave the line please. One second please.

The call handler is clearly confused and concerned and repeatedly implores Kivimäki to stay on the line while she rings other departments to escalate the threat. He urges her to check Lizard Squad's Twitter feed and find out if someone on board under his name has a bomb. The calls and the tweets worked. Perhaps the most provocative of the latter was one showing Smedley's name and a video of the 9/11 planes crashing into the World Trade Center. The response and the diversion apparently cost American Airlines $13,217 in personnel, maintenance and stopover costs. It cost the US Air Force approximately $15,000 to scramble the fighter jets. But this wasn't the end of Kivimäki and co's campaign against Smedley. They had found a new punchbag.

Three days later, Kivimäki hacked into Smedley's LifeLock account. LifeLock is a service that protects your identity by monitoring your credit, bank account, social security number and other personal information, and alerting you to any suspicious activity. But the customer service team didn't seem to find it suspicious when Kivimäki called up pretending to be Smedley and got every security question wrong. The now seventeen-year-old had found the executive's social security number and that was enough. He pretended to have forgotten his password for the account and once the customer service rep had reset the password Kivimäki logged in and had all of Smedley's identity information at his fingertips. Within hours he and his gang had applied for new bank accounts with the details and carried out false credit applications affecting Smedley's credit rating and creating an enormous administrative nightmare for him to set everything right. Lizard Squad accounts also tweeted out screenshots from inside the account saying they 'love Smedleys LifeLock account'.

And still that wasn't the end. Smedley's family home was swatted multiple times and on 16 September 2014 he tweeted that someone had sent him a picture of his dad's gravestone in San Diego, smeared with an unknown substance. 'You will be found,' he tweeted back.

As with Blair Strater, it's unfair to say that all this hurtful harassment was the work of Kivimäki alone. But one of his Lizard Squad friends from the time told Bloomberg that he in particular seemed to be spurred on when a victim fought back. 'If they don't retaliate, then Julius gets bored and then we move onto a new person.'[13] But if someone put up a fight, he could get fixated and come after them again and again.

The John Smedley plane incident was headline news around the world, making some of Lizard Squad worried about the heat it was bringing to the gang. In early September – days after the incident – they posted a LulzSec-style retirement message onto PasteBin. 'We've been called everything from an organized criminal "gang" to complete assholes, really we are just a bunch of guys with too much free time.' 'Goodbye,' they wrote, adding links to all the news articles about them at the bottom of the page like little trophies. The notice included a list of hacker aliases including 'ryan' which in this case was Kivimäki. At the bottom of the page they also posted a strange endnote: 'PS: chF was never a part of Lizard Squad, just a friend.' Many took this for what it was – an attempt to clear this individual of any responsibility. Perhaps one of the boys who was most worried or had the most to lose from an arrest. But determined to find this individual – and after a long search and weeks of being bounced around various other people – I was finally given his up-to-date social media account details.

'How did you find me?' was the first thing he replied, angry that someone had given me his handle. It was a good sign that I had found the right person. After years of talking to hackers and wannabe hackers, I've learned that the ones who are most shy are usually the ones who have the most to say. And the most to lose by talking to reporters. ChF opened up eventually, saying that he has moved on from that 'teenage shit' and is living a normal life now. He answered most of my questions, albeit tersely and with a healthy dose of disrespect for journalists. He said he was young during the Lizard Squad days – only fourteen or fifteen. 'I got scared after Zeekill did the bomb threat to Smedley's plane, like a jackass. So I told the guys to write that bit about me in the retirement note to try to disassociate myself.'

He didn't want anything to do with that stunt – it took things too far and he was scared that the FBI would kick his door in. He wasn't a fan of Zeekill and hadn't been happy about him being brought into the group at all. 'Zeekill had a bad rep for being a snake. He was a different breed,' he says. He also says Zeekill didn't really do much hacking in the gang and took credit for other people's work. Behind the scenes ChF says he continued being a part of the gang and enjoyed it when things really 'popped off' for Lizard Squad shortly after the Smedley incident, especially after he set up an interview with the gang and popular YouTuber Keemstar. ChF proudly says this was one of the things that really propelled them to online infamy. The attention the crew were getting for every DDoS attack was scary at the time but he had a 'teenage invincibility mentality' so enjoyed every moment. The note about him in the retirement post was of course nonsense. He was too deep into it by then and despite Zeekill's influence and the threat of police action, he went along with it all. It shows us how hard it is to leave these groups. It's not just the stunts, hacks and hoaxes – it's the hours-long video calls and text chats. The shared risk and adrenaline reward.

So in spite of their publicly announced retirement and internal concerns, Lizard Squad didn't simply disappear. At the same time as the big public attacks, some of the gang were also pursuing their own grubby little private campaigns. Kivimäki, for example, relentlessly harassed an American girl who had broken off contact with him. It's not known what kind of relationship they had had but as she was in Norwalk, Connecticut we can assume it was at most some sort of online romance. Kivimäki made a swatting call to the local police pretending to be her 'unstable' father. He said he wanted to kill himself and her. And when the call handler said that they had arrived at the family home, Kivimäki made the sound of gunshots on the call to spur the police into action. All because she didn't want to talk to him any more.

Harassing and scaring girls who don't want to talk to them any more seems to be common behaviour for these often lonely, immature and repressed boys. We saw it with Mir Islam in UG Nazi and here again with Kivimäki. Shortly after Kivimäki targeted the Connecticut girl, another of the Lizard Squad delinquents who was based in Canada and called himself 'Obnoxious' went after a woman in Arizona. The cyberstalking got so bad that she was forced to withdraw from her semester at the University of Arizona because she became so anxious under his constant threats to her and her family. On 16 September 2014 after she repeatedly rejected him, Obnoxious called the Tucson police to prompt a swat of her home, claiming he had shot his parents with an AR15 rifle, had bombs and would kill the police if he saw any marked vehicles.

Obnoxious, who was seventeen at the time and wasn't identified to press, shared news articles online about this swat and others he inflicted on the family, apparently bragging about them. He used a software program to send the young woman 218 text messages in quick succession. He hacked her university email account and tweeted out her family's personal information, including their social security numbers, and called companies to try to cancel their utilities and internet. The young student wasn't the only girl Obnoxious targeted. Local news reports from *Tri City News* said he terrorised six young, female gamers and their parents across the US.[14]

Allison Nixon says this kind of behaviour towards women is something she has come to expect from this internet subculture. 'There's a pattern that these communities lose their minds in the presence of a woman,' she says. Allison thinks it could be this toxic attitude that explains why there were and are so few female hackers in these communities, especially back in this era. As soon as you disclose that you are a girl you get abused or treated badly. 'It means there's no opportunity to seek communal connections and bonds that you need with fellow cyber criminals to share techniques, ideas and workload,' she observes.

The anonymous nature of hacking makes getting accurate statistics difficult but one study by Royal Holloway University in 2021 gives us a rough picture of the gender imbalance in cybercrime.[15] Researchers carried out detailed profiles of 100 of the 303 people convicted of cybercrime in the UK between 2008 and 2018 and found only three of them were female. As the researchers wrote in their paper, 'the vast majority of hackers in this project are men, and all of the semi-skilled or high-skilled individuals are male'. Another study of hundreds of international cyber criminals convicted in the United States found that 94 per cent of them were male.[16]

Misogyny in male-dominated online environments is not a new phenomenon and has its roots right back in the early days of the internet. The nerdy message boards populated by early adopters in the 1990s were invariably dominated by men, and as the internet became more accessible the idea spread, particularly in anonymous forums, that anyone who said they were a woman was probably lying. The phrase 'there are no women on the internet' became a go-to joke thrown around whenever someone claimed to be female. In some spaces such as 4chan, identifying as a woman would prompt users to ask for evidence. Catchphrases like 'TITS or GTFO' (send a picture of your tits or get the fuck out) would be spammed underneath an apparently female poster's messages. This was a sexist trope of course, but weirdly it was also a protective measure as many men were indeed pretending to be women in these spaces to get more attention or perks (see Kayla from LulzSec for example). Of course, as the internet spread far and wide, this adage became quickly outdated. Especially on social media sites where women and girls are usually the early adopters. But the misogyny continued and nowhere more so than in gaming. This was never more apparent than in 'Gamer Gate' which exploded during the time that Lizard Squad was active – August 2014.

Gamer Gate was a widespread harassment campaign against women involved in the gaming industry. It started out as an attack on a female game developer by her angry ex-boyfriend, but morphed into a mass campaign against any female who expressed an opinion about gaming online. Unknown abusers sent physical threats to women, forcing them to flee their homes. Events had to be cancelled. Untold harm was done to the careers and confidence of many women. I couldn't find any direct link between Lizard Squad and the Gamer Gate thugs but it's notable that both groups were active at the same time. Both were a loosely organised band of mostly boys and young men with no leader and no coherent message or motive.

Both wanted to inflict hurt and harm for their amusement, pleasure and power.

On 1 December 2014, Obnoxious was arrested by Canadian mounties and jailed for sixteen months for harassment and for other swatting and hacking offences. A reporter in court said the teen smirked during the proceeding, drumming his fingers on his knees and pumping his leg. According to the *New York Times* he was interviewed at length by a social worker, a psychiatrist and a psychologist, who confirmed that his childhood had been marred by an abusive father and a mentally ill mother.[17] The psychiatric report noted that he had essentially no remorse: 'His description of the pleasure he gets from causing humiliation and harm . . . is suggestive of quite significant emerging psychopathic traits.'

Sometime after Obnoxious was arrested, Lizard Squad tried to disown him, claiming that he wasn't part of the core gang.[18] Whether or not that was the case, losing Obnoxious certainly didn't slow them down. They were about to launch the attack that made them truly hated around the world by tens of millions and would finally cause the group – and with it this era of teenage hacking – to crash and burn.

//10
Christmas is cancelled
25 December 2014

The Andersons are Christmas traditionalists. Dan says it's more his wife Paige than him, but secretly he also loves all the fuss. So there they were on the sofa in their pyjamas in front of the twinkling Christmas tree before the sun had risen over a chilly morning in Buffalo, USA. Thirty-two-year-old Dan was proud and smug as he handed over his gift to Paige – a 'fancy new Kindle Voyage'. She loved it. Then it was his turn, and he excitedly ripped into the wrapping paper watched over by his confused dogs – one of which was tellingly named after Dan's favourite computer-game character (Vivi from *Final Fantasy*). As the present revealed itself, the avid gamer saw the instantly recognisable and much-loved logo – it was a brand-new PlayStation 4. The console was still in its first year of release and the ultimate top tier gaming machine. Straight away he unpacked it, rigged it up to the TV and switched it on. The plan was to get it fired up and download *Little Big Planet 3* to play for a few hours before meeting up with family. Paige had been looking forward to it since she bought the new console – the couple loved the game's earlier versions on the old consoles. However, it wasn't to be. 'We didn't even make it as far as starting to download the game because it wouldn't let me log in to PlayStation Network,' Dan said. 'Nothing was online at all, so we couldn't even try and download games.' Disappointedly they headed out for the day's events and couldn't try again until that evening when they discovered that the network was still down. A $400 gift they couldn't play. Dan had to work the next day too so he couldn't even try it then. He was gutted.

Some 550 miles north in Toronto, sixteen-year-old Mustafa Aijaz was pumped. Christmas Day – particularly the evening – was the best game time of the year. It's always been a bit of a holiday within the holiday for serious players. The tradition revolves around a phenomenon called 'Christmas Noobs'. At Christmas, so many new players receive new games and consoles that online games are flooded with a tidal wave of new gamers who often fumble their way through the top games and act like cannon fodder for the waiting legions of seasoned veterans. Mustafa and his mates were skilled at *Call of Duty: Advance Warfare*. With the rest of their families crowded round the TV or in a turkey-induced coma, Mustafa and his group of mates from around the world logged onto their Xboxes and excitedly chatted as they prepared for their marathon all-night gaming to begin. 'We were all ready for a night of easy wins, quick XP (experience points) farming and were looking forward to levelling up like crazy.' So, they waited like crocodiles anticipating herds of migrating buffalo to enter the river. But just as the bullets started flying they were all unceremoniously chucked out of their matches and knocked offline. 'None of us could log back in and Party Chat was down too, so we couldn't even talk to each other to figure out what was happening,' Mustafa said. The fallout hit gamers like a tidal wave and Mustafa, like thousands of others, took to Twitter to find out what was going on and vent his frustration.

It was all over social media: a group of hackers called Lizard Squad, who had already built up a sizeable 120,000 followers on social media, were bragging about their massive DDoS attack on Xbox Live and PlayStation Network – the crucial services that linked tens of millions of gamers to the Microsoft and Sony servers. Mustafa had seen that the group had already carried out smaller-scale attacks and had for weeks been taunting and threatening a big attack. Apparently it was all linked to some silly and incomprehensible spat with a rival but minor hacking group called 'Finest Squad'. Mustafa was angry but also fascinated by the attack and the incredible reaction online. 'The fallout was instantaneous. People were furious,' he said.

PlayStation Network at the time had about 110 million subscribers and Xbox Live had roughly 48 million. Xbox was back to normal within twenty-four hours – on Boxing Day. But PlayStation struggled for longer. It didn't just affect existing subscribers either. Before you can use any new games, consoles or vouchers you need to register them via the gaming company's servers. It was a catastrophe for the games industry, especially Sony which had already been having a tough time after a different cyber attack the previous month. (This earlier attack was linked to North Korea, which had been angered by the company's recent controversial film *The Interview* in which Kim Jong Un is assassinated.)

Services were down around the world. Error messages in dozens of languages were being posted as screenshots on YouTube and Twitter. One Saudi gamer posted a lengthy workaround in Arabic that went viral but sadly didn't actually work. There was nothing anyone could do until the engineers at Sony and Microsoft figured it out or Lizard Squad stopped the attack.

What baffled Mustafa and others the most was why these Lizards, who were likely gamers themselves, wanted to take out gaming services and become hated the world over. They had clearly planned it for this Christmas period to cause maximum annoyance, and they seemed to have no care for the trouble they were in. Late in the evening on Boxing Day, an interview with two of the hackers was aired on BBC Radio 5 Live. They showed zero remorse for the impact they'd had on people around the world. Why would they go on national radio with their real voices and attempt to paint themselves as the good guys? Surely this was a massive OpSec risk that would land them in jail?

The next day – 27 December – was the day I was tasked with 'getting a Lizard' on the evening bulletin at Sky News. My first move was to listen back to that BBC radio interview and I was stunned by the bravado of these boys. The late-night Northern Irish presenter Stephen Nolan is well known for being a fierce and outspoken interviewer when required. And he had not held back on Lizard Squad who were horribly arrogant and unremorseful about the disruption they were causing. The two hackers called themselves 'Member 1' and 'Member 2' and started by blaming Sony and Microsoft for having poor cybersecurity and failing to defend against the attack. Member 1 spoke softly and slowly with a foreign accent. Perhaps from northern Europe, I thought at the time. He was young but came across as sure of himself and cocky. 'We're also doing it to amuse ourselves,' he admitted, adding that the anger the group had received online was 'funny'. Member 2 was a less confident speaker and less sure of his place in the story. He was more serious and insisted more forcefully but just as unbelievably that the hack was about raising awareness. He spoke with a south-east-English accent and said he was twenty-two.

Member 2 contradicted himself many times. He claimed the hack was all planned but then said it had been carried out on the spur of the moment. He said they did it to highlight security problems but then admitted that the gang had since accepted $300,000 worth of cloud storage vouchers from controversial internet entrepreneur Kim Dotcom to make them stop. Stephen Nolan's reply to this was savage: 'This wasn't about exposing security at a company at all was it? It was just dirty grubby greed.' In another contradiction, Member 2 seemed to suggest that he wasn't actually part of the gang; he was just helping 'them' sell the vouchers.

Softly spoken Member 1 didn't say much, except to warn at the end that they weren't going to stop their attacks until companies improved their security. He added that even if the police found him, they would only come and look at the computer for a while and realise there was nothing on it connecting him to these attacks. 'They'd have to let me go,' he said arrogantly.

After listening to the interview, I began my hunt for a Lizard to talk to us on air. It took hours of trawling Twitter and speaking to dozens of wannabes and fakes but I eventually succeeded in finding contact details for Member 2 – a man called Vinnie Omari.

I sent him a message and then obsessively refreshed my inbox in between doing dispatches on Sky News about the hack. He finally got back in touch to say that he might be open to talk. He was coy about telling me anything about himself but said that the BBC radio interview had gone badly and that he had been 'mislabelled' as one of the hackers. He claimed that he was in fact just a communications person for them – 'a mouthpiece' as he put it to me. He said he wasn't involved in the hack and wanted to make sure this was made clear in my report. I sensed regret in him and a lot of fear that he would be in trouble with the police. He said he would talk but only if I portrayed him as a 'well-connected member of the hacking community and an analyst'. In an amazing stroke of luck, it turned out that he lived in Twickenham – just a few miles from the Sky News studios in west London. He agreed to come to us for the interview. He was pale, skinny, wore all black and talked fast. He was at pains to distance himself from Lizard Squad but left the studios promising that Member 1, who was apparently called 'Ryan', would be in touch. I had no idea at the time of course that this 'Ryan' was Kivimäki and that he already had such a storied career as a teenage cyber criminal. It was later that afternoon – at around 3 p.m. – that Ryan made contact via Skype. Just in time for us to edit our conversation with him into our news piece.

He looked very young and pale, with a shaved head and soft features. In spite of everything he was polite and seemed in no rush. He wanted to be there and didn't need any persuading. But he was also utterly unremorseful and arrogant, struggling to stifle a smirk throughout the interview. He said one of the Lizard Squad group was only thirteen years old (I now think that was a lie but it's true that ChF was around fourteen when he was in the group). When I started by asking him why he wanted to ruin Christmas for tens of millions of people, he gave me the same boilerplate answer that Nolan had got from him, adding 'these companies make tens of millions every month from just their subscriber fees and they should have more than enough funding to be able to protect against these attacks'. We went back and forth for about fifteen minutes without him giving any hint of regret or awareness for how many people had been affected by his stunt. 'I'd be worried if those people didn't have anything better to do than play games on their consoles on Christmas Eve and Christmas Day. I mean, I can't really say I feel bad. I might have forced a couple of kids to spend their time with their families instead of playing games.'

The interview blew up online, with more than a million views on YouTube and thousands of comments on Twitter, where many four-letter words were hurled at the Lizards. PlayStation and Xbox also received a torrent of abuse. As did John Smedley, who had to patiently remind angry gamers over and over again that PlayStation Network was nothing to do with his department. It took another twenty-four hours for Sony to acknowledge the attack. Later they would offer a five-day extension to players' subscription periods and 10 per cent off as compensation. The resulting bill for the company must easily have been in the millions.

Kivimäki went on to speak to other reporters, sometimes calling himself Ryan Cleary. In one interview and debate on YouTube channel DramaAlert he is implored by Kim Dotcom to stop the silly hacker rivalries that were impacting so many innocent people. 'Hackers used to be respected, they used to have a magic about them,' Kim says, accusing Lizard Squad of harming the image of hackers around the world with their actions. Kivimäki's response is fascinating: he laughs it off as old-fashioned thinking: 'It's wrong to connect groups like Lizard Squad with, for example, L0pht from a couple of decades back. There's really no connection with the hacking groups of today and the hacking groups of two decades ago. The meaning is totally different now.'[1]

The Christmas 2014 DDoS incident has gone down as one of the – perhaps *the* – most disruptive cyber attacks ever by an NPT group. It certainly affected more people than any other such attack – either before or since. Every major outlet reported on it, and it was breathlessly discussed on news programmes around the world. To this day, a decade later, the attack is cited as a cautionary tale. In 2023, cybersecurity company Threatpost put the hack on its list of the worst holiday season cyber attacks and urged organisations to better protect themselves from hackers trying to maximise damage when employees and companies have their guards down.

Although many security experts angrily railed against the media's portrayal of Lizard Squad as 'sophisticated', people grudgingly came to accept that the Christmas attack *did* have a big beneficial impact on cybersecurity and the gaming industry. There's little doubt that this was not the group's motive – despite their clumsy attempts to claim so in interviews. But it was a wake-up call. Security website SecurityAffairs wrote a 'lessons learned' piece by dissecting my interview with Kivimäki. 'We need to change the approach to cybersecurity. Many experts only consider threats from cyber criminals or state-sponsored hackers . . . almost all people considered Lizard Squad script kiddies . . . this approach is totally wrong,' they wrote.[2]

The Christmas attack is also cited in research papers, dissertations and PhDs written at universities in the US, Italy, Portugal and UK. One thesis submitted at the prestigious US Naval Postgraduate School cited the attacks as an impactful use of what they called Radical Leveling Technologies (RLT) – powerful hacking tools or techniques that users can leverage to produce national or international impacts without the need for significant technological expertise: 'Many find it surprising that Microsoft, a major cyber-security software provider, was defeated by a small group of bad actors using tools that cost less than $500. But this is the impact of RLT: the ability to create leverage and change the balance of power in unanticipated ways.'[3]

Some, including Allison Nixon, go as far as to argue that the attack was one of the key catalysts that spurred the development of DDoS protection services. Whenever a cyber threat develops, dozens of companies soon pop up to make a fortune from offering their protection services and the 2014 attack became a great marketing tool for firms. The size of the attack unleashed on that day would be shrugged off by most modern sites but DDoS attacks are still commonplace and are getting more powerful. Expensive protection services are now a must-have for any organisation that needs to stay online. The attacks also started something of a cybercrime trend – many Christmases since have seen attempts to cause havoc with DDoS attacks. It's become such a tradition that in 2024 Europol unveiled an international law enforcement operation to take DDoS services down in December: 'The festive season has long been a peak period for hackers to carry out some of their most disruptive DDoS attacks, causing severe financial loss, reputational damage and operational chaos for their victims.'

At the time of Lizard Squad's attacks, the general public was stunned. Despite the previous four years of NPT chaos, there was little awareness of the power that could be wielded by these otherwise amateur attackers. There might have been a vague feeling in the zeitgeist that 'hackers in hoodies in their bedrooms' were increasingly causing problems, but this attack was immediate, unmissable and easy to understand. It was of course also easy to get angry about. Over the next couple of days I came back to the story with follow-ups about the fallout as other Lizard Squad members spoke to YouTubers about the so-called 'drama'. But the big thing the newsroom kept asking me was 'when would these kids be arrested?'

Vinnie Omari was the first. On New Year's Eve he was raided by the South East Regional Organised Crime Unit, which collared him on suspicion of cyber fraud offences committed between 2013 and 2014. It looked like the raid was for other alleged offences involving PayPal fraud but the search warrant, which later surfaced online, also referenced the Christmas DDoS attacks. 'They took everything. Xbox One, phones, laptops, computer USBs, etc.,' Vinnie told reporter William Turton from *Daily Dot*.[4]

After he was released on bail, Vinnie and I stayed in touch. He was very helpful to me as I tried to learn about the world of hacking and for the next couple of years, we would talk a lot and even went out for a pizza once. He reinvented himself as a bodybuilder and personal trainer, but I felt genuinely sorry for him as the police kept him in a state of limbo for years while he was on bail. This is often the case with teenage cybercrime as computer forensic work is time consuming and these crimes are not prioritised in the same way as violent physical offences. Time and again teenagers caught up in cybercrime, even lower-level stuff than Lizard Squad, are kept waiting as the cogs of justice grind along with little to no urgency. Is it any wonder that some of them are pulled back into the world before they have a chance to serve a sentence or be given their punishment?

Eventually Vinnie was cleared of all wrongdoing, including for the Christmas Day attacks. According to him he was always just a Lizard Squad figurehead. Shortly after he was cleared he told me he had got a job in IT security at the Houses of Parliament. The job (the existence of which I could never confirm) was short-lived and Vinnie moved abroad where he is now running 'multiple businesses' and regularly posts glamorous pictures of his luxury lifestyle and love of earning (and spending) bitcoin. I interviewed him for this book in July 2024 but he became upset that I was also talking to Urharmless, who he had a big falling out with and considers a fraud (Urharmless says the same about Vinnie, naturally). Sadly, Vinnie refused to talk to me any further.

After Vinnie's arrest, other Lizards were taken out too. On 16 January 2015 police announced that they had arrested an eighteen-year-old in Southport, near Liverpool. They didn't give a name but reporters at the *Daily Mail* identified him: 'The "quiet" teenager, named locally as Jordan Lee-Bevan, was arrested during a raid at his semi-detached home in Southport, Merseyside, today, with officers seizing computers as he was taken away in a police car.'[5]

Cyber reporter Brian Krebs identified him as the prolific hacker known as 'Jordie', 'EvilJordie' or 'GDKJordie'. Lee-Bevan was accused of gaining unauthorised access to computer material and knowingly providing false information to law enforcement agencies in the US. He was also charged with swatting after being linked to the ISIS Gang swats mentioned earlier.

So the FBI finally got all the delinquents they had wanted from ISIS Gang. But, as ever, it took years for Lee-Bevan to face justice. He pleaded guilty in 2018 to the swatting counts and was sentenced to sixteen months in prison. There's no mention of the Christmas Day attacks in reporting about the trial. There's also no mention of another high-profile hack against US broadband provider Cox Communications in 2014, which was carried out by a hacker calling themselves 'Evil Jordie'. That hack cost the firm a fine of $600,000. Lee-Bevan has not come up again in my research so it appears that he got himself back on the straight and narrow after his time in jail.

Despite Vinnie and Jordie's arrests, Lizard Squad limped on for a bit, performing minor but sickening hacks to try to stay in the news. On 26 January 2015, they hijacked the website of Malaysia Airlines, redirecting users to a notice that read 'Hacked by Cyber Caliphate' alongside the words '404 – Plane Not Found'. A 404 error code is what comes up when a website page can't be connected to ('page not found'). So 'Plane Not Found' is a tasteless reference to the loss of Malaysia Airlines Flight MH370 which had disappeared a year before with 239 people on board. The group also hacked Taylor Swift's Twitter account and posted for her 50 million followers to follow

@veriuser and @lizzard. The tweets were live for only a couple of minutes and the accounts were swiftly suspended. In a further bid to remain newsworthy, the Lizards also took credit for a major Facebook outage and were by now so infamous that the company was forced to issue a statement dispelling their claims.

The last Lizard attack worth mentioning took place in February 2015, when they redirected visitors to the website of computer manufacturer Lenovo to a slideshow of pictures of Ryan King (AKA Starfall) and Rory Andrew Guidry (AKA KMS). You might be wondering why these two were given such pride of place despite not actually being in Lizard Squad. Well, just as with Kivimäki using Ryan Cleary's name, this was Lizard Squad trying to embarrass King and Guidry, who were apparently now enemies of the gang. In fact, it turns out KMS was on some sort of mission to bring the group down, along with a hacker forum that Lizard Squad was heavily involved with called Darkode. KMS was apparently the person who had stolen and leaked all the information about Lizard Squad's DDoS service, LizardStresser.[6] This was the tool that the group had used to carry out the Christmas attacks, and they went on to offer it up for hire. For the princely sum of $129.99 a month or $500 for 'lifetime' usage, you could use the tool to take down a website for eight hours at a time.

According to a report in *Daily Dot*, KMS may have actually been an FBI informant, who eventually helped police take down Darkode and arrest a dozen of its core members.[7] But the same series of raids also saw KMS get arrested himself in July 2015 in Opelousas, Louisiana, for various hacking offences.[8] He was sentenced a year later to one year and a day in prison. While I was writing this book, news filtered through the hacking community that KMS had died at the age of thirty-seven. His family didn't say how. The memorial page online showed a tall smartly dressed man with a thick black beard standing unsmiling next to his family. 'He was always interested in learning and sharing knowledge with others in IT communities and was a professional in information security,' his family wrote.

The news of his death shocked and upset many in the community who looked up to him a great deal. The eulogy page was quickly filled with dozens of people sharing fond memories of him, with many openly writing about hacks they had carried out together. Some of the tributes ended with the words 'Hack the Planet'. It's not clear if KMS carried on criminal hacking late into his short life but it's clear he was still very much part of the community.

In 2016 Zachary Buchta from Maryland was also arrested for his role in Lizard Squad and another group called 'PoodleCorp'. According to the *Chicago Tribune*, the nineteen-year-old sobbed in the dock as he was sentenced to three months in prison and ordered to pay back $350,000 in restitution to victims. As a boy he had been warned in 2014 about his criminal path by police who had caught him carrying out minor cybercrime activity. But he was undeterred and even changed his Twitter profile at one stage to @fbiarelosers to taunt the cops.

At the same time that Buchta was arrested, Dutch police raided and arrested another nineteen-year-old. Bradley van Rooy, who used the names 'Uchiha' or 'UchihaLS', was accused of conspiring with other members of Lizard Squad to operate websites that provided cyber-attack-for-hire services, facilitating thousands of DDoS attacks and trafficking stolen payment card account information for thousands of victims.

Bradley was put on bail for two years. He was eventually given a two-year suspended sentence and 180 hours of community service. The vast majority of charges against him were dropped as they had taken place when he was a minor. He ended up being convicted of the DDoS-for-hire operation and handling stolen credit cards. He was also found guilty of running a service called phonebomber.net, through which customers could pay $20 to have victims harassed with repeated phone calls. I tracked him down and he openly talked about that period of his life, which he had put behind him a long time ago. He says that it was actually a Lizard Squad friend who made and ran the phonebomber.net service. But Bradley is sanguine about having been convicted of something he didn't do. As he says, he was let off for other acts that he did commit. 'I'm now twenty-seven and I see the damage that I did and understand that there could have been a higher punishment,' he says. 'But then I also see that I was just a kid and I had a troubled time at school and just fell into the hacking life after meeting the wrong people when I was playing the game *Runescape*.'

Like so many kids who head down the criminal path, Bradley was a curious boy intoxicated by the thrill of learning new skills. Once he was told about a trick by someone on a group chat, he would try it and then ask 'what else can I do?' It snowballed for him, turning from curiosity into financial gain. 'You don't think about the harm you're doing with your dumb actions,' he says.

It's fascinating that Bradley's journey and words track so perfectly to the experiences of hackers speaking to the NCA hundreds of miles away in the UK. It's as though there is a universal constant, whereby a subset of gamers in every generation is pulled into cybercrime in exactly the same way. There are literally billions of gamers in the world, so these people represent only a tiny fraction. But it seems to be inevitable and cyclical as hacker groups rise and fall. The differentiating, and more important aspect though, is how these boys and young men react when they cross the line and are caught. There is no pattern here. It completely varies depending on parental guidance, police action and the individual's appetite for risk. Bradley never went back to cybercrime after his arrest. He completed a degree in computer networking with a view to getting into cybersecurity but ended up becoming wealthy through trading cryptocurrency instead. He bought a house and helped his struggling family out and now mostly plays computer games and looks after his dog Indra.

But what of Julius Kivimäki AKA Member 1 AKA Ryan AKA Zeekill?

Surely, after appearing on TV and radio admitting that he was part of the gang, he too would be rearrested sharpish? Well, many organisations ran excited stories about him being raided and detained on around 1 January 2015. But no one thought to ask the Finns if it was true. A reporter at Finnish broadcaster YLE did ask the cops and it turned out that officers did indeed visit Kivimäki to interview him but they 'did not arrest him – contrary to reports in the international media'. It's not clear why they took no further action, but perhaps when the teenager confidently said that police would find nothing on his computer, he was right. 'They'd have to let me go,' he had cockily asserted. If so, maybe his earlier HTP-related arrest had taught him to cover up his tracks more effectively. Or maybe he hadn't taken as much of a leading role in the DDoS attacks as he had claimed.

For Finnish cybercrime cop Antti Kurittu, seeing Kivimäki on TV was especially galling. 'I remember watching your Sky News interview,' he told me 'and just thinking "wow, this guy is not even trying to cover up his crimes. He's just a different sort of person."' By then Antti was up to his eyeballs on other cyber cases. He had handed over to prosecutors the lengthy HTP investigation report that he had started in 2013. It was up to them to put it to the courts and up to other cops to start a new case against the teenager if the evidence was there.

#

So, Member 1 of Lizard Squad was free to carry on with life while he waited for the Finnish legal system to run its course. And Kivimäki didn't simply wait around. In May 2015, according to Bradley van Rooy, Kivimäki and Vinnie Omari travelled to Amsterdam and convinced Bradley to come and hang out with them in the city, not far from his Dutch home town. Bradley had only joined Lizard Squad in the aftermath of the Christmas Day attacks but had got to know Kivimäki very well online. The three Lizards had a fun time drinking and eating out. Kivimäki was out to enjoy himself and splash his cash. He had brought a fortune in bitcoin with him to spend in

Amsterdam and in Hong Kong where he was travelling on to afterwards. According to Bradley, Kivimäki showed him a Trezor wallet, which is like a USB stick used for storing details of your cryptocurrency wallet. It contained around 215 bitcoins, which were worth about $50,000 at the time. It was an incredible amount of money for a seventeen-year-old to be carrying around. But bear in mind that the same amount of bitcoins would be worth $20.7 million in 2024. Kivimäki told Bradley that this was just his travel money. 'He had real "fuck you" money but I knew the types of things he was doing in hacking so it wasn't that surprising,' Bradley said, refusing to give any more details. This could potentially explain why Kivimäki didn't seem to get back into any public hacking gangs after the fallout from the Christmas Day attacks. He clearly had something else going on that was far more lucrative and under the radar.

It wasn't until three months later in July 2015 that Kivimäki faced the music for his hacking with HTP. And it was no doubt a sweet melody to his ears. He was found guilty of the rather preposterous total of 50,700 instances of aggravated computer break-ins. It made for great headlines around the world, but what it actually meant was that the courts had counted one instance for every computer that he had enslaved into the HTP botnet. He was also found guilty of his part in HTP's hack of Massachusetts Institute of Technology's email system which gave them several hours of control over all the messages sent across the university's mailing system. He was also convicted of other offences including data breach, money laundering and being in possession of, and using, stolen credit cards. For all of these offences, he was handed a two-year suspended sentence and ordered to forfeit 6,588.88 euros as the proceeds of his money-laundering activity. If he had been an adult he could have got years behind bars, but as a minor and first-time offender he served no time in prison. So Kivimäki, just a few weeks from his eighteenth birthday, remained free. He began calling himself the 'Untouchable Hacker God' on Twitter. One of the Lizard Squad Twitter accounts celebrated the news: 'All the people that said we would rot in prison don't want to comprehend what we've been saying since the beginning, we have free passes.'

It was a shocking triple whammy. First, Kivimäki was a previous offender and on bail when he outed himself as one of the Christmas hackers. Second, the conviction had not taken those attacks into account at all. Third, the sentence was comically lenient compared to the headline-making crimes. Brian Krebs wrote a reaction article on his website titled 'Finnish Decision is Win for Internet Trolls'. The danger in a decision like this, he said, 'is that it emboldens young malicious hackers by reinforcing the already popular notion that there are no consequences for cybercrimes committed by individuals under the age of eighteen.'

Krebs also talked to Kivimäki after the conviction, finding him unsurprised at being let off with no jail time. 'During the trial it became apparent that nobody suffered significant, if any, damages because of the alleged hacks,' he told Krebs. In Kivimäki's interview with Finnish publication *Long Play* a year later, he again brushed off his conviction, saying that 'conditional doesn't mean anything at all if you don't commit new crimes'. He adds that it took him a couple of days to even hear about the sentence as he was busy travelling abroad at the time. He even struggles to recall exactly where he was.

Other cybersecurity commentators were concerned about the message the sentence sent to other young would-be hackers. Speaking to the BBC, Professor Alan Woodward from the Surrey Centre for Cyber Security pointed out that 'if I were another hacking group and saw someone attract a suspended sentence for over 50,000 hacks, some of which caused significant damage, I don't think it would cause me much concern'.

Perhaps the most furious of all was Sony executive John Smedley. He took to Twitter to vow that this was not the end. 'I'm coming for you Julius,' he posted, adding that the hacker was 'a sociopath and will get what's coming to him'.[9] He threatened to launch a civil lawsuit against Kivimäki and posted a long, impassioned comment on Reddit about why the sentence was a miscarriage of justice. 'This guy is the worst kind of bad news,' he said. He detailed all the DDoS attacks that he blames Kivimäki for, describing the grief it caused for gamers and the economic damage it did to the companies that make and run games. He outlined the emotional impact that Lizard Squad and Kivimäki had had on him too. 'This shit is real to my life and my family's life and I'm sure as hell not lying down for it for a second,' he wrote.

As for Antti Kurittu, he admits it was a disappointment but not a surprise. In spite of working so hard to get the conviction he was still expecting Kivimäki to receive a soft punishment because of how the famously lenient Finnish system works. He had a feeling it wouldn't be the last he heard of Kivimäki. 'That guy was not going to be deterred, you could just tell.'

#

A year after Kivimäki's sentencing, in a bizarre coincidence, Antti bumped into the hacker in Amsterdam. It was April 2016 and Antti was walking through the departures lounge of Schiphol Airport when he passed the by-then eighteen-year-old who was sitting typing on his phone. Antti did a double take, gobsmacked to see him. It was so surreal that they both found it amusing and took a selfie. After a short chat Antti asked Kivimäki if he was now 'staying out of trouble'. Kivimäki replied 'of course' but when Antti asked him for a contact email address he made one up with '@FBI.gov' at the end. They laughed and went their separate ways.

But, as Antti predicted, The Untouchable Hacker God would be back eventually. Four years later he was. And this time he had a new alias: 'ransom_man'.

//11
Vastaamo implodes
2020

'There are only two types of companies – those which have been hacked, and those which are going to get hacked.'

So goes the beloved maxim of cybersecurity sales people trying to sell us their companies' latest and greatest products. It is of course true. In a pessimistic sort of way. In the last five or so years since the rise of prolific, Russian-speaking ransomware gangs, organisations have been hit week in week out. There are so many organisations crippled by these criminals that it's impossible to report on all of them and futile to try to keep up.

Those same sales people will have you believe that these cyber attacks will cost you your business. But in truth, it's very rare for a cyber attack to be fatal. I've reported on countless cases when I thought one might be but most of the time the company recovers, albeit with a big financial hit and a herculean effort from staff. But ransom_man's attack on Vastaamo was fatal.

If you search online for 'companies that collapsed after a cyber attack', Vastaamo is very likely to be on the list.[1] And it isn't a long list – maybe running to only a dozen companies because, in many cases, there are other exacerbating factors that pushed the organisation over the edge. But with Vastaamo there is a distinct cause (ransom_man) and effect (collapse).

Why?

Well, there are two ways in which a victim organisation suffers from a hack – operationally and reputationally. Operational impacts are the things we see: blank computer screens, services offline, long queues of angry customers, deliveries upended, appointments cancelled, projects delayed. Most of the time these effects are painful but short term. If a company can recover quickly, communicate well, and prove they weren't complacent about their security then their reputation can be saved and the company can limp on until it fully recovers.

In some cases, however, the operational impact alone can be fatal. This was the case for UK company Code Spaces, which went from being a healthy and growing platform for hosting computer coding projects to full collapse in just twelve hours. An unknown hacker managed to sneak into the firm's computer network in 2014 (there's that tumultuous year again) and hit it with repeated DDoS attacks while also trying to blackmail them for money. When the firm refused to pay, the vindictive attacker started deleting every database he or she could find. For hours the company's IT team tried to kick them out of the computer network but the criminal kept a foothold and didn't stop deleting files and folders until the company was left with nothing. The hacker had drained the lifeblood from Code Spaces. Without the coding projects that the company was hired to protect and manage – there was no business. As the CEO put it in the final message on its website: 'Code Spaces will not be able to operate beyond this point, the cost of resolving this issue to date and the expected cost of refunding customers who have been left without the service they paid for will put Code Spaces in an irreversible position.'

Thankfully it's rare for this kind of devastation to result purely from operational impacts. Take a similar attack on Intercontinental Hotels Group (IHG) in 2022. Hackers tried to carry out a ransomware attack on the UK-based firm which runs 6,000 hotels around the world, including the Holiday Inn, Crowne Plaza and Regent brands.

The organisation's cybersecurity team managed to stop and contain them inside a small part of the network. But out of spite, the criminals deleted as many databases as they could get to before they were kicked out. Booking systems went down and customers were unable to use some of the company's apps. But IHG got through it. They handled customer complaints, came up with workarounds and warned investors about the disruption through the London Stock Exchange, which saw the share price take a hit. But it has since climbed to nearly double what it was. The hack caused huge operational impact but minor reputational impact. There was no customer data stolen and aside from a few weeks of annoyance for consumers, the damage and real suffering happened inside the firm and its franchisees as staff struggled their way through the issues. Size was of course a factor here as IHG had a steady stream of customers that ensured money continued to flow through the business.

When ransom_man hacked Vastaamo the attack wasn't an issue operationally at all. The actual cyber attack wasn't even noticed at the time. But reputationally it was catastrophic. After all, Vastaamo was a company built on one thing – trust.

Ville Tapio, Vastaamo's CEO, who has dark deep set eyes and thick eyebrows, blames his IT team for the breach and the police for how badly the fallout was handled. When he called in the National Bureau of Investigation (NBI) he trusted them to do what was best for the company and the victims whose data still hung in the balance. He says they locked him out of all decision-making – he didn't know what was being said in emails sent under his name. He accepts that the NBI had to manage a 'tactically tricky' situation, but says they clearly failed because the hacker was provoked into publishing the information and then extorting victims directly. 'In my opinion, in retrospect, the company's legally responsible persons should not be excluded from decision-making in such situations, and the police should not use the victims' identities for secret negotiations with criminals.' The NBI did not respond to my requests for a comment.

According to Ville, his cooperation and his trust in the NBI cost him dearly. Only one week after the extortion investigation began, the NBI filed a criminal complaint against him, accusing him of a data protection violation. It was the start of his downfall as head of the company and led to the board removing him from the position of CEO. His staff were kept completely in the dark about what was happening. According to one admin worker, who wanted to remain anonymous, Ville's sudden absence was a mystery and very confusing at the time. Of course, this was made even worse when ransom_man went public a few days later and everything blew up. 'It was awful when the phones started ringing, and they didn't seem to stop 24/7,' she said. 'Customers were desperate and calling for help and threatening to hurt themselves if they didn't get access to their therapy notes. And Ville was nowhere to be seen,'

This administrator had worked at the company for years and regularly spoke to the CEO but was not given any insight into what was happening. In the days before the hack erupted she had an inkling that something had happened after overhearing snippets of conversation between members of the IT team. When ransom_man went public the company was plunged into total chaos. She was tasked with answering the phone helplines set up to handle customers but was given no guidance about what she could and couldn't say. 'People were so angry and there was very little I could tell them other than try to calm them down,' she recalls.

It's an experience shared by others, including therapist and Vastaamo regional manager Nora Lindgren who first heard about the hack from one of her clients. She had to try to stay professional in front of her clients and the staff she was responsible for. 'I had no answers for either side and we were all working day and night trying to help customers when we ourselves were completely out of the loop.' For the first three days, everyone was in a state of high tension, waiting to see if the hacker would carry out his threat and publish all the data. 'We were really afraid for the clients and ourselves,' Nora says. Then of course everything was dumped online and it got even worse, with hundreds of calls every day. 'It felt like an avalanche on the necks of ordinary workers,' she says. Nora is clearly still angry that Vastaamo executives had three weeks to plan some kind of crisis guidance before the hacker went public but they did nothing. Clients were demanding to see what their therapists – including her – had written about them and she helped them all individually. But at the same time she felt like a victim too. The notes were only ever written for herself as a memory aid to help the therapy sessions be productive. Now they were open for the world to see.

Another therapist, Anja Snellman, described being in the office when customers descended in large numbers for help. 'There were a dozen or so clients waiting in the lobby when I arrived and they wanted to see their records right away,' she told Finnish newspaper *Helsingin Sanomat*.[2] 'They asked who I was and when I admitted that I was working there, they almost attacked me. It was a scary moment.' Some of the clients seemed suicidal and took out their anger on employees. All the time she, like Nora, felt horrible that her professional notes were now exposed. 'They were our words, like diary entries that were stolen.' Some staff broke down in tears in the office as they dealt with distressed and angry clients. She is still ashamed of the company's response to the crisis.

Ville Tapio agrees that the way his company reacted wasn't good enough but claims it was not his fault. His dismissal wasn't announced until 26 October, by which time the leaderless company had already drifted into a complete communication crisis. 'I completely lost the ability to influence any of the company's decision-making and communications. I wasn't allowed to speak to the media, or even participate in internal staff briefings, even though I was still the largest individual owner of the company.' But Tapio wasn't just dismissed as CEO, he was sued by the parent company, which accused him of failing to protect customer data and misleading the firm about the extent of another data breach that was only now coming to light.

When Vaastamo commissioned cybersecurity specialists Nixu to investigate the hack, the resulting report revealed that the company's database had been breached at least twice. The first time was by ransom_man in 2018, after which he had held on to the data for two years before launching his extortion attack. But Nixu also found that someone else had got in in 2019 too. The hacker, thought to be unrelated, had broken in and tampered with the database, deleting at least some of it and potentially downloading a copy before posting an extortion note on the system for IT staff to see. Nixu found that someone at Vastaamo had restored the database from a backup, deleted the ransom note and fixed the security flaws. This whole mysterious episode had happened in one day in March 2019 and was only ever disclosed as a minor data-loss incident to authorities. All this happened in the build up to a multimillion-euro deal between private equity firm Intera Partners and Vastaamo. Intera now says it was kept in the dark while in the process of buying Vastaamo. This was the secret reason for Ville Tapio's unceremonious dismissal from his own company.

On 28 October the new parent company also obtained a court order to confiscate assets worth almost 10 million euros from the Tapio family to reduce the risk of them trying to hide, destroy or give away their property before any settlement could be reached. Ville's mother Nina, who was a psychotherapist herself, and father Perttu, who was a priest, founded the company with him before stepping back to let their son run it. A lawsuit followed which didn't conclude until a settlement was reached in April 2023.

The settlement details must remain a secret for fifteen years as per the court arrangement so neither Ville Tapio nor Intera will say how much money was paid in apparent compensation to Intera. But it's likely to be in the millions. His parents were also ordered to return part of the purchase price too. No other detail is given but

Ville has always vigorously denied any cover up of the 2019 breach and it was never proven in court. He also insists that the buyers of his company had the same information as he did when they went ahead with the purchase. Intera Partners refuse to go into details about the court case but sent me their blanket statement: 'If we had been aware of the data breach at Vastaamo in March 2019 and the prior deficiencies in safeguarding customer information, we would never have proceeded with the acquisition.'

Tapio's IT managers, Sami Keskinen and Ilari Lind, have remained silent. Their pictures adorned the 'about us' page of the Vastaamo website but Keskinen's LinkedIn profile has been scrubbed of his involvement in Vastaamo and Lind now has no online presence at all. I couldn't get either man to respond to my messages.

To add a further twist, Keskinen and Lind had come to Ville Tapio during the chaos of the hack crisis with a confession. Before beginning work at Vastaamo they had been criminally investigated in connection with a different incident at a previous company. 'They told me they had been suspected and both detained in pre-trial detention for data breach and data theft just a few weeks before they started working at our company in 2015,' Tapio claims. The pair hadn't been charged with anything back then, but Tapio thinks they only decided to tell him after they had found out that Antti Kurittu was looking into the breaches at Vastaamo. Antti had been involved with the investigation into the previous case in his role as a Security Specialist for the National Cyber Security Center and they were perhaps worried that he and Nixu would be biassed against them. Tapio remains furious about the revelation and says he would never have hired the pair had he known that there were potential issues. He squarely blames them for the Vastaamo breach, claiming that it was their responsibility to ensure the system was secure. The therapy company's IT systems were woefully protected. The patient database was left directly exposed to the internet and unprotected for fifteen months. There was no firewall stopping people accessing it from any computer in the world. So, by using common internet scanning tools, anyone could have found it and attempted to break in. Even worse – there was no password used to log in. It wouldn't have taken ransom_man long to find the database in 2018. It would have taken even less time for him to load it up and have the private, personal and sensitive details of 33,000 therapy patients at his fingertips. He even bragged about this point on the forum when he went public with the attack:

> USER 135982231: 'The system was unsecured. The login password was root:root'

In total it took just four minutes for ransom_man to carry out his silent heist. It's still not known how or why the database was left open to the internet and so poorly protected, but Tapio blames his IT team for altering the security settings at some point from around November 2017 until March 2019. He assumes it was to make it easier for them to get in and carry out tasks remotely from home. 'I personally perceive the patient data leak as more of an internal abuse than an external hack. I find it incomprehensible that the police and the prosecutor have not been interested in finding out these internal actions and responsibilities in more detail,' he says. Tapio argues that it was impossible for him as CEO to have had the time and technical understanding to have prevented the security lapses. But Nixu's report found other mistakes and insufficiencies with Vastaamo's IT network that should have been bread and butter for any responsible organisation. Some of these red flags should have been picked up by Vastaamo's IT team, and would have been spotted easily by an external auditor had the company paid one to come and give the firm a once over. Tapio says he did this in 2017 – before the database security was changed – and that they gave everything a clean bill of health and procedures were adequate. Then for some unknown reason everything unravelled later that year. The next time things were checked externally was in May 2019 by Intera Partners who sent some experts in as part of their due diligence for purchasing the company. They uncovered some minor cybersecurity deficiencies at the time which were promptly fixed ahead of the deal. But that was of course after all the damage had already secretly been done.

Regardless of who is to blame for the horrendous lapses in security that allowed the breaches to happen, those lapses – or rather the revelation of them – were fatal for Vastaamo. Operationally, the company might have been able to build back and keep going. But reputationally, it was game over. The company took a thundering hit when ransom_man struck but arguably it was the unearthed security lapses and the way the firm handled the fallout that delivered the killer blows.

Tapio insists that the company's collapse might have been preventable had he been allowed to stay at the helm but ultimately Vastaamo filed for bankruptcy in February 2021. In December 2021 a 608,000 euro fine was issued to the company by the Deputy Data Protection Ombudsman for the European Union for failing to protect customer data and failing to disclose the 2019 breach. The fine could have been higher had the company still been active but the decision was taken to issue the lowest possible financial sanction so as not to reduce the funds available for other claims relating to the firm's bankruptcy, such as potential compensation for damages. The judgement described the negligence as 'extremely serious' and 'long lasting'.

Ville Tapio was convicted in the District Court of Helsinki for data protection violations under the EU's General Data Protection Regulations. He was sentenced to a three-month suspended prison sentence in April 2023 after being found guilty of not anonymising or encrypting the personal data processed at Vastaamo. When delivering the verdict, the court heard that this failure was particularly reprehensible due to the highly sensitive information his company was responsible for storing. Prosecutors had pushed for a nine-month suspended prison sentence for Tapio because they accused him of being grossly negligent in relation to information security and data protection. Both sides have since lodged appeals against the conviction.

Meanwhile, what was left of Vastaamo was sold off to a company called Verve, which took on its debt and the potential compensation packages yet to be decided by the courts. Verve agreed to carry on employing Vastaamo staff, though by that time many of them had left or gone on sick leave after the events of winter 2020. Nora was one of the first therapists to leave. She couldn't handle the emotional toll that the incident had taken on her – three years went by before she felt able to talk fully about that time. The thing that comes across when speaking to her and other therapists and patients is that Vastaamo was genuinely providing a worthwhile service and had a really good thing going before the hack. Ransom_man didn't just harm the victims he extorted, he also destroyed an important public service that was making a difference. Now he was set to face justice in what would be the largest criminal trial in Finnish history – but there was still time for him to throw in one more twist of his own.

//12
Untouchable Hacker God caged
2024

On Friday 19 January 2024, Julius Kivimäki took to the witness stand in Espoo, just west of Helsinki.

The moment was highly anticipated. His trial had been going on for months by this stage but this was the first time Kivimäki (now using his adult name Aleksanteri) would tell his side of the story. Every twist and turn of the hearings so far had been covered in the Finnish press by a few dedicated legal reporters, but on this day the courthouse was heaving, with a large crowd of journalists from Finland and beyond. The US media outlet Bloomberg had sent a team as part of plans to write an in-depth feature about the case and I had travelled from London to witness events while on annual leave from my job at the BBC.

I arrived at the courthouse bleary-eyed after being awoken at 4 a.m. by the metallic grating and scraping of snow ploughs on the Helsinki streets beneath my hotel room. Finland was in the middle of a large dumping of snow and as the hearing start time approached people made their way up to the courthouse on slippery pavements. You could tell the foreigners like me from a mile off as we shuffled cautiously along in poorly planned footwear. The locals seemed to barely notice the treacherous conditions as they tap-danced gracefully up the steps of the building. This was the largest case yet to be held at West Uusimaa District Court's giant modern courthouse, which had opened in mid 2022 and still felt brand new. But as the largest case in Finnish history in terms of the number of victims, this was always going to be a major event for any courthouse, old or new.

The design of the building is sleek, with huge columns of brick framing dozens of elongated windows that pour light into the waiting areas outside of the courtrooms. Inside it's airy, spacious and no-nonsense. There weren't enough seats outside the room for all the press, so everyone stood around waiting for the intercom to call us all in. I was told we would be able to film the first few minutes of the hearing. This is a common practice in Finland and I'd seen clips of Kivimäki at the start of previous hearings he'd attended. Some clips showed him smiling and seemingly enjoying the attention. In one he grins while inexplicably holding up a copy of L. Ron Hubbard's *Dianetics* – a pseudoscience self-help book seen as a precursor to Scientology. That clip was sent around the bemused cyber community with enthusiasm, partly because of the startled and embarrassed reaction of Kivimäki's lawyer Peter Jaari who was sat next to him at the time.

So, minutes before the hearing started, I prepared myself for the strange novelty of filming a defendant inside a courtroom. In the UK it's illegal to take pictures in the corridors of a courthouse, let alone inside a hearing. When the intercom sounded, we all piled into the large wood-panelled room, our cameras rolling or clicking as soon as the door opened. Kivimäki was sitting in the far corner, looking down intently at a laptop and trying to ignore the dozen or so cameras that were soon within a couple of feet of his cherubic face. His wispy golden hair was combed back over his head and he wore a black T-shirt and grey hoodie – another oddity for me. Defendants in all court cases I'd been to before had worn smart clothing – usually suits. He furrowed his brow as camera flashes went off in his face, but never looked up from his computer. I filmed him on my phone for about a minute and wondered if he would recognise me from all those years ago on Skype. But I also felt extremely awkward. The room was utterly silent and anyone who wasn't filming or taking pictures was staring at Kivimäki, watching for any reaction. In spite of everything I knew about him, he was still innocent until proven guilty and this side of the Finnish court system felt exploitative to me.

Presiding over events was lead judge Ilkka Lahtinen, who was sitting alongside two other judges on an elevated row of seats situated next to Kivimäki's witness desk. In Finland almost all cases are decided upon by judges and not a jury – perhaps a reason for the reduced need for in-court privacy. Lahtinen called order and everyone took their seats to let the hearing begin. The courtroom had been designed to be fully multimedia-friendly, with screens on each desk and cameras and microphones trained on the speakers. But none of these devices had been turned on so people had to strain to hear the softly spoken Kivimäki over the tip tapping of reporters on their laptops. There were about fifty people in the room and dozens more watching remotely. A cinema screen in Helsinki had been co-opted since the start of the trial to play a live feed of the hearings to any of the victims who wished to attend. To ensure their privacy, the location of this auditorium was, and remains, a secret. Many of the victims we've heard from in this book were sat in front of that screen listening and watching Kivimäki speak for the first time.

Kivimäki's lawyer Peter Jaari started the questioning. Kivimäki answered the long list of preplanned questions slowly and calmly, making himself smile with small jokes. While he talked, he lightly swiped on the touchpad of his laptop, apparently moving the mouse around unconsciously. He described how he started experimenting on computers from the age of three and first discovered hacking after learning how to cheat in *Minecraft* aged ten. He dropped out of school early and got involved in games cheats forums that led him down a bad path, carrying out hacks as a member of teenage gangs not realising the damage he was doing. It was all just for the excitement and 'felt like a video game', he said. He claimed his main skills as a hacker were as a networker – both with people and knowing his way around IT networks. He wasn't good at programming, he claimed, contradicting what he had told cops in that boastful interview at DEF CON as a fifteen-year-old.

Around the time he was doing criminal hacking, he told the courtroom that he also earned money as a white-hat hacker, finding vulnerabilities in computer code and reporting them to companies. He said, for example, that he had received about 3,000 euros from Google after finding a security hole in their internet browser Chrome. But this has been called into question by some experts, including Antti Kurittu who wonders if Kivimäki may have taken credit for someone else's discovery. Kivimäki insisted to the court that he stopped hacking after a short time because it was 'limiting his life'. No one gets rich from such an activity, he said.

At the age of sixteen, he moved to Barcelona, where he said he did IT consultancy to fund his jet-set lifestyle. He said he moved to London just before the pandemic in 2020 where he lived with a friend and his girlfriend. Two women are mentioned in court papers. Kivimäki has spoken to press about getting married and even having a child but nothing about this was brought up in the hearings. I've spoken to Finnish reporters who have also tried and failed to verify the details of this side of his life.

We can flesh out Kivimäki's time in London a smidge more by going to the police investigation report. While living in the city he owned two expensive apartments – one of which he called his spare. During this time he had an idea for a cybersecurity business called Scanifi which he started setting up with a friend. It would scan the internet for historic vulnerabilities and sell the information to insurance companies. The prosecution used this information as a weapon against him, arguing that it was precisely a tool like Scanifi that might have helped him find the unsecured Vastaamo database. One of his partners in the business was an American called Gus Naughton who Kivimäki was very close to. In a police interview in Seattle in March 2023 (attended remotely by DCI Marko Leponen) Naughton said Scanifi was a great idea that they worked on for about a year but never actually launched – Naughton and the others had severed contact with Kivimäki as soon as the company servers were seized by Leponen's team on that whirlwind morning in October 2020. They assumed that Kivimäki had become involved in criminal activity again and were disappointed in him. 'We thought he'd turned things around,' Naughton said.

Naughton had first come across Kivimäki on IRC chat channels in around 2013–14, where he knew him only as Zeekill or Ryan C, and kept his distance thanks to the hacker's reputation for being unhinged. But years later in 2019 they bumped into each other again online and became good friends. Kivimäki seemed to have become more mature, discussing ideas for Scanifi and a luxury travel service he was eager to launch. At one point in summer 2022 – just months before the Interpol Red Notice was put out for Kivimäki's arrest – he invited Naughton on an all-expenses paid trip to Saint-Tropez bankrolled by a luxury travel company he had links to. Naughton's Instagram Stories videos from the time show him wide-eyed and beaming from ear to ear at expensive restaurants and cruising around in a Mercedes singing Red Hot Chilli Peppers songs. Kivimäki is seen in the background of a couple of clips, less excited about the luxury surroundings. He was apparently used to the high life. In one clip he is coaxed awkwardly into singing 'Bohemian Rhapsody' with Naughton in a large kitchen. A young and pretty woman with long dark hair joins in – perhaps Kivimäki's girlfriend or wife at this point.

Back on the stand, Kivimäki denied any involvement in the Vastaamo data theft or the extortions. He claimed to have heard about it from Finnish news websites and the Ylilauta message board. He admitted that he had shared a link to patient information on a discussion forum on his account and said he regretted that. He described the cyber attack as a low crime and insisted that it wouldn't make sense for him to have done it because he didn't need the money. He added that he was surprised the blackmailer didn't ask for a higher ransom. He only learned that he was a suspect when his Scanifi server went offline, and he realised it had been seized by police. It was a pretty big surprise, he told the court. He also accused the police – Marko Leponen in particular – of lying at various points in their investigation. Kivimäki's main gripe was that the police had no reason to arrest him in absentia and issue the Interpol Red Notice because they were already in touch with his lawyer Peter Jaari. They could have just organised to question him in the normal way instead of going to the lengths they did. This was the reason he didn't come home to Finland and chose to carry on living in Paris under fake names. He says he was worried he would not get a fair trial as the police themselves weren't acting fairly. This accusation against Leponen had been issued by Kivimäki before on Twitter and in press interviews from prison a few months before the trial. Leponen says he didn't contact Jaari as he wasn't Kivimäki's official lawyer at that time. Police had no obligation to search for Kivimäki's lawyer, he insists.

After his days giving testimony in court, Kivimäki reapplied to be let out on bail and the judges agreed – much to the dismay of concerned prosecutors who argued that he was a flight risk, and proceeded to lodge an urgent appeal against the decision. In the meantime he was let out on Monday 5 February. Keen to arrange an interview, I managed to get a number for him from his lawyer and Kivimäki replied to my first text on Tuesday 13 February. 'Hi Joe, I'm very well, making breakfast,' he said. After that he read all my texts but didn't reply to any of them. Then he disappeared. Not just from me – from everyone.

On Friday 16 February the prosecutors won their appeal to get him detained again for the remainder of the trial. There was just too much risk that he would flee and try to leave the country and no one knew how much bitcoin he had stashed away to fund an escape, they successfully argued. So, Kivimäki was ordered to return back to the police for detention, but instead he stopped answering phone calls and wouldn't tell anyone where he was. After trying and failing to get hold of him over the weekend and on the Monday, the police were forced to issue a search notice for him. Kivimäki was once again a wanted man. The story made the headlines in Finland and on tech outlets. It seemed a farce to many that this could have happened again after Kivimäki's storied history. The news tore through cybersecurity communities – a group chat Mikko Hypponen was on exploded with anger. 'We couldn't believe they let him out and I was certain he would try to leave the country,' he said.

As part of his bail conditions Kivimäki wasn't allowed to leave the Espoo area and was ordered to be available at a certain address (he gave his parents' house) between 7 p.m. and 8 a.m. every day of the week. Plus, he had to report to the police department three times a week and be reachable from a certain phone number if necessary. Police confirmed to news outlet *HS* that he had not complied with the orders and they had no idea where he was. Kivimäki meanwhile told *HS* over Signal messages: 'I'm not missing. I haven't run away and I will definitely be in court.' He claimed to still be in Espoo and promised to show up for his next mandated appearance the following week. But he refused to hand himself in or say where he was. It was a remarkable move for a defendant trying to win over a court and prove his innocence. But when you take into account his previous decade of interaction with the law, it's all very much in keeping with The Untouchable Hacker God. Peter Jaari confirmed to me at the time that the news stories were true but that he was confident his client was not on the run. As he told *HS* at the time, 'I don't know where he is. I urged him to register, but his message was that we will see him at the district court next week at the latest and I trust that he will appear there, if the police do not catch him earlier.'[1]

The police did not take any chances. Marko Leponen was once again put in charge of the manhunt. They figured that Kivimäki must have rented a place to stay and – given that he had managed to get somewhere at such short notice – they theorised that he had used Airbnb. Once again the key piece of information came from Kivimäki himself – he had published a picture of an expensive bottle of champagne on the Ylilauta website. Officers managed to get clues from the furniture in the background to locate the exact Airbnb that he was holing up in. When they knocked on the door of the apartment in Kruununhaa, Helsinki, Kivimäki answered. They sighed in relief and immediately rearrested him. It seemed he had received help from people in his close circle who had paid for the apartment and given him a virtual credit card.

He'd been missing for over a week. The whole thing was horribly embarrassing for the courts and annoying for police who once again had to spend time and resources tracking him down. It also saw interest in the case reach new heights, prompting even more press to turn up the following Tuesday when Kivimäki returned to court for the final stages of live evidence before the judges retired to consider their verdict.

They had much to consider. As well as the evidence heard in the trial, they also had to take into account the 2,200-page report submitted by Marko Leponen and his officers.

#

Months before the trial had begun Marko would sit up at night wondering if the evidence would be strong enough to get the conviction. He knew he had the right guy but, as ever with the legal system, he also knew that the case had to be proven beyond all reasonable doubt to secure a guilty verdict. The press and his superiors were constantly asking for updates and wondering when the investigation report would be completed. To outsiders, Kivimäki seemed so obviously the culprit that they presumed it would be easy to prove. But Marko and his team needed to make the case watertight.

Kivimäki's name had been put on the shortlist of potential suspects early on after his aliases such as 'RyanC' had been found linked to the Vastaamo.tar file that ransom_man had accidentally leaked, and on the servers that had been seized in October 2020. Experts were certain that ransom_man had to be Finnish due to the blackmail emails and the intimate knowledge of Finnish internet culture. Digital forensics also showed that ransom_man had searched the patient notes in Finnish for terms like 'famous', 'police', 'paedophilia' and 'rape fantasy'. The words matched the types of notes he released online in the initial batches.

Ransom_man's so-called TTPs (tactics, techniques and procedures) also matched up with what the police knew about Kivimäki and his teenage hacking days. Experts noted the sarcastic and offensive file names and passwords found on the servers. For example, the folder name for the patient data was called 'therapissed/patients/directory'; email addresses linked to the server were called things like anussucker@cs.email and fuckfuckfuck@cs.email; and references were also found to other phrases such as 'lulzsecryan', 'Niggers1' and 'ihateblackpeople'. Seeing some of these puerile terms in the investigation report and hearing them used in the serious setting of the courtroom was surreal.

The next major leap forward for Marko came when IP addresses linked to Kivimäki's home addresses in London (from where the extortion had taken place in 2020) and Barcelona (where the hack had been carried out in 2018) were found amongst the seized server logs. 'But that still didn't get us to 100 per cent,' Marko recalls. So he and the team 'kept digging and digging and digging'. One of the major hold-ups was waiting for internet companies to respond with information. One large US tech giant, which Marko wouldn't name, took two and a half years to get them information that ended up being a key piece of evidence, linking Kivimäki to the server used to send the extortion emails to Vastaamo patients. 'It was very frustrating but we get used to it in cybercrime investigations,' Marko says, laughing at the absurdity of it. Until that point the team had had evidence proving Kivimäki was involved in stealing the data and extorting Vastaamo but not the final and cruellest step in the criminal scheme.

The case was now strong, but there were still pieces missing so Marko decided to organise a two-day conference at the headquarters of the National Bureau of Investigation, bringing together all the departments involved in the case.

In April 2023 fourteen officers, all equipped with different skills and expertise, sat in a large meeting room fuelled by sandwiches and 'hundreds of litres of coffee' and went through everything. It worked brilliantly – people would describe what evidence they had accumulated and what bits they were missing, then another team would raise their hands and say, 'Actually we do have that detail'. Over two days the puzzle was almost entirely completed. The process was exhausting but by the end there were only a few pieces missing and none of them vital. 'It was really exciting because this was the first point when I saw our whole case and understood what we have and how everything connects,' Marko says.

As well as the main investigation team, a further 200 officers had the gargantuan task of processing the thousands of individual criminal complaints lodged by Vastaamo victims – all on top of their normal police work, and all against the deadline of the impending trial date. 'Many people missed many holidays and time with their families to get everything done in time,' Marko says. Once his investigation report was complete he called in the prosecutors, Pasi Vainio, Bo-Niklas Lundqvist and Harri Mäkelä, to begin preparing for trial. Without any prior experience in cyber cases they at first found it daunting to try to convey such detailed and complex evidence to the non-specialist court. Marko describes them as phenomenal. 'They learned to speak fluent cyber and then found a way to portray everything clearly and in plain language.' The Vastaamo case had been a monumental and hugely costly operation for police and other public sector bodies. According to estimates the crisis response, police investigation, trial preparation, international manhunt, local manhunt and the trial itself cost Finland's public purse at least 4 million euros.[2]

The verdict came in at exactly 2 p.m. on 30 April 2024.

Instead of calling everyone back to court, the authorities uploaded it to the court's website for all to download. The twenty-six-year-old was guilty on all counts. The judges said that no individual item of evidence had been sufficient on its own to prove that Kivimäki was guilty but that they had come to their decision by taking everything into account as a whole. He was convicted of aggravated data breach, almost 9,600 counts of aggravated invasion of privacy (relating to named individuals who specifically pressed charges), more than 21,300 counts of attempted aggravated extortion (for the emails he was confirmed to have sent), and twenty counts of aggravated blackmail (for the people who paid his ransom). 'Taking into account Vastaamo's position as a company producing mental health services, Kivimäki has caused great suffering or the risk of it to the interested parties,' the verdict said.

Marko says the written document shows the judges had completely understood the complex and intertwined arguments and evidence. He points to four key pieces of information that sealed Kivimäki's fate:

1. The servers used to carry out the hack, extortion and blackmail were linked to Kivimäki's own bank account. The machines were hired with the same bank details he used to reserve a hotel room and spend money on an Only Fans subscription.
2. Only a small number of people – Kivimäki and some of his friends and Scanifi colleagues – had access to these servers and police were able to show that his private login keys were used at

the time of the cyber attack to access the server. Marko says his team were about 90 per cent certain of this point but Kivimäki got them to 100 per cent after admitting it to them in an interrogation. In court he tried to backtrack on this, which further raised this point as a red flag against him.

3. The IP addresses used in the crimes were linked back to Kivimäki. Most notably the extortion emails were sent using his internet connection at 70 Horseferry Road – a tall apartment building in a sought-after and famous street in London where a small flat can cost around £4,000 a month. He lived there with his girlfriend and a friend.

4. Police were able to link Kivimäki to a personal account on Ylilauta from which posts were made that betrayed inside knowledge of the crime. Marko is particularly proud of his team for the way they managed this. On an otherwise anonymous photograph posted under the account, his officers noticed that you could see someone's fingers holding a bottle of water. Using novel forensics techniques investigators were able to zoom in and enhance the image and then match the fingerprint swirls seen in the picture with Kivimäki's own. 'It was unbelievable, but it shows that you have to use every measure you know, and try those you don't.'

There were other pieces of evidence that also swayed the verdict. Remember that 0.01 bitcoin that Marko's team paid ransom_man during their negotiations with him – ostensibly to check that they had set up their payment system correctly? Well, perhaps the 'cherry on top' of the case was the way in which Marko's team tracked that bitcoin through the blockchain until it eventually landed in Kivimäki's own bank account. It was part of a group of payments apparently mixed in with the twenty ransoms he was sent. In court Kivimäki disputed the accuracy of the blockchain tracing but could not explain where the other payments had come from or remember who the people were whose names were used to make the poorly laundered payments to him.

Despite appearing cool, calm and even aloof at times during his trial, prosecutors noted that Kivimäki's story kept changing. 'When the proof has progressed. Kivimäki has clearly tried to reconcile to the evidence,' prosecutors argued. The judges agreed. However, it's also notable that every one of the convictions in the court's verdict starts with the words: 'Kivimäki, *alone or together with unknown persons*'. There is a strong suspicion that he worked with another hacker or hackers on at least some of the process but police were never able to prove it. Kivimäki criticised the prosecution for not working hard enough to find the people he claims carried out the hack and extortions but he never mentions any names. Of course, it seems extremely unlikely, even impossible, that Kivimäki didn't know himself who the perpetrators were if it wasn't him. It's also important to note that in the past Kivimäki had no qualms about pulling in other names and blaming other people for being involved in cybercrimes with him. Has he become loyal in his later years and started protecting his co-conspirators? Or is he just lying and did it all alone?

Which brings us to another big question: why did he do it?

It's plain from his lifestyle (not to mention monumental legal fees) that the twenty-six-year-old Kivimäki is rich – probably very rich. His wealth was, as we've heard, a chief angle of his own defence – why would I try to extort Vastaamo and then its customers for money if I'm already rich? It's a logical argument and one I have puzzled over during the writing of this book. Kivimäki's Lizard Squad buddy Bradley van Rooy (AKA Uchiha) has a theory that it was never really about the money: 'It must be where Julius gets his buzz or he might have just been bored. Of all the people from our hacking days that could have done something like this – it was Julius. He was always okay with me, but there was always a careless attitude in him.'

One word that keeps coming up from other people in Kivimäki's orbit is 'sociopath'. According to *Psychology Today* a sociopath is someone who:

exhibits a pattern of antisocial behaviours and attitudes, including manipulation, deceit, aggression, and a lack of empathy for others. Sociopathy is a non-diagnostic term, and it is not synonymous with 'psychopathy', though the overlap leads to frequent confusion. Sociopaths may or may not break the law, but by exploiting and manipulating others, they violate the trust that the human enterprise runs on.[3]

None of the people who used this description for Kivimäki are psychologists and it can be irresponsible to throw around terms like this without expert analysis. But I bring it up at this point as a potential explanation for the inexplicable actions we've seen from this enigmatic criminal.

Antti Kurittu agrees that Kivimäki stood out even among teenage hacking gangs for being uncaring and callous. 'I don't think he was ever interested in cybersecurity that much,' Antti told me when we met in Helsinki during the trial. 'I think he was just interested in causing mayhem to people's lives. And he found a way that he could do that without risking damage to his facial bone structure, basically: from behind the computer.' I suggested to Antti that this was a sign of cowardice but he disagreed. Kivimäki never really shied away from putting his name and face to attacks. 'I'd just say that he is uncaring to a degree which is difficult to understand. He is more of a nihilist, I think, than a coward.'

Another insight comes from Kivimäki's friend and Scanifi business partner Gus Naughton. At the end of Naughton's interview with police in Seattle the cops were about to press stop on the recorder when they asked if there was anything else he wanted to add. 'I think he needs help,' Naughton said about his friend, who was by this time in prison awaiting trial. 'I think he needs help to find his own way in this world. I don't know if he did this and if he did then that's terrible. But he's a very clever, misguided person.' Naughton also says that Kivimäki had confided that he and their other Scanifi partner Alex Vanderport were his only real friends.

Regardless of his mentality and motive, the judges gave Kivimäki very close to the maximum possible sentence – six years and three months in prison out of a possible seven. But his time inside will be reduced to around half because Kivimäki has not served a prison sentence during the past five years so, incredibly, he's treated as a first-time offender under Finnish law. This seemed absurd to many commentators. Kivimäki was far from a first timer. He had been convicted in 2015 for his HTP cybercrimes and went on to be implicated in many more criminal schemes. I was also surprised to find out during the trial that he had received a second conviction in 2019 which hadn't ever been covered in the press.

This conviction was related to the harassment in 2014 of John Smedley, Agent Brogan and the unnamed US girl. While these crimes were being investigated, Kivimäki had been arrested and remanded in custody. Twice. And he was also charged with swatting his alleged former HTP team mate Nathan Nye. This was new and huge information to me, highlighting how little Kivimäki cared about getting into trouble with the police and how ineffectual being on police bail is as a deterrent for people like him. This discovery also helped me make sense of a Skype call clip in which Kivimäki jokes to the others on the call that jail was 'kind of shitty – only like a 4 star prison. You had to make your own food. It was terrible – the room service sucked.' The clip was recorded in the middle of December 2014, and I now realise that it must have been made not long after Kivimäki had been released from police custody on bail. This was less than two weeks before he came on Sky News to brag about the Christmas Day attacks. Perhaps the fact that he was already on bail for the harassment offences might explain why police didn't pursue him for his involvement in those gaming attacks – they already had their hands full pursuing him for the HTP offences of 2013 and the harassment campaigns of 2014.

It took years for Kivimäki to stand trial for the 2014 offences. In August 2018, when the call went out for him to appear, he couldn't be contacted as he was abroad. The trial started in 2019 regardless and he was convicted, prompting a protracted appeal process that didn't conclude until November 2022. In the end the Helsinki Court of Appeal sentenced him to a ten-month suspended prison term and a fine of 480 euros. He was also ordered to pay Agent Brogan's parents $3,000 each for the 'considerable fear, insecurity, and suffering' that he had caused them. So it was largely another slap on the wrist for The Untouchable Hacker God. You can see why the news was overlooked and ignored.

One thing that the Vastaamo case judges took into account in his 2024 sentencing was Kivimäki's agreement in principle that he would pay compensation in relation to some of the thousands of claims from victims, which were to be addressed in a separate civil case (still not resolved at the time of writing). It seems bizarre for a defendant who was pleading not guilty to agree to compensate the victims of a crime that he insists he didn't commit. But it's true that during the trial Kivimäki agreed to pay 4,000 victims an undisclosed sum if he was found guilty. That's on top of any potential claim for compensation that might be made by Vaastamo itself, although that seems unlikely to be forthcoming now that the company is bankrupt. One woman who paid Kivimäki's ransom and suffered a great deal, reportedly secured 6,500 euros in compensation but that appears to have been a one-off. So far only a small number of the victims appear to be engaging in the process of litigation, perhaps because so many are nervous about coming forward. Tiina Parikka says winning some form of compensation will do little to heal the wounds the affair has caused. When I met her in a cafe near Helsinki she talked about how there are still members of the public who question whether or not anyone even deserves compensation: 'People sometimes ask me what's the harm with all this – it's only stolen data, it's not violence. But so many people were affected by this in so many ways, and still, it's far from being over. Thirty-three thousand people are a lot of victims and it's affected our health, and some have been targeted with financial scams as well as using the stolen data.'

Further attacks have become a problem for many Vastaamo victims. In June 2024, for example, a warning was issued by Finland's data protection agency about a scam involving personal data released during the Vastaamo hack.[4] It appears that cyber criminals had made use of the stolen personal identity codes and physical addresses to put together a phishing email that looked like it was from the government and was designed to convince the recipient to click on a link and log in to a scam website.

Salla was one of those who received the email and luckily brushed it off as a fake – probably thanks to her new-found interest in cybersecurity. She watched many of Kivimäki's court appearances from the secret cinema space reserved for victims. At first, she says she and others would arrive and sheepishly sit down to witness the hearings but that over time they had started talking and a few dozen of them had become friends, opening up about their experiences. 'I didn't need to explain how I felt, they already knew,' she says. She and the victims she is close to were impressed with the work of the police and prosecutors but Salla said the trial itself was emotionally draining. The worst moment for her came when prosecutors described how Kivimäki had searched through the data to find the most salacious and dramatic therapy notes to grab more attention for his extortion. 'That day was one of the hardest. I couldn't sleep for a few nights afterwards, I felt almost haunted. Those poor people, nobody deserves this, nobody. No matter what kind of things they battled with.'

Another victim – Antti Laulajainen – says the trial emotionally broke him again. 'Kivimäki's attitude was appalling. He had no empathy and no guilt at all,' Antti says. There was further anger when a Finnish blogger claimed that Kivimäki was playing solitaire on his laptop during one hearing. It was never confirmed but even the rumour was enough to cause upset among the victims. You can hear in Antti's otherwise softly spoken voice how raw the anger still is. The most triggering part of the trial for him was when some of the victim impact statements were read out and the court held a minute's silence for the people who had allegedly taken their lives over this. 'It just tipped me over and I couldn't stand up for a long time and just cried.' He relapsed at this point and he has still not recovered. 'I totally closed out after that and have been suffering from PTSD ever since.'

There weren't many victims who came to the court cinema. When the court sent out a survey to check on interest, around 500 people replied to say they would like the opportunity to view proceedings so a large venue was reserved but after the first few weeks it became clear that only a dozen or so were turning up. The busiest day saw around thirty people walk in. No doubt everyone had their own reasons for staying away. One victim – Sami Laiho – told me he avoided it as he knew it would just make him angry. Sami is a high-profile cybersecurity expert who went to Vastaamo twice with his ex-wife. He has never been overly worried about the way in which his private marital issues were made public but he and his wife have spent untold hours trying to protect themselves from further identity theft and fraud. 'It's a ridiculous legal system in Finland and I already felt so bad about the hack that I didn't want to go there and put myself through it to hear him get a sentence that I knew would be so short,' Sami said. As a cybersecurity worker and a Finn, Sami knew all about Kivimäki and felt utterly disillusioned with the fact that he was being tried as a first timer after already being let off with lenient sentences. His view has not changed now that Kivimäki is behind bars. 'He's been cheating the system all this time and he'll do like two years in jail then come out after doing this horrible crime and he's got a huge amount of bitcoin stashed away too. The whole thing is just so unfair.'

During the trial we were given a potential hint at where some of Kivimäki's alleged bitcoin riches might have come from. Working for news outlet *Suomen Kuvalehti* (*SK*), journalist Aarno Malin reported that evidence uncovered in the Vastaamo case may have inadvertently revealed that Kivimäki was heavily involved in another criminal enterprise.[5] Using a legitimate website on the mainstream internet, criminals redirected people looking to buy drugs with bitcoin on the darknet to their own fake darknet sites that looked like real marketplaces but in fact took their money instead. The scam reportedly earned 2 million euros for whoever was behind it. I asked Marko Leponen about the allegation and he said his police force weren't able to open an investigation into it as no one had complained. 'We don't have any victims,' he said with a shrug. You almost have to take your hat off to Kivimäki – or whoever is behind the scheme – it's a perfect crime. Kivimäki denied being involved when asked by *SK*.

But there is one other investigation that police have successfully launched as a spin-off from the money-laundering side of the Vastaamo case. Information unearthed by the investigation in January 2024 seems to have handed cops a major new lead on a separate cryptocurrency-related case involving another suspect in Estonia. They have now opened a new investigation which may lead to new charges against Kivimäki.

As for Kivimäki himself, the now twenty-seven-year-old is appealing his conviction and sentencing but as it stands, he'll be behind bars until summer 2026. I've written to him three times while he's been in jail to see if he wanted to talk to me for this book but he has never replied. He's serving his time in Vantaa Prison just northeast of Helsinki where prisoners can wear their own clothes, take part in carpentry classes and visit the gym for an hour a day. The Untouchable Hacker God is also allowed on the internet.

But he has to apply each time.

And a warden watches over every move of his mouse.

//13
The baton passed

Kivimäki is the most notorious hacker to come out of the 2010–15 NPT gangs. As we have seen he was shaped by this period and helped shape it. These were formative years for him and many other hackers in many senses, and this time was probably the most active period in history for youth cybercrime gangs. The period came to an end when Lizard Squad fizzled out and things went quiet. No one really knows why, but the most likely explanation is that the police had eventually collared the right people to dampen the spirits of this wave of juvenile hackers. Any of the big names like Kivimäki who were still out there went to ground with more secretive (and profitable) ventures. Or perhaps they were aged out or mature enough to realise that shouting about your hacks was no longer a good idea. Teen hacker gangs fell from the headlines. The cyber world was busy dealing with Russian spy hackers trying to disrupt US elections (2016), destructive crypto worms launched by North Korean government hackers (2017) and the rise of organised crime ransomware gangs (from 2018). When people talked about 'teenage hackers in hoodies in their bedrooms' during this period, it felt as though the stereotype had become outdated and wrong.

But that was naive. Yes, there weren't any attention-seeking groups taking on tech giants and plastering their logos online any more. But teenage boys were still active in this arena, they were just staying below the radar. In fact it wasn't until a few months before the Vastaamo crisis that I was reminded these types of gangs were still out there and prepared to risk it all for online clout. And bitcoin.

Just after 10 p.m. on 15 July 2020 a strange tweet popped up from tech billionaire Elon Musk. He said he was feeling generous and would double the bitcoin of anyone who sent some to his wallet. The tweet showed all the telltale signs of a so-called 'giveaway scam' – scammers impersonate a celebrity and promise to give away free bitcoin to whoever sends them some. They are easy to spot but when they are carried out on an account with tens of millions of followers like Musk's, the fraudsters were bound to fool a small number of people. It seemed at first as though this was something that would get shut down very quickly. But then a very similar tweet was posted by Kanye West. Then Kim Kardashian West. Then Uber. Then Apple. Bill Gates. Barack Obama. Joe Biden.

Twitter was in chaos, not knowing what had happened or how to restore control of the accounts to their rightful owners. For about three hours people didn't know who was going to be hacked next. It's estimated that over a hundred million people saw the scam adverts which were posted to 131 accounts. A total of $110,000 was successfully sent to the scammers' wallets by an estimated 320 victims (many more transactions were blocked by fast-thinking crypto exchanges). It was described as the worst ever hack of social media and once the chaos was over, Twitter CEO Jack Dorsey tweeted saying 'we all feel terrible this happened'.

One of Dorsey's staff, who was on the coalface of combatting the hack, was Yoel Roth, Head of Trust and Safety. For him it was nearly twelve hours of bedlam as he and his team tried to contain and deal with the cyber attack. It wasn't until 5 a.m. that he shut his laptop. He sat on the floor of his home office in San Francisco leaning against the wall after a final call with lawyers about how they were going to handle the fallout. The 'Great Twitter Hack' as it became known was unprecedented and in a few hours everyone from the police to

THE BATON PASSED

politicians would be asking how on earth such an influential company could have been so badly exploited. They would also want to know which hacking gang could have humbled the tech giant.

Yoel knew pretty early on who had done it. A group of young men and boys had been plaguing the website – and him – for years. In fact, in 2019, this community of low-skilled but persistent, creative and vindictive hackers had gone so far as to make an industry out of hijacking high-value usernames and selling them through a site and community called OG Users. OG stands for 'original' or 'original gangster'. 'I found these types of accounts and username stealers to be a particularly repellent corner of the internet,' Yoel said. He also felt that having these kids active on Twitter represented a larger threat than just the nuisance of stealing accounts, so he led a fightback by Twitter and a coalition of other sites to ban a large number of these problematic people and their IP addresses. As a result Yoel soon found himself on the receiving end of a harassment campaign. 'They doxxed me and tried to swat me but the cops were able to stop it,' he said.

The gang also called in a bomb hoax to Twitter HQ pretending to be Yoel but completely mispronounced his name. He had to change his number after receiving non-stop abusive phone calls and messages on his personal phone. 'This was as persistent and as aggressive an adversary as I had seen in all of my years dealing with Russian troll farms and Chinese disinformation,' he said.

When this same gang carried out the Great Twitter Hack, Yoel's team was very quickly able to pull together a report about what had happened based on their familiarity with how these boys worked and in some cases who they were. It turns out that they'd managed to trick an employee into handing over access to the powerful internal tool used by staff to manage every customer account. The hackers had used all the social engineering tools in the NPT toolbox to get in but also got lucky with the person they chose to trick. They also planned their attack during the Covid-19 lockdowns when Twitter employees were working from home and less sure of IT procedures. Once they had successfully gained access to the internal control panel, they could take over any account they wanted. At first they targeted the big ticket accounts that would sell well in the OG Users community, then they got greedy and launched the mass bitcoin giveaway scam through the most famous accounts they could find.

Like previous hacking groups, they were not great at covering their tracks and it took just two weeks for the US Department of Justice to charge three people – twenty-two-year-old Nima Fazeli (AKA 'Rolex') of Orlando, Florida, nineteen-year-old Mason John Sheppard (AKA 'Chaewon') of the United Kingdom, and seventeen-year-old Graham Ivan Clark (AKA 'Kirk'), of Tampa, Florida. Clark and Fazeli were jailed and went on to serve short sentences. As part of my work for the BBC, I went to Mason Sheppard's house in the seaside town of Bognor Regis. He didn't want to talk and unbelievably, as of writing in early 2025, his case is still open and unresolved. I think, but have not been able to confirm, that he is still fighting an extradition request to the US. Another hacker – Liverpudlian Joseph James O'Connor (AKA 'PlugwalkJoe') – was also prosecuted for his involvement in the Great Twitter Hack and other cybercrime incidents before and after. He was successfully extradited to the US and is serving five years in prison.

Yoel Roth is conflicted about these boys and men. 'I wouldn't say I have admiration for these kids because, frankly – fuck them. But what they showed was that you can spend millions and millions of dollars on all the advanced security software and doodads under the sun, but humans are always the most vulnerable part of an organisation and they had the persistence to make the most of that.'

The Great Twitter Hack was a moment when teenage hacking activity bubbled back up to the surface. It was a stupid smash-and-grab style of attack that could quite easily have been worse had they had more of a plan. And once again the pattern of criminal behaviour is undeniable and arguably predictable by now. In fact, it's remarkable that after witnessing so many previous crime waves, security professionals and the public at large can still be shocked by the ability – and the desire – of these kids to carry out this kind of attack. But hacking remains as addictive as ever to teenagers, as is shown by the last – and perhaps the wildest – of the case studies explored in this book.

#

What happens when you combine the brash bravado of Lizard Squad with the professionalism of an organised cybercrime outfit? You get Lapsus$.

No company seemed to be safe from Lapsus$. They hit Microsoft, Uber, Revolut, Okta, Samsung, Rockstar Games and BT/EE. They were so successful that in 2023 the US Department of Homeland Security issued a lengthy report that asked 'how organizations could expect their programs to perform against well-resourced cybercrime syndicates and nation-state actors' when these same richly resourced cybersecurity programs could be so easily breached by a 'loosely organized threat actor group, which included several juveniles'.[1]

Lapsus$ began bragging about their hacks in late summer 2021, determined to embarrass the biggest firms they could find and shout about it on their Telegram channel. But they also tried new things and took social engineering to extremes. The gang of British and, allegedly, Brazilian hackers used 'SIM swapping' techniques to take over accounts and get access to company networks. SIM swapping works by exploiting the procedure you use to get your mobile phone number back if you lose your handset and SIM card. Hackers trick a mobile phone network provider into transferring the victim's phone number to a new SIM card that they control. It's a brilliant way to get around the security measures that tie your phone number to your email and password – so-called two-factor authentication – and bears similarities to what we saw CosmoTheGod do to hack into the email account of the Cloudflare CEO.

SIM swapping is not a Lapsus$ invention – it was used extensively by OG Users too. But Lapsus$ threw in another new technique called 'multi-factor fatigue'. It works like this: Lapsus$ would steal a username and password for a big tech company and try to log in. They would then find their path blocked as a multifactor prompt was sent to the employee's phone. If that prompt was a text message, the gang would perform a SIM swap to get the code sent to their own phone instead. But if that person received their prompt codes via an app on their phone, Lapsus$ would just repeatedly try to log in over and over again for hours until that person became fatigued by the multiple requests and clicked accept. And they tended to carry out these attacks late at night to increase the chances of an employee giving in. It worked many times.

Lapsus$ quickly became the new bogeyman of the cyber world – the gang seemed to be young and immature but also creative, relentless and brazen. They were also unusual in that they operated in English and Portuguese and attacked Brazilian, Portuguese and South American targets as well as US multinationals. They were prolific, but also didn't seem to be that bothered about money. They would hold data ransom and ask for payment from the companies but not really press that hard or chase it. 'Lapsus$ seemed to work at various times for notoriety, financial gain, or amusement, and blended a variety of techniques, some more complex than others, with flashes of creativity,' said the Department of Homeland Security report. Which, of course, sounds all too familiar by this point in our story.

Eventually, in March 2022, the City of London Police arrested seven people between the ages of sixteen and twenty-one, who were allegedly involved with the group, and another person was arrested in Brazil later that year. But the arrests were just the start and it turned out the police had no idea what type of hackers they had uncovered.

Detective Inspector Mike O'Sullivan led the Lapsus$ investigation for City of London Police. Launched after Lapsus$ hacked

London-based BT/EE in late 2021, it was the largest investigation since his unit was created in 2014, involving dozens of officers from the UK's National Crime Agency and the FBI. The BT/EE hack was a massive mobile phone SIM swap operation that saw Lapsus$ use their access to the phone company to steal SIM details from hundreds of customers in order to sift through them and steal cryptocurrency from as many victims as possible. Across the country hundreds of crypto accounts were being logged into by people who weren't the owners. Hundreds of text messages containing security codes for those accounts had been pinging on phones that weren't in the account owners' hands. Tracking where all of these redirected security text message prompts had landed, Mike and his team identified twenty-nine different devices all registered to the UK. The names of two boys came up rapidly: Arion Kurtaj, who was sixteen and another boy, who was fifteen (and cannot by law be named because of his age). They were both arrested and had their houses searched and computers and phones seized. Kurtaj was in Oxford and the younger hacker in London.

But around a month after their arrests, Lapsus$ struck again. This time the target was the microchip and software behemoth Nvidia. The gang stole 1 terabyte of data, including a significant amount of sensitive information about the designs of the company's graphics cards and the usernames and passwords of more than 71,000 Nvidia employees. The group threatened to release this data if Nvidia didn't meet a series of demands. Mike and his team saw the hack in the news while they were up to their eyeballs investigating the BT/EE hack.

Alarm bells rang – the methods used in the hack seemed similar in style to those used by the two boys they had released on bail. This hunch was right – Kurtaj and his accomplice had got hold of new computers, got back onto the gang's Telegram channel and picked up where they left off. They were both rearrested. This time Mike called in a specialised forensics search team normally reserved for murder inquiries to comb the boys' homes in case they had any devices hidden away. The team searched every cranny with endoscopes and probes and took away any internet-connected devices they could find. Had the boys been over eighteen at this point they would have been jailed, but as they were underage the police had no choice but to bail them again. 'If we think someone is a danger to society then we try to get them remanded in custody, but this is very difficult with juveniles as the welfare of the child is always important,' Mike says. Further adding to the complex safeguarding situation was the fact that both boys are autistic – Kurtaj acutely so. The police tried to find a hospital bed which they could check him into to keep him under loose surveillance but nowhere was available.

Kurtaj's second arrest became a big story when some rival hackers published a dossier of his personal and private information online. The doxxing claimed that he was known as 'White' and was the leader of Lapsus$. The unknown aggressors also claimed that he was sitting on a stash of bitcoin worth $14 million. I called his father when the story broke and his confusion was palpable: 'I had never heard about any of this until recently. He's never talked about any hacking, but he is very good on computers and spends a lot of time on the computer. I always thought he was playing games.' He probably was, at first.

With Kurtaj's details out there, unwanted food deliveries started arriving at his home. Ominous online videos showed people outside his house filming his street. Police became worried for his safety. They didn't, and still don't, believe that the sixteen-year-old was a crypto multimillionaire, but that didn't stop others from doing so. Kurtaj wouldn't tell them if he had received any threats to his safety but they took precautions. Local police in Oxford carried out a 'target hardening' operation installing stronger doors and locks and a CCTV system in his home. But then his mother received a death threat by email. Mike and his team sprang into action and took Kurtaj and his mother into police protection. Interestingly, Mike now thinks

THE BATON PASSED

that the threat email came from Kurtaj himself as the sender's email address has since been linked back to him. Mike guesses that he had received threats online, but that since he couldn't admit that he was back on the internet he had sent the anonymous threat to his mother to prompt the police to help.

Kurtaj and his mother were put into a Travelodge in Bicester – not far from Oxford. At first they shared one room but the seventeen-year-old complained and was given his own room. Mike and his team were now understandably nervous. They couldn't keep him under surveillance because it would be a breach of the Human Rights Act and they couldn't station officers outside his door as it would have drawn too much attention. So all they could do was wait and hope that he had learned his lesson as his younger accomplice had done.

But Kurtaj hadn't.

In the days after the death of Queen Elizabeth II on 8 September 2022 many of the officers in Mike's team had to be diverted to royal funeral duties. That was when Kurtaj struck again from his hotel room. His next target was the ride-hailing giant Uber. Acting either alone or with help from his Lapsus$ buddies, Kurtaj used a multi-factor fatigue attack to get into an Uber contractor's account. For Mike, there was one detail, released by Uber, that convinced him Kurtaj was at it again. 'I saw the stuff about the hacker posting an image of a penis to the internal staff websites and I thought – yep – that's Arion isn't it?'

However, once again Mike was left with a difficult decision – they would need solid evidence to prove that it was Kurtaj and convince the Crown Prosecution Service to let them take a juvenile into custody and that could take weeks or months. So instead they waited and prepared to swoop in when they could be certain of getting irrefutable evidence. Sure enough, just a few days later, Kurtaj and Lapsus$ carried out their most high-profile attack yet. It was against Rockstar Games, makers of the third biggest computer game ever – *Grand Theft Auto V*.

Kurtaj raided Rockstar's servers to steal ninety unseen and unfinished clips from the company's hugely anticipated follow-up game, *Grand Theft Auto VI*. He also broke into the company's internal Slack messaging system and messaged all staff: 'if Rockstar does not contact me on Telegram within 24 hours I will start releasing the source code'. Rockstar didn't cooperate, and Kurtaj posted the clips and source code to a GTA forum under the username 'TeaPotUberHacker'. The clips spread like wildfire, with YouTubers making videos and poring over them for hints about the forthcoming game. The closely guarded secret that the game would have a female lead character for the first time in the franchise was spoiled by the leak. And some fans unfairly criticised the unfinished visuals in the stolen clips. It might not seem much but in the gaming world there is no bigger story than *GTA VI* and Lapsus$ had thrown a chaos grenade into what was the most secretive of productions. In its written evidence Rockstar told the court that the hack had cost the company $5 million to recover from, plus thousands of hours' worth of staff time.

Detective O'Sullivan had no choice but to attempt the arrest as soon as possible in case Kurtaj struck again. He and four officers waited outside his hotel room door. They were poised for the moment that Kurtaj next came online under the Lapsus$ user profile they guessed was him. As soon as they saw the user was active on the public Telegram channel, they swiped a room card and swooped in. Kurtaj was lying on his bed with an iPhone in his hands. He jumped up, locking the phone and trying to stash it under a pillow. On his TV he was watching a fishing video on YouTube thanks to an Amazon Fire Stick that he had plugged into the back of the set. Bingo – not one but *two* bail violations as he was caught using two internet-connected devices. Mike and his team took him into custody and began a more thorough search. As well as the Fire Stick they discovered a Bluetooth mouse and keyboard. This was how Kurtaj had got himself back online and been able to carry out the Uber and Rockstar hacks. Having a computer was too big and risky for him in case the police dropped in, so he had effectively turned his TV into a giant monitor, linked by Bluetooth to his mouse and keyboard and connected to the internet via the Amazon Fire Stick. He was easily able to gain remote access to his hacking tools and servers through the hotel TV. The police still have no idea how he got hold of the Fire Stick and other accessories.

Kurtaj remained firmly in custody until the end of the Lapsus$ trial. I was in court for some of the big days including the sentencing, live-tweeting much of the proceedings, and I got another insight into the wealth and immaturity of this community when someone sent me a private message offering me £1,000 to take a picture of Kurtaj in the dock. I declined, reminding the person that it was illegal to take photographs inside UK courthouses.

Kurtaj's accomplice, who was seventeen years old by the time of the trial, was sentenced to an eighteen-month Youth Rehabilitation Order, including intense supervision and a ban on using VPNs. He and his mother, who had been sitting next to him for the whole trial, seemed relieved. Doctors deemed Kurtaj unfit to stand trial due to his autism so, unusually, the jury was asked to determine whether or not he had committed the alleged acts – not if he had done so with criminal intent.

Kurtaj and his accomplice are not the only hackers with autism in this story and there are many more with the diagnosis in the history of hacking. Autism, and particularly Asperger's Syndrome, has featured as a defence in many high-profile hacking cases including with Gary McKinnon, Lauri Love, Adam Mudd and Ryan Cleary. London barrister Ben Cooper has represented many autistic hackers and spoken about the pattern he sees in his clients. He has said that generally they're not really thinking consequentially. 'They get carried away, in the middle of the night, on their computers. Most of them are extremely lonely guys who have no friends, maybe kicked out of school, some of them have mental health problems and are very much on their own, and so this is their one opportunity to have a community.'[2]

In spite of the wealth of anecdotal cases, there's not enough evidence to conclude that autistic kids are more likely to be cyber criminals. There does appear to be strong evidence that certain autistic traits like attention to detail and systemic thinking can lead to increased hacking skills. But of course being a skilled hacker doesn't necessarily lead to cybercrime. In fact, some research suggests that having autism is likely to make an individual more rules-based and law abiding than the rest of the population. The societal stereotype is so strong though that academics have researched the topic numerous times in the last ten years and so far, all seem to have reached the same conclusion – yes it's possible that there's a link between autism and cybercrime but more research or data is needed.

The issue of autism certainly added to the complexity of the jury's task in the Arion Kurtaj court case. Not only were they asked to set aside questions of criminal intent, they also had to arrive at a verdict without knowing quite what it might mean for this young man with complex needs. It had already been a long complicated trial, conducted at the height of the London summer, and I often felt sorry for the jurors – normal people repeatedly being taken through hours and hours of hideously detailed cyber forensics. At one point I looked over and saw that two of them had fallen asleep. The judge promptly and smoothly called a recess to allow everyone to get a coffee. At the end of the trial though, the jury agreed with the prosecutors. The court heard that Kurtaj had shown no signs of remorse or any urge to stop committing cybercrime. Prison staff also said he had been violent while in custody with dozens of reports of injury and property damage. The judge sentenced him to an indefinite hospital order – he will remain at a secure hospital for life unless doctors deem him no longer a danger to the public. Even then, the decision would need sign-off from a series of other authorities before he could be released.

It's not known how much money the two hackers actually made from their attacks – both refused to share the keys for their seized bitcoin wallets with police. But one figure we do know is $10 million – that's the estimated damage the hacks did to companies and individuals. Detective Inspector Mike O'Sullivan says that figure could have been reduced if the police had been able to deal with the boys differently. 'Our youth justice system is set up to deal with dangerous kids who are committing sexual and violent offences, not those committing cybercrime and fraud. But, if you look at the harms of some of these attacks they are pretty significant. People are losing life savings and it's enough to put people over the edge.'

The detective's frustration is echoed by the report released by the US Department of Homeland Security in 2023. In several jurisdictions, a perpetrator's juvenile status 'can yield lighter penalties and less severe consequences that may encourage young cyber criminals to re-offend,' it reads. In the report it is estimated that Lapsus$ most likely had a core of eight to ten members. With the two Britons dealt with and a Brazilian man in custody that still leaves many at large.

Lapsus$ itself quickly disbanded, but there are rumours that at least one if not more of the Lapsus$ lads smoothly transitioned onto the next and still active community of cyber criminals.

'The Com', as it calls itself, is short for The Community. It's a sprawling hacker subculture organised across a large network of hundreds of private Discord servers, Telegram channels and self-hosted forums. It's full of all manner of cyber criminals and cybercrime. Allison Nixon, who spends a lot of time tracking The Com says there are constantly groups and individuals competing for dominance, money and clout. It's not just hacking either. One hacker who knows the scene well told me: 'The Com is just youth gang culture online.'

Worryingly, physical attacks have become a key weapon in the armouries of these gangs in the last two years. 'Offline violence is growing, particularly with criminal versus criminal,' Allison says. 'Doxxing and swatting is no longer enough. They're less successful as police are wiser and it's not intimidating enough. So these hackers are paying people to throw bricks into their enemies' houses on the other side of the world.' Each attack is celebrated with a video or picture posted away from the eyes of mainstream internet users and police. In one video, a man fires shots into a house in Pennsylvania while shouting 'Justin Active was here'. Justin Active is, as Brian Krebs reported on his website,[3] the nickname of a prominent player in cyber criminal communities, who has vehemently denied knowledge of, or participation in, the shooting. In another video the same attacker botches an arson attack, throwing a homemade Molotov cocktail at a smashed window but missing it. No one was hurt in either incident and the attacker was found and jailed.

For Allison, the escalation from swatting to bricks, petrol bombs and bullets has been horrible to watch. But she says it was also inevitable when you're dealing with kids who are high on the power and money that hacking can bring. 'You're already paying someone to carry out an attack, so why not pay them more to do worse things? It's a logical next step.' The iconic novel *Lord of the Flies* springs to mind. Give unsupervised boys enough freedom and often things can get heated. Throw in bitcoin and the potential for online fame and they can get out of hand. It's also significant that this is all happening in private channels online – no longer on the public sites like Twitter. Discord, Telegram and private forums with membership vetting are hard to access for journalists, researchers and police. And completely alien for parents to understand.

At first, these instances of offline violence were only played out as a kind of civil war within The Com – much like the hacker rivalries of the past. But things began to change in 2023 when we started getting reports of physical threats to everyday cybercrime victims. One of the splinter groups that emerged from The Com is known as 'Scattered Spider' or 'Octo Tempest'. This is the group that one or more of the at-large Lapsus$ boys apparently moved onto. Researchers at Microsoft say Scattered Spider used threats of real-world violence to try to get login details from employees of their victim organisations: 'In rare instances, the group resorts to fear-mongering tactics, targeting specific individuals through phone calls and texts. These actors use personal information, such as home addresses and family names, along with physical threats to coerce victims into sharing credentials for corporate access.'[4]

The Microsoft report included screenshots of a flurry of text messages sent to one employee that said: 'if we don't get your login in the next 20 minutes were [sic] sending a shooter to your house.' Another message minutes later said: 'ur wife is gonna get shot if you don't.' Microsoft says these types of threats are rare but obviously the fear is that they may increase until someone gets hurt.

Scattered Spider are best known for an audacious hack of casinos in Las Vegas which brought down slot machines, check-in computers and even hotel room keycard systems. The victim was hotel and casino giant MGM Resorts. Videos showed gambling terminals out of order and mammoth queues of people trying to check in, check out or cash out as staff struggled to work without computers. In a filing to the US Securities and Exchange Commission MGM said the attack cost the company more than $100 million in direct and indirect costs.

In another strange new development the Scattered Spider crew were observed to start coordinating and working with one of the most notorious Russian-speaking ransomware gangs called 'BlackCat' or 'ALPHV'. Researchers say this is something of a first as professional cyber criminal groups have not previously mixed with amateur youth gangs. Plus the language and cultural barriers were enough of a block. But not any more, it seems, as they can both offer each other increased capabilities and therefore profits. Scattered Spider uses social engineering and language skills to hack into places. BlackCat provides experience, malware and a platform for extortion.

The Scattered Spider hackers were quickly identified by researchers as being young culprits, likely from the UK or the US, and there was a huge amount of frustration in the cybersecurity world that no arrests were being made. But in a flurry of charges in November and December 2024 the US announced that six males aged between nineteen and twenty-five have been accused of various Scattered Spider-linked crimes. One of them is a twenty-two-year-old from Scotland who is alleged to have been hacking for years before his arrest. A seventeen-year-old from Walsall in England was also arrested earlier in the summer.

But apparently that wasn't the end of the story for the Walsall boy. A month after being cuffed for his alleged involvement in Scattered Spider, it appears he was rearrested. (Well, police wouldn't confirm at the time of writing that it was the *same* boy, but he was the same age and came from the same town, and Walsall is not known as a hotbed for hacking.) This time it was for allegedly carrying out one of the biggest hacks of the year in Britain – presumably while still on bail for the earlier charges. The victim this time was Transport for London (TfL), the company responsible for trains, tubes and buses in the capital city. The vehicles kept moving, but for weeks customer services such as live train times were offline and it was impossible to apply for some annual passes.[5] TfL's 25,000 members of staff were also unable to log in to their work computers until they each carried out an in-person security check. Staff were given time slots to turn up to offices and show their passes before being allowed to reset their passwords. Long queues could be seen outside the offices for days in a rare visual sign of the impact of cyber attacks.

As far as we know at the time of writing, the TfL hack did not involve any physical threats, but other sections of The Com subculture are now infamous for carrying out despicable sexual and physical violence. Members of the group called '764' have used hacking and threats of violence to make girls send them naked pictures, bragging in their channels about what they've managed to get girls to do. Some victims have been very young. The group share this content despite knowing that it amounts to child sexual abuse. In fact they seem to revel in this added element of danger. Police have described this particular corner of The Com as 'a network of violent extremists who seek to normalise the production, sharing and possession of child pornography and gore material to desensitise and corrupt youth toward future acts of violence.'[6] Arrests have been made in the US, UK and Romania but notably hacking and cybercrime has not featured in the cases. 764 is far removed from hacking culture and only interested in causing harm. This type of abuse could never be carried out in the glare of the giant social networks – but it can flourish if not challenged in these hidden communities dominated by lonely pubescent boys with no strong moral role models.

Victims of the larger Com collective have told reporters that they've been forced to harm themselves on camera, injure their pets or carve cutsigns into their own bodies.[7] Violent kidnappings and home invasions targeting large holders of cryptocurrency are also being linked to this group which police have described as an 'online violent terror network'.[8] This is how *Wired* characterised these young hackers in its year-end summary article 'The Most Dangerous People on the Internet in 2024':

> Even in an age of state-sponsored Chinese cyberspies, Russian hacker saboteurs, and ransomware gangs, nihilistic young hackers remain a constant in the darker corners of the internet. And few of those corners are as dark as the ones frequented by the Com. The loose movement of online trolls and criminals who operate under the Com banner in channels on Telegram and Discord, many just in their teens, engage in some of the most despicable digital crimes possible.[9]

Physical violence represents a horrible escalation of the activity we've seen in this book. But I think it's important here to remind ourselves that this is still a rare aspect to teenager cyber delinquency. Teenage hackers are (as the sub-title of this book states) hijacking the lives of normal people not with bricks and bullets but with a keyboard and mouse. It's easy to be distracted by the threat of physical violence, but we would be doing a disservice to the victims we have heard from if we didn't acknowledge the real-world suffering already being done by the cyber criminals and cybercrimes. Scattered Spider, The Com, 764 – whatever the group and whatever the means, this is an evolution of the same pattern of behaviour. The main difference now is that these groups can no longer be called NPTs – Noob Persistent Threats. This has been going on for years and everyone – from police and cyber defenders to parents and school teachers – should know that this new hacker culture has become pervasive, corrupting and dangerous.

The rise and fall of LulzSec, HTP, UG Nazi, ISIS Gang, Lizard Squad and Lapsus$ has left its mark on internet culture and these boys have not stopped passing the baton, each time slightly changing their tactics. They no longer shout about their crimes across public social networks. But the one-upmanship is seemingly worse than ever and with physical attacks and children being targeted even the low moral bar that once existed appears to have dissolved into the ether. The Hacker Manifesto is all but forgotten. In fact only one of the hackers interviewed for this book mentioned it to me, during a long discussion about the ethics of hacking. A Lizard Squad hacker pasted some lines of The Mentor's poem to me speaking fondly of the essay as inspiration. But even he admits that those ideals have been completely lost now in the case of most of the hackers he has met. 'I don't think the modern iteration of the hacking scene is anything like the older cats,' he said.

There will be people frustrated by reading this bleak thesis. There are no doubt kids out there learning how to hack who will live fulfilling lives and careers making the online world a better place. I've met some of them myself and it's brilliant to see. Experimenting kids playing and exploring computing will go on to be the future Steve Jobs or Bill Gates. I'm not disregarding that. Without boys and girls pushing the boundaries, we will fail to develop The Next Big Things that have helped the human race launch wondrous technologies.

THE BATON PASSED

But as we have seen, youth hacker culture has tipped far into the negative and it's not good for anyone. On the hacker matrix we heard about, the groups seen since LulzSec can only be characterised as Chaos–Evil.

#

I have a little rule when I do a news interview: always finish with a nice question at the end.

It helps to end on a positive note and makes the interviewee feel everything has gone well even if the preceding exchange has been serious or abrasive. I never expect to get anything useable or interesting from the last question. It's just an aesthetics thing. When interviewing Detective Mike O'Sullivan about his work on Lapsus$, my final question was about how gratified he felt after taking down this harmful cyber gang which had been wreaking such havoc around the world. I expected him to say he felt very proud of his work. But his answer surprised me and encapsulates the problem that we face as a society with teenage hackers. 'There's nothing to be proud about when you're locking up kids,' he said. 'Arion Kurtaj doesn't have a future now and it's hard to feel proud of this. I'm there to protect the public but sometimes that means doing something that just feels horrible.' It's a hard truth about handling teenage cybercrime.

So what can be done to prevent boys from stumbling onto this path?

It's something I've asked everyone I've spoken to in my research for this book. Part of the answer seems to lie with policing. Allison Nixon says police have become more effective at arresting the most important players, but need to be even more aggressive and fast to make a dent in these groups. 'Only the government can take the action necessary to stop this, by arresting the perpetrators who are the core drivers and recruiters in this activity.' She points to Kivimäki as a great example of this type of young influential cyber criminal. She said more needs to be done to join the dots between attacks and groups to find out who are the loudest and most powerful kids. They should be approached in the same way that cartels are, she argues.

That approach is much harder in cybercrime, where everyone is spread around the world and hiding behind aliases. But it doesn't help that information sharing between police forces seems to be far from complete. This was most pronounced for me during my research into Kivimäki's complex and storied history with Finnish police. It took me months to find out about his multiple arrests, detainments and charges as each individual police department seemed unsure of the history. It surprised me that these officers didn't seem to have detailed knowledge of the investigations carried out by their colleagues in other divisions. It could be that they had simply forgotten the intricacies and had moved on to other cases. But evidently Kivimäki was passed from section to section over the years he was being investigated. Even now, the latest fresh investigation into him isn't being carried out by Marko Leponen or any of the teams who have previously dealt with him – it's a new team and a new investigation. This seems like a system that only helps the cyber criminals.

Another possible solution to curb teenage cybercrime is to hand out harsher sentences and find a stronger way to handle juveniles post arrest. It's a difficult balance of course as we don't want to lose talented young hackers to an overly draconian justice system when they could otherwise be put to good use later as desperately needed cyber defenders. We also don't want to get too heavy handed and inadvertently destroy the futures of kids who just began venturing down the wrong path or got chatting to the wrong people online. There is no doubt a huge disparity between how young men and boys are being dealt with around the world. This might be leading to confusion about how serious cybercrime is. Kids are getting mixed messages about what happens when they break the law online.

Which brings us on to a suggestion that was made to me time and time again. It's so often brushed off as an easy and clichéd suggestion but really it does have merit: education. Detective Chief Inspector Marko Leponen said it best: 'We need to teach children how the internet works and where the lines are. Every young person knows that if you kick a person it's a crime but the harm is not seen in cyber so these teenagers don't understand the consequences and the evil of their actions.' There will always be bad apples – the criminals that *know* what they are doing is wrong and just want to hurt people. But without a doubt, a decent chunk of teenage cybercrime is carried out by curious kids who don't know the hassle, harm and hurt they are causing.

There are some programmes and campaigns that seem to have moved the dial a bit in recent years. The professionalisation of bug bounties has been a big win as young people can sign up to, and earn real money from, ethical hacking. Find a bug in a website or system, responsibly disclose it through companies like Hacker One and Bugcrowd, earn money. The millionaire bug bounty hunter I mentioned earlier in the book – Santiago Lopez – told me that having the option to earn good money in this way definitely helped him resist the temptation to earn money through illegal hacking. Perhaps we need to showcase more role models like him and others who are young, successful and rich.

There are also regular campaigns run in the UK by cyber authorities to get kids – increasingly girls – interested in cybersecurity from a young age. Hacking competitions and games are being held regularly to sift talent and show children the potentials of a life on the right side of cyber. Another on–off campaign by the National Crime Agency and others is to take out paid adverts on Google and YouTube to warn kids that certain things like DDoS tools are illegal if used maliciously. When someone searches for 'stressers', for example, they are met with a warning.

Police in many countries including the Netherlands, a nation that punches above its weight in cybersecurity (and cybercrime), also run rehabilitation workshops for low-level criminals to learn the law and how they can use their skills for good. The Hack_Right programme is time consuming and expensive for the authorities. Only about ten kids a year can undertake the highly tailored course. But organisers say that none of the young people they've helped have gone on to reoffend.

The fourth and final potential solution is to put more of the emphasis on parents. Some of the victims would definitely place a hefty portion of blame on the parents of hackers. John Smedley, for example, tweeted shortly after Kivimäki had been given his first suspended sentence, saying that 'his parents need to be held accountable for his actions'. As a parent of three young boys myself I do worry about how I'm going to police their activity online as they get older. I hope to be more clued in than most thanks to my job and interests, but I am also under no illusion that it's going to be anything but a huge challenge to stay on top of their lives online.

Things are improving as monitoring and safeguarding are being made easier. Apple and Google in particular see the value (both financially and ethically) in developing more and more tools for parents to access information about what their kids are doing on tablets, phones and laptops. Governments in the West are increasingly pushing for more safeguards to protect children online from harmful sites and content including potential bans on children under sixteen going on social media. After more than two decades of growth without consequence, social media platforms are feeling the pressure and are increasing safety measures and moderation to protect kids. It's still a wild west out there but things are far better than they used to be for parents trying to keep kids on the straight and narrow.

Blaming parents of teenage cyber criminals is a natural response. But it's also a somewhat blinkered and maybe even classist approach. This was a view that I'd not considered until a BBC interview I did with a New York lawyer, Carrie Goldberg, who specialises in lawsuits against online platforms that harm children. She argues that pointing the finger at parents for not monitoring everything their kids do online is the privilege of educated and middle-income or high-earning families. It doesn't take into account the lives of single mums or dads who work more than one job on tough shift work. Blaming these parents for not policing their kids online seems unfair and ultimately reductive.

Also, let's face it – no matter how hard we try, technology is generational. We all eventually get left behind.

Which brings me to my final thought as I look ahead to the future. In 2021 Mark Zuckerberg changed his company's name from Facebook to Meta and the world went mad over the idea of 'the metaverse'. Analysts, venture capitalists and tech bros predicted we would all soon be living in some form of metaverse – living, working and playing in a fully immersive online environment. The idea has faded from the headlines lately, replaced by excitement (and fear) about artificial intelligence. But Zuckerberg and others are still building their vision and in some areas the idea is gaining steam. Just look at the staying power of metaverse-style games like *Roblox* and *Fortnite*. Each has hundreds of millions of players a month and users are no longer just playing. They're hanging out and going to concerts and earning in-game currency and trading items with each other. The players are mostly children who are all interacting largely unsupervised. The first time I put on a virtual reality (VR) headset it was noticeable that the vast majority of players seemed to be young boys. This has got even more pronounced lately since Meta reduced the minimum age of users to just ten years old in the US and Canada. That's right – reduced. While other online platforms are being urged to increase minimum age, Meta is now encouraging ten-year-olds to get stuck in. Put on a VR headset now and you are met with a wall of screaming kids, jumping about and dominating every nook of this new frontier in tech. While most of us are nonplussed about VR and 'the metaverse', kids are embracing it. In 2022 there were more Meta Quest headsets sold than Xboxes[10] and no doubt Apple's own nascent headset will make VR more popular too.

Young people have always, and will always, colonise new online spaces first with little scrutiny or supervision from grown-ups. More than ever kids are being left to their own devices. Literally. Who knows what cybercrime will look like in the metaverse or whatever new perplexing platform is dreamt up next. Without any action we're already enabling the cyber criminals of the future as we struggle to understand or keep up.

THE END

Acknowledgements

I would like to take this space to thank some people who made this – my first book – a reality. My agent Caroline Hardman for believing in the idea. Publishing and storytelling gurus Katie Bond and Celia Hayley for taking it on and helping me craft and shape it. I'd also like to thank all the contributors who took time to tell me in such detail and with such honesty about the events in these pages – especially those who would rather forget about the trauma they endured. And I'd like to thank my closest advisor – my wife Sophie – for her unwavering support, guidance and expert criticism. Oh, and my mum because she will get mad if I don't thank her! Plus, in a bizarre twist she ended up in court in Finland with me to witness Kivimäki's trial and she came up with some of the best descriptive lines for the scene.

Thanks lastly to you for reading the book.

Endnotes

Preface
1. https://www.statista.com/outlook/tmo/cybersecurity/worldwide

Chapter 1: An accidental arrest
1. https://actu.fr/ile-de-france/courbevoie_92026/courbevoie-appelee-pour-violences-conjugales-la-police-arrete-un-criminel-international_57121782.html

Chapter 2: Ransom_man strikes
1. https://x.com/veikkoeranti/status/1330781861874966528
2. https://yle.fi/a/3-11896654
3. https://assets.sophos.com/X24WTUEQ/at/c949g7693gsnjh9rb9gr8/sophos-state-of-ransomware-2023-wp.pdf

Chapter 3: I got the email
1. https://www.economist.com/europe/2024/04/04/the-secret-behind-the-worlds-happiest-country
2. https://www.wired.com/story/ransomware-hospital-death-germany/
3. https://healthitsecurity.com/news/hackers-demand-ransom-from-patients-after-breaching-florida-clinic#:~:text=January%2010%2C%20 2020%20%2D%20Current%20and,who%20hacked%20the%20clinic's%20 server
4. https://x.com/kirsipiha/status/1320091258505887745
5. https://x.com/anttivesala/status/1320077773340352516
6. https://www.is.fi/digitoday/tietoturva/art-2000006704088.html

Chapter 4: The rise of Zeekill
1. https://aleksanteriKivimäki.com/
2. https://www.longplay.fi/pitkat/hakkerin-etiikka

3. https://steamcommunity.com/id/zeekill

Chapter 5: Hacking for retweets
1. https://www.youtube.com/watch?v=0tEnnvZbYek&t=212s
2. The Hacker Manifesto, © Loyd Blankenship, was first published in *Phrack Magazine* on 18 March 1986; https://phrack.org/issues/7/3
3. https://www.youtube.com/watch?v=0tEnnvZbYek&t=208s
4. https://phrack.org/issues/31/5.html
5. Joseph Menn, *Cult of the Dead Cow: How the Original Hacking Supergroup Might Just Save the World* (New York: PublicAffairs, 2019)
6. Geoff White, *Crime Dot Com: From Viruses to Vote Rigging, How Hacking Went Global* (London: Reaktion Books, 2020)
7. https://www.theguardian.com/technology/2011/jun/24/inside-lulzsec-chatroom-logs-hackers
8. https://web.archive.org/web/20110719150237/http://freze.it/5S
9. https://thenextweb.com/news/50-days-of-lulz-the-life-and-times-of-lulzsec
10. https://www.reddit.com/r/AMA/comments/2rdwgm/i_am_avunit_ask_me_anything/
11. https://www.youtube.com/watch?v=HXXoO0FwUKQ
12. https://www.youtube.com/watch?v=swISFM2eXds
13. https://www.theguardian.com/media/2011/jul/18/sun-website-hacked-lulzsec
14. https://www.bbc.co.uk/news/technology-22526021

Chapter 6: Hacking for power – and bitcoins
1. https://www.youtube.com/watch?v=Rn2cf_wJ4f4
2. https://www.forbes.com/sites/parmyolson/2010/12/24/ddos-attacks-on-visa-mastercard-were-symbolic-more-to-come/
3. https://www.nationalcrimeagency.gov.uk/who-we-are/publications/623-cyber-crime-report-crest-nca/file
4. https://pastebin.com/aiqfELhE
5. https://wiki.hackforums.net/RyanC
6. https://archives.fbi.gov/archives/news/stories/2008/february/swatting020408

7. https://www.splinter.com/haunted-by-hackers-a-suburban-familys-digital-ghost-st-1793852060

Chapter 7: Zeekill arrested
1. https://www.linode.com/blog/linode/security-incident-update/
2. https://web.archive.org/web/20240725193940/https://www.gironsec.com/blog/2013/03/reversing-a-botnet/

Chapter 8: Addicted to hacking
1. https://www.youtube.com/watch?v=AcZzqaSlJns
2. https://krebsonsecurity.com/2013/03/the-world-has-no-room-for-cowards/
3. https://www.dictionary.com/e/slang/edgelord/
4. https://blog.cloudflare.com/post-mortem-todays-attack-apparent-google-app/
5. https://www.forbes.com/sites/andygreenberg/2012/05/22/hackers-impersonate-web-billing-firms-staff-to-spill-500000-users-passwords-and-credit-cards/
6. https://www.wired.com/2012/09/cosmo-the-god-who-fell-to-earth/
7. https://garwarner.blogspot.com/2016/07/hacking-carding-swatting-and-ocd-case.html
8. https://krebsonsecurity.com/2016/07/serial-swatter-stalker-and-doxer-mir-islam-gets-just-1-year-in-jail/
9. https://www.buzzfeednews.com/article/josephbernstein/tomi-masters-down-the-rabbit-hole-i-go

Chapter 9: Hacking to harm
1. https://www.ibtimes.co.uk/fbi-hunting-uk-isisgang-hackers-over-us-terror-threats-1465403
2. https://www.thetimes.com/article/hackers-threaten-school-massacres-hdrgsnnvpwk
3. https://www.bbc.co.uk/news/technology-47771925
4. https://www.justice.gov/usao-ks/pr/ohio-gamer-sentenced-deadly-swatting-case
5. https://apnews.com/article/crime-police-shootings-kidnapping-wichita-1dc334273f81d08053dd4caa227023b7

CTRL+ALT+CHAOS

6. https://www.justice.gov/usao-md/pr/catonsville-man-pleads-guilty-conspiracy-swatting-incident
7. https://news.sky.com/story/first-ever-uk-swatting-sentence-passed-after-man-shot-in-face-by-armed-unit-due-to-hoax-call-13118559
8. https://www.thecourier.co.uk/fp/news/angus-mearns/171671/im-going-to-prison-gamer-who-called-down-havoc-on-angus-friends-house/
9. https://www.scotland.police.uk/what-s-happening/news/2024/may/man-jailed-following-fraud-hearing-at-airdrie-sheriff-court/
10. https://www.dailyrecord.co.uk/news/scottish-news/crypto-currency-fraud-victim-vows-27208789
11. https://arstechnica.com/information-technology/2015/01/a-hacked-ddos-on-demand-site-offers-a-look-into-mind-of-booter-users/
12. https://x.com/j_smedley/status/503513012527845376
13. https://www.bloomberg.com/news/features/2024-04-22/a-massive-therapy-hack-shows-just-how-unsafe-patients-files-can-be?embedded-checkout=true
14. https://www.tricitynews.com/local-news/coquitlam-teen-admits-to-swatting-3011654
15. https://regmedia.co.uk/2021/04/12/techreport-jamescrawford.pdf
16. https://vc.bridgew.edu/cgi/viewcontent.cgi?article=1012&context=ijcic
17. https://www.nytimes.com/2015/11/29/magazine/the-serial-swatter.html
18. https://pastebin.com/BMSpLPJY

Chapter 10: Christmas is cancelled

1. https://www.youtube.com/watch?v=PGTbttD91pI&t=149s
2. https://securityaffairs.com/31565/cyber-crime/lizard-squad-interview.html
3. https://apps.dtic.mil/sti/tr/pdf/AD1009289.pdf
4. https://www.dailydot.com/unclick/lizard-squad-vinnie-omari-arrested/
5. https://www.dailymail.co.uk/news/article-2913619/British-teenager-18-arrested-connection-Christmas-cyber-attacks-Playstation-Xbox-networks-joint-FBI-British-investigation.html
6. https://www.dailydot.com/unclick/darkode-fbi-informant-kms-

7. Ibid.
8. https://www.justice.gov/usao-wdla/pr/opelousas-man-charged-participating-major-computer-hacking-forum
9. https://x.com/j_smedley/status/618923473549725696

Chapter 11: Vastaamo implodes

1. https://assured.co.uk/2023/closed-for-business-the-organisations-who-suffered-fatal-cyber-attacks-that-shut-their-doors-for-good/
2. https://www.hs.fi/suomi/art-2000009378000.html

Chapter 12: Untouchable Hacker God caged

1. https://www.hs.fi/suomi/art-2000010237782.html
2. https://www.iltalehti.fi/kotimaa/a/6713542a-7c01-4c54-9cd0-6d288b99e1ef
3. https://www.psychologytoday.com/gb/basics/sociopathy
4. https://www.suomi.fi/news/watch-out-for-scam-messages-pretending-to-be-from-suomi-fi-do-not-click-on-the-links-in-the-message
5. https://suomenkuvalehti.fi/paajutut/uudet-tiedot-yhdistavat-vastaamo-syytetyn-huijauksiin-tor-verkossa-onko-aleksanteri-Kivimäki-dnstats/?shared=1288285-55987891-500

Chapter 13: The baton passed

1. https://www.cisa.gov/sites/default/files/2023-08/CSRB_Lapsus%24_508c.pdf
2. https://www.newstatesman.com/spotlight/2017/10/will-prison-deter-autistic-teenager-hacking
3. https://krebsonsecurity.com/2022/09/violence-as-a-service-brickings-firebombings-shootings-for-hire/
4. https://www.microsoft.com/en-us/security/blog/2023/10/25/octo-tempest-crosses-boundaries-to-facilitate-extortion-encryption-and-destruction/
5. https://www.theguardian.com/uk-news/2024/sep/23/fallout-from-tfl-cyber-attack-is-slow-burning-and-potentially-costly?CMP=Share_iOSApp_Other
6. https://www.justice.gov/opa/pr/member-violent-764-terror-network-sentenced-30-years-prison-sexually-exploiting-child

7. https://www.wired.com/story/764-com-child-predator-network/
8. https://www.justice.gov/opa/pr/arizona-man-associated-online-terror-network-arrested-production-child-sex-abuse-material
9. https://www.wired.com/story/the-most-dangerous-people-on-the-internet-in-2024/
10. https://www.thevirtualreport.biz/data-and-research/65297/quest-2-vr-headset-outsells-xbox-series-xs-consoles/

Index

A

Advanced Persistent Threats (APTs) 109–10, 112
Aijaz, Mustafa 154–56
'aivpot' (hacker) 96
Al-Bassam, Mustafa ('tflow') 33, 65, 127
Amazon 64, 119
Amazon Fire Stick 210, 211
American Airlines flight bomb threat (2014) 144–5, 146
Amet, Asan (Kivimäki) 2
Anderson, Dan and Paige 153–4
AnonOps (DDoS attackers) 75–6, 77, 80
Anonymous ('hacktivists') 60–1, 62, 115
anti-gay campaigns 124
AntiSec (hacking group) 81
Apple 202, 222
Argentina 127
Ars Technica 114
ASCII (American Standard Code for Information Interchange) 78
Asperger's Syndrome 77, 211
Associated Press 14
AT&T 58, 119, 121
autism 77, 90, 98, 211–12
'Avunit' (elusive hacker) 65

B

bank accounts 34, 37, 147, 191, 192
Barr, Robert ('Veri'/'Verified') 90, 139–40, 163
Barriss, Tyler 137–8
BBC News xi, 14, 181–2, 222–3
BBC Radio 5 Live 155–7
Bebo 60
Bellagio Hotel, Las Vegas 93, 95, 98, 102
Biden, Joe 202
bipolar disorder 128
Bitbo calculator 43–4
bitcoin 21–2
    as ransom payment 7, 12, 15, 83, 95, 142
    rise of 84, 167
    stash 5, 187, 208
    wallet 22, 28–9, 43–4, 45, 117, 140
Bittiraha (cryptocurrency exchange) 45
black-hat hackers 40, 50, 85, 127
Black Swan events 110
BlackCat/ALPHV group 215
Blankenship, Loyd ('The Mentor') 55–7, 218
Blizzard 143
blockchain 43, 66, 192
Bloomberg 181
bomb hoaxers 86, 117, 125, 134, 138, 140–2, 144–6, 150, 203
booters/stressers 112–13
Boston Convention and Exhibition Center 134

bot herder 104
botnet (robot network) 104–6, 167
Brazil 205, 206, 213
breaches, data 31–2, 62, 81, 105, 118, 176, 179
Brennan, John 125
Brogan, Kevin and Judith 141–2, 196
Brogan, Ryan 92, 93, 94, 97, 102, 142–3, 195
BT/EE 205, 207
Buchta, Zachary 164
bug hunting 127
Bugcrowd 221
Burrows, Nathan 92, 97, 102
Buzzfeed 129

C

Call of Duty 116, 137, 154
Canada 111, 149, 223
casino hacks, Las Vegas 215
Catsquad (hacking group) 133
Central Intelligence Agency (CIA) 63, 115, 125
'Chaewon' (Mason John Sheppard) 204
Chaos Computer Club (ethical hacking group) 57–8, 59
chats, online group 68–71, 76
ChF (linked to Lizard Squad) 148–9, 158
Chicago Tribune 164
China 112, 203
Christmas DDoS attacks (2014) ix, 153–9, 163
City of London Police 206–7
Clark, Graham Ivan ('Kirk') 204
Cleary, Ryan 66, 103, 158, 163, 211
cloud service providers 103, 112, 119
Cloudflare 119–21, 205
CNN 14

Code Spaces 172
ColdFusion, Adobe 104
Computerworld 83
The Com (The Community) 213–14, 216–17, 218
Cooper, Ben 211
cosmetic surgery clinic hack, US (2020) 32
'CosmoTheGod' (Eric Taylor) 116–18, 121–3, 124, 125–8, 205
Covid-19 pandemic 27, 32, 36, 203–4
Cox Communications 162
credit card fraud 102–4, 105, 164
Cruise, Tom 125
cryptocurrency 44, 45, 58, 140, 165, 167, 207, 217
cryptojacking 81–2
Cult of the Dead Cow (US hacking group) 58, 59
cutsign 131, 217
Cyber Intelligence Sharing and Protection Act (2011 proposed bill) 115–16
cybersecurity experts 15, 38, 50, 109–12, 120, 127, 159, 171, 221
cyberstalking 128, 149–50
'Cyberzeist' (hacker) 118
'Cyphereus Prime' (Jack Levin) 82–3, 97

D

Daily Dot 161, 163
Darik's Boot and Nuke (DBAN) 141
darknet websites 11–13, 39, 199
Darkode 163
DarkReading 83
DarkTower Threat Intelligence 128
data-leak sharing forums 47
Davis, Jake ('Topiary') 67–8
'Deathbolt' (hacker) 103
'Declaws' (Jamie Sales) 139

INDEX

DEF CON (hacking conference) 91–2, 95, 97
Dexter (TV series) 125
Discord 69, 213, 217
Distributed Denial of Service (DDoS)
  AnonOps attack 75–6, 77, 80
  attacks 63–4, 105, 114, 126, 143–4, 149, 172
  Christmas attacks (2014) ix, 153–9, 161, 163
  Code Spaces 172
  development of 160
  LizardStresser (DDoS service) 163, 164
  tools 84, 95, 96, 112, 221
  UG Nazi attack 115
'Dorkslavz' (hacker) 96
Dorsey, Jack 60, 202
Dotcom, Kim 156, 158
doxxing 75, 80, 125, 203, 208
DramaAlert (YouTube) 158
Düsseldorf Cyber Incident (2020) 32

E

'edge lord' culture 9, 114–15
Elizabeth II, Queen 209
encrypted files 24, 65–6
end-to-end encryption 65–6
Eranti, Prof Veikko 9
Estonia 199
eTeknix 143
Europol 160
Eve Online 111
Exposed.su website 124–5, 128

F

F-16 fighter jets 144
F-Secure 49, 50, 51
Facebook (now Meta) 40, 60, 163
Fancy Bear (Russian hacking unit) 110

Fansign 131
Fazeli, Nima ('Rolex') 204
Federal Bureau of Investigation (FBI) 87, 93–8, 102, 122, 125–6, 141, 162, 207
Financial Times 14
Finch, Andrew 138
Finland 2–6, 27, 112, 181–2
forensics, cyber 22, 67, 100–1, 161, 189, 192, 207–8, 212
Fortnite 223
4chan 9, 119, 120
Fox (US) 62
France 1–2
Fusion 90

G

Gamer Gate (harassment against women) 151–2
Gaskill, Shane 137–8
Gates, Bill 125, 202
General Data Protection Regulations, EU 179–80
Germany 32, 57–8
Giron, Joe 106
Glastonbury 63
Gmail 119
Goldberg, Carrie 223
Google 82, 119–20, 121, 221, 222
Google Chrome 184
government, Finnish 35–6, 41
Grand, Joe 58
Grand Theft Auto (GTA) 209–10
Great Hacker War, The 79
Great Twitter Hack 202–4
'@GreatestGamerEver' (Xbox account) 118
grooming, online 76
Guardian 14, 63
Guidry, Rory Andrew ('KMS') 102, 163–4

235

H

Hack The Planet (HTP) 77–84, 96–8, 102–6
  arrests 166, 167
  attacks 117, 167
  background 74–5
  Kivimäki and 93
  zines 78–81, 86
hacker groups 57–8, 58–9
Hacker Manifesto (Blankenship) 56–7, 59, 74, 218
Hacker One 221
Hackers (1995 film) 73–4, 77, 102
HackForums 84, 95, 96
Hack Right programme 222
hacktivists 60–1
Hadžipašić, Amir 46–7
Halminen, Laura 38–41
Hanon, Matt 123
hate speech 9
helpline, crisis 37–8
Helsingin Sanomat (HS) 38, 175, 187
Helsinki Cyber Crime centre 2–6
Highlandtitles.com 103
Homeland Security, US Department of 205, 206, 213
hospitals 31–2
hosting companies 23
Hubbard, L. Ron, *Dianetics* 182
Human Rights Act, UK (1998) 209
Hypponen, Mikko 15–16, 17, 18, 43–7, 49–51, 187

I

'The Ice King' (hacker) 96
ImageShack 80–2, 83, 84, 97
influencers, social media 15
Instagram 33, 185
Intera Partners 176, 177, 179
Intercontinental Hotels Group (IHG) 172–3

Internet Protocol (IP) address 23, 112, 189, 203
Internet Relay Chat (IRC) system 62–3, 68, 74–5, 80, 95, 110, 132, 185
Interpol 3, 185, 186
The Interview (2014 film) 155
Ireland 111
ISIS Gang 134, 135–7, 140–1, 162
Islam, Mir ('JoshTheGod') 118, 123, 125, 127–9, 149
Islamic State of Iraq and Syria (ISIS) 134
ISPs (Internet Service Provider companies) 76

J

Jaari, Peter 182, 183, 186, 187
Jabber (messaging service) 117
Jay-Z 125
'Jordie'/'EvilJordie'/'GDKJordie' (Jordan Lee-Bevan) 162
'JoshTheGod' (Mir Islam) 118, 123, 125, 127–9, 149
journalists 38–41, 112–14, 128, 155–9, 162, 168, 181, 199, 219
Justice, US Department of (DoJ) 115

K

Kardashian, Kim 125
'Kayla' (hacker) 66
Keemstar 148
Keskinen, Sami 177
King, Ryan ('Starfall'/Sarah King/'Vypor') 92–8, 142, 163
King, Sarah (was Ryan King) 95, 96–7, 98
'Kirk' (Graham Ivan Clark) 204
Kivimäki, Aleksanteri Julius Tomminpoika x, 2–6, 49–51
  'AntiSec' and 81
  arrested and convicted 166–9

INDEX

attends DEF CON 91
avoids arrest 165–6
in court 181–99
harasses girls 149, 195
HTP member 74–6, 93
influences 66–7
interviewed by Sky News 157–9,
    166, 220
joins Lizard Squad 141–3, 145–9
Nixon on 219
rise of xii–xiii, 23, 47
'sociopath' 194
stolen card purchases 102–3, 118
Strater family pranks 85–91
swatter 125
see also aliases: Amet, Asan;
    ransom_man; Ryan; RyanC;
    Untouchable Hacker God;
    Zeekill
Kivimäki family 49, 52, 94, 100, 222
'KMS' (Rory Andrew Guidry) 102,
    163–4
Knowles, Beyoncé 125
'Kottizen' (hacker) 75, 76
Krebs, Brian, 112–14, 128, 162, 168
Krebs on Security (website) 112
Kurittu, Antti 18–23, 99–101, 106–7,
    166, 169, 177, 184, 194
Kurtaj, Arion 207–12, 219
Kutcher, Ashton 125

L
L0pht (hacking group) 58, 59, 159
LadBible 65
Lahtinen, Ilkka 183
Laiho, Sami 198
Lanza, Adam 123
Lapsus$ 205–214, 218
Laulajainen, Antti 34–5, 197–8
League of Legends 143
leak sites 12, 13, 46–7, 142–3

Lee-Bevan, Jordan ('Jordie'/
    'EvilJordie'/'GDKJordie') 162
Legion of Doom (hacking group) 57
Lenovo 163
Leponen, Marko 3–5, 23–5, 38, 185,
    186, 188–92, 199, 221
Levene, Brandon 109, 110
Levin, Jack ('Cyphereus Prime')
    82–3, 97
LifeLock 146–7
Lind, Ilari 177
Lindgren, Nora 174–5, 180
LinkedIn 62, 82, 88
Linode 103–4
Little Big Planet 3 153–4
Lizard Squad (hacking group) ix–x,
    130, 131–4, 141–52, 154–69, 201,
    218
LizardStresser (DDoS service) 163
logos 61, 78, 114
lolcow culture 90
London Stock Exchange 173
LongPlay magazine 53, 168
Lopez, Santiago 127, 221
Love, Lauri 211
LulzSec (hacking group) 60–8,
    78–81, 117, 127, 132
Lundqvist, Bo-Niklas 190

M
McKinnon, Gary 211
Maclean, DCI Andy 140
Mäkelä, Harri 190
Malaysia Airlines website hack
    (2015) 162
malicious software 12, 51, 94, 105,
    106
Malin, Aarno 199
Marin, Sanna 36
Massachusetts Institute of
    Technology 167

237

Masters, Tomi 129
media coverage 14, 155–9
'Member 1' (Kivimäki) 156–7
'Member 2' (Vinnie Omari) 156–7, 161–2, 166
Menn, Joseph 58
Meta (previously Facebook) 223–4
MGM Resorts 215
Mibbit (IRC chat service) 80
Microsoft x, 117, 155, 160, 205, 214–15
Middleton, Reggie 140
Minecraft 53, 183
Monsegur, Hector Xavier ('Sabu') 65, 127
Moss, Jeff 'The Dark Tangent' 92
MSM Messenger 60
Mudd, Adam 211
Mueller, Robert 125
multi-factor fatigue technique 206
Musk, Elon 88, 202
MySpace 60

N
National Bureau of Investigation (NBI) 173–4
National Crime Agency (NCA) 76–7, 84, 165, 207, 221
National Cyber Security Center (NCSC) 21, 177
Naughton, Gus 185, 194–5
Naval Research Laboratory, US 12
Netflix 119
Netherlands 112, 221–2
Newsnight (BBC) 68
Next Web, The 64
Niinistö, Sauli 35
Nixon, Allison 109–12, 120, 131–2, 142–3, 150, 160, 213–14, 219–20
Nixu 18–19, 22, 99, 176, 177
Nmoto, Satoshi 84

Nolan, Stephen 156–7
Noob Persistent Threats (NPTs) 109–12, 121, 128, 132, 143, 145, 160, 201, 218
North Korea 32, 201
Nvidia 207
Nye, Nathan 195

O
Obama, Michelle and Barack 125, 202
'Obnoxious' (hacker) 149–50, 152
obsessive compulsive disorder (OCD) 128
O'Connor, Joseph James ('PlugwalkJoe') 204
OG Users ('original gangster') 203, 204, 206
Ohisalo, Maria 35
Okta 205
Omari, Vinnie ('Member 2') 156–7, 161–2, 166
Operation Card Shop (FBI bust) 122
OpSec (Operational Security) 19–20, 110
'OsamaTheGod' (Troy Woody Jr) 118, 123, 127–9
O'Sullivan, DI Mike 206–9, 210, 213, 219
Oswego, Illinois 85–91

P
Page, Larry 82
Parikka, Tiina 27–9, 196–7
Paris 1–2
PasteBin 78, 120, 121, 147
PayPal 75, 102, 112, 161
Pearson, Edward 106–7
Pepe the Frog cartoons 9
Philippines 128–9
phishing 34, 197

INDEX

phonebomber.net 164–5
Phrack magazine 57
Piha, Kirsi 33
PlayStation 4 153–4
PlayStation Network ix, 143, 144, 154–5, 158
'PlugwalkJoe' (Joseph James O'Connor) 204
PoodleCorp 164
Portal 53
Prince, Matthew 119, 121
Protect Children charity 33
Psychology Today 194

R
Radical Leveling Technologies (RLT) 159–60
Raiskio, Jenni 42
ransom_man (Kivimäki) 7–26, 28–31, 33, 36–47, 169, 171–80, 189, 192
ransomware 12, 32, 201, 215
Rasimus, Jesse 46, 47
Reddit 14, 169
Revolut 205
'rilWrruren' (hacker) 96
Roblox 223
Rockstar Games 205, 209–10
'Rolex' (Nima Fazeli) 204
Romania 217
Roose, Kevin 90
Roth, Yoel 202–3, 204
Royal Holloway University (2021 study) 150
Runescape 165
Russia xi, 105, 110, 112, 125, 201, 203, 215
Ryan (Kivimäki) 3, 67, 75–6, 82–3, 103, 157–9
Ryan ('Urharmless') 69–70, 90, 131, 139, 140, 141, 161

'RyanC' (Kivimäki) 84, 185, 189
Ryley, John ix

S
'Sabu' (Hector Xavier Monsegur) 65, 127
Sales, Jamie ('Declaws') 139
Salla (ransom_ man victim) 36–7, 38, 42, 197
Samsung 205
Sandy Hook Elementary School Shooting (2012) 123–4, 137
'Satan' (hacker) 133
Saudi Arabia xi, 155
saunas, Finnish 27
scammers 84, 95–6, 140, 197, 199, 202, 204
Scanifi 184–5, 194
Scattered Spider/Octo Tempest group 214–16, 218
Scientology, Church of 60, 182
Scottish Cup Final (2016) 139
Securities and Exchange Commission, US 215
SecurityAffairs website 159
Serious Organised Crime Agency, UK 63
764 group 216–17, 218
Sheppard, Mason John ('Chaewon') 204
Signal app 34, 187
Sim Park 111
SIM swap attack/techniques 140, 205–7
Sky News ix, xi, 156–9, 166
Skype 68, 70–1, 89, 132, 141, 157, 183, 195
Smedley, John 144, 145–8, 158, 168–9, 195, 222
Snellman, Anja 175
Snowden, Edward 92

239

social media 15, 33, 39–40, 59–60, 151, 154–5, 158, 222
   see also individual platforms
sociopath (definition) 194
Song, Dug 59
Sony x, 155
Sophos 13
South America 206
South East Regional Organised Crime Unit 161
spam 20, 34, 151
'Starfall' (Ryan King) 92–8, 142, 163
Steam (games platform) 53
Stop Online Privacy Act (2011 proposed bill) 115
Strater, Amy 88–9, 90
Strater, Blair 85–91, 95
Strater family 86, 87–9
stressers/booters 112–13, 221
suicide 42
Suomen Kuvalehti (SK) 199
Surrey Centre for Cyber Security 168
swatting 137–40
   attacks 134–5, 147, 149–50, 162
   harassment technique 87, 125–6
   Krebs and 113–14, 128
   Nye and 195
Swift, Taylor 162

T

Tapio family 176
Tapio, Ville 10, 14, 15, 20–2, 173–80
tar files 16, 42, 189
Taylor, Eric ('CosmoTheGod') 116–18, 121–4, 125–8, 205
Team Speak 68
teen cybercrime research 109–12, 120–1
Telegram 205, 210, 213
Tesla 88

'tflow' (Mustafa Al-Bassam) 33, 65, 127
'The Mentor' (Loyd Blankenship) 55–7, 218
The Onion Router (Tor) 12, 14, 16, 17
Threatpost 159
Toivonen, Dr Heidi 30–1
'Tommy' (ISIS Gang) 135–6, 140–1
'Topiary' (Jake Davis) 67–8
Torilauta 11, 13–14, 15, 16, 18, 46
Transport for London (TfL) 216
Trezor wallet (cryptocurrency) 167
Trump, Donald 125
TTPs (tactics, techniques and procedures) 189
Turton, William 161
Twitch 143
Twitter (now X) 60–4
   asking for help on 44
   complaints on 144
   Davis and 67
   Great Twitter Hack 202–4
   hacked accounts 88, 122, 124, 146, 162–3
   HTP and 78
   Musk on 202
   rise of 59
   Smedley on 168
   UG Nazi 120
   Vastaamo thread 14, 33, 36, 39, 40, 41

U

Uber 202, 205, 209
'Uchiha'/'UchihaLS' (Bradley van Rooy) 164–5, 166, 166–7, 193
UFC (Ultimate Fighting Championship) 115
UG Nazi (Underground Nazi Hacktivist Group) 103, 114–16, 117–23, 125, 127, 130

INDEX

Ukraine xi, 105
UNICEF Finland 33–4
United Kingdom (UK) 111, 205, 217
United States (US) 32, 58, 62, 112, 134, 217, 223
Untouchable Hacker God, The (Kivimäki) 3, 4, 167–8, 169, 181–99
'Urharmless' (Ryan) 69–70, 90, 131, 139, 140, 141, 161
US Air Force 144, 146

V

Vainio, Pasi 190
van Rooy, Bradley ('Uchiha'/'UchihaLS') 164–5, 166, 166–7, 193
Vanderport, Alex 195
Vastaamo cyber attack (2020) 2–6, 7–26, 27–47, 171–80, 185, 189–91
'Veri'/'Verified' (Robert Barr) 90, 139–40, 163
Verve 180
Vesala, Antti 33
Viner, Casey 137
virtual reality (VR) 223–4
Visa 75
'Vypor' (Ryan King) 142

W

Walker-McDaid, Robert 138–9
WannaCry hack (2017) 31–2
Warner, Gary 128
West, Kanye and Kim Kardashian 202
West Uusimaa District Court, Espoo 181–2
Westboro Baptist Church (extremist pressure group) 124

White, Geoff, Crime Dot Com 62
white-hat hackers 40–1, 46, 47, 50, 127, 184
WHMCS (web host) 121
WikiLeaks 61, 63, 75
Wired magazine 14, 122, 217
WithSecure 16, 18, 50
  see also F-Secure
Woodward, Prof Alan 168
Woody, Troy Jr ('OsamaTheGod') 118, 123, 127–9

X

X-Factor, The 62
X (was Twitter) 15, 59, 83
  see also Twitter (now X)
Xbox 116–19, 137, 158, 224
Xbox Live ix, 154–5
'XIX' (hacker) 93, 104

Y

YLE (Finnish broadcaster) 166
Ylilauta 7–11, 13, 14, 188
YouTube 65, 133, 144, 148, 155, 158, 160, 210, 221

Z

ZDNet 75–6
Zeekill (Kivimäki) 49–54
  AnonOps and 75–6, 77
  arrested 99–107
  Blair and 86
  group chats 69, 71
  LulzSec and 79
  Naughton and 185
  powerful player 3, 80, 83–4
  scamming users on HackForums 84
  'Starfall' and 92–8
Zuckerberg, Mark 223

241